Franz Schultheis, Erwin Single,
Raphaela Köfeler, Thomas Mazzurana
Art Unlimited?

Franz Schultheis is Professor of Sociology at the University of St. Gallen and President of the Fondation Bourdieu. He is co-editor of Pierre Bourdieu's writings.
Erwin Single studied sociology, communication sciences and journalism and works as a freelance journalist in Berlin.
Raphaela Köfeler studied International Affairs at the University of St. Gallen.
Thomas Mazzurana studied Business informatics and Sociology. He is a research associate at the Institute of Sociology at the University of St. Gallen.

Franz Schultheis, Erwin Single,
Raphaela Köfeler, Thomas Mazzurana

Art Unlimited?

Dynamics and Paradoxes of a Globalizing Art World

Translations by James Fearns

[transcript]

Published with the support of the Swiss National Science Foundation.

Translated with the support of the Dr. h.c. Emil Zaugg Fund
of the University of St. Gallen.

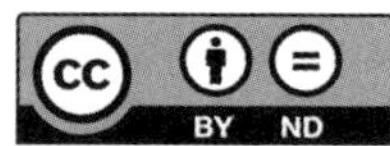

Bibliographic information published by the Deutsche Nationalbibliothek
The Deutsche Nationalbibliothek lists this publication in the Deutsche Natio-
nalbibliografie; detailed bibliographic data are available in the Internet at
http://dnb.d-nb.de

© 2016 transcript Verlag, Bielefeld
Cover layout: Kordula Röckenhaus, Bielefeld
Cover illustration: Thomas Mazzurana, Shanghai, May 2014
   (Long Museum West Bund, Shanghai). © Thomas Mazzurana.
Typeset by Justine Haida, Bielefeld
Printed in Europe
Print-ISBN 978-3-8376-3296-5
PDF-ISBN 978-3-8394-3296-9

Contents

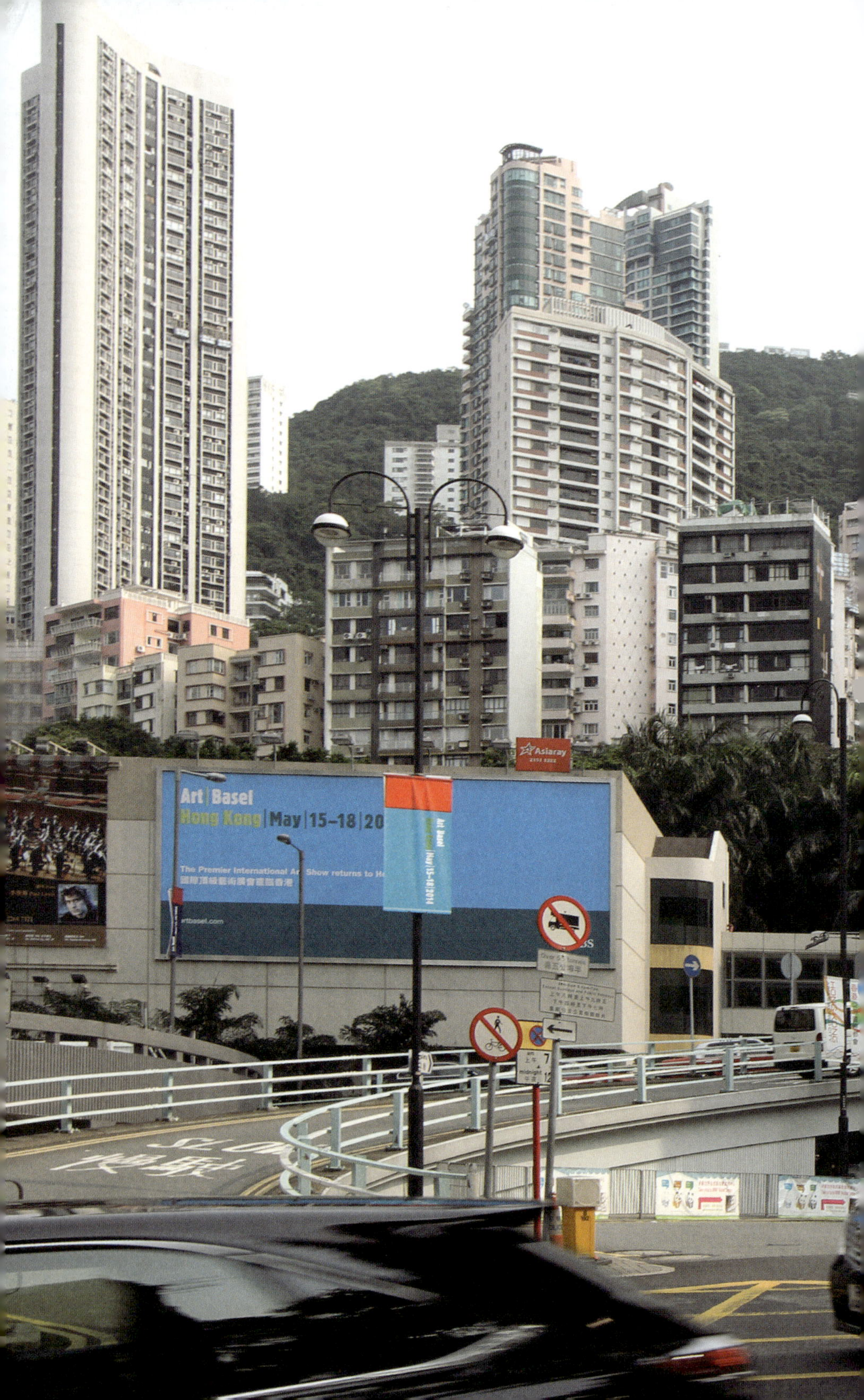

Asiaray
Art | Basel
Hong Kong | May | 15–18 | 20
The Premier International Art Show returns to Ho
artbasel.com
Art Basel | May 15–18 | 2014

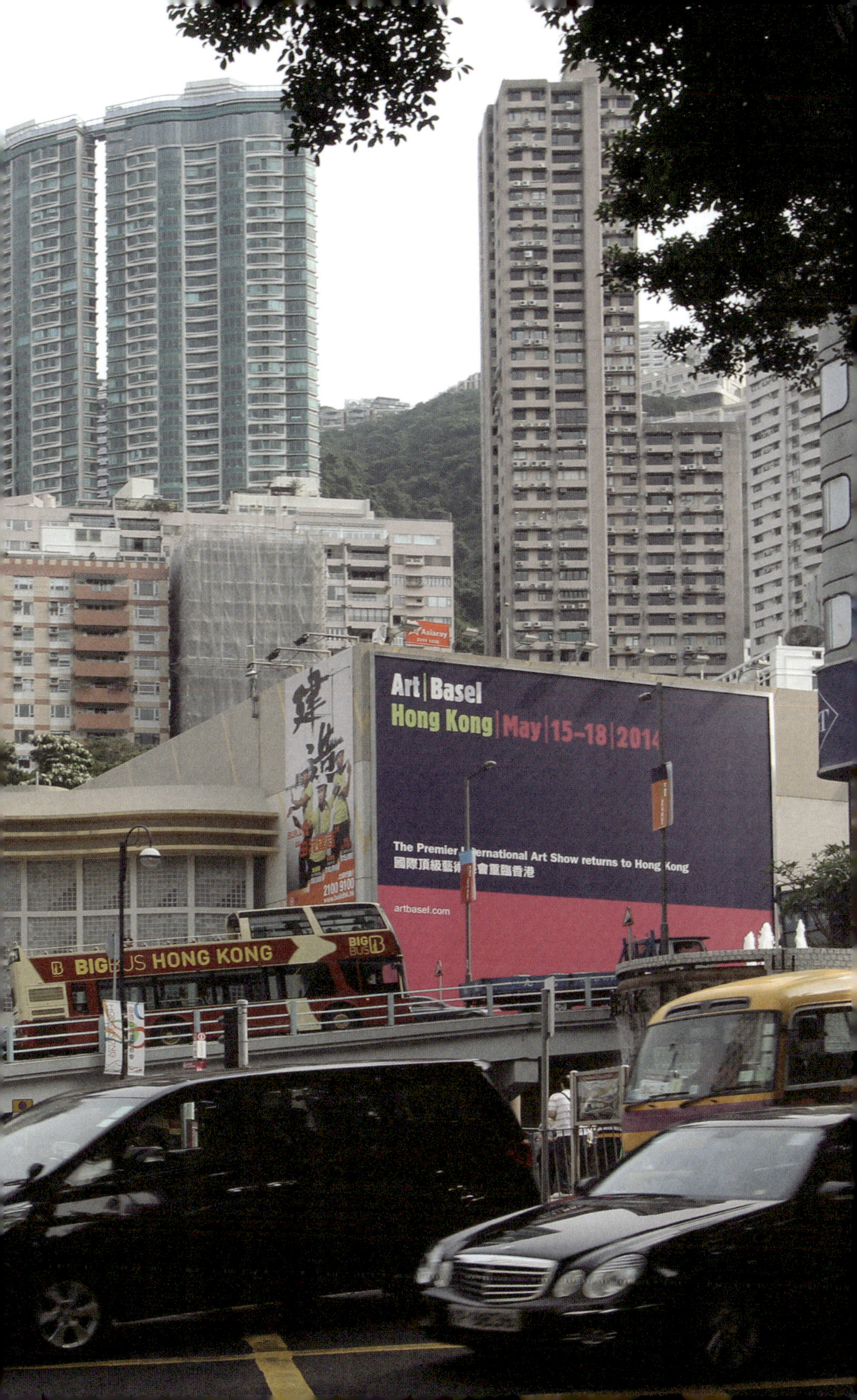

Art | Basel
Hong Kong | May | 15–18 | 2014
The Premier International Art Show returns to Hong Kong
國際頂級藝術盛會重臨香港
artbasel.com
Asiaray
2100 9100
BIGBUS HONG KONG
BIG B

Preface

The talk about globalization is omnipresent today. The topic has also been eagerly taken up and discussed in the art world in recent years. The discourse turns primarily upon the global expansion of the production, distribution and reception of contemporary art on the world map of art. Regions which have until quite recently only enjoyed a peripheral existence are advancing more strongly onto the international stage and are thus moving into the center of attention. The focus is on the question of the emergence of these local and regional art markets and art forums, which are situated so far away from the established centers of art in the USA and Europe.

But the overall effects of the phenomenon of globalization on art, the art market and the art world have hitherto remained largely unexplained. Depending on the perspective adopted globalization is understood to be a hegemonial form of "territorial occupation", the conquest of new art markets by the powerful actors on the market from the Western art metropolises, the assertion of the economic and cultural "mainstream" which evolved historically in these centers, or a leveling down and "homogenization" of cultural goods tailored to meet this "dominant taste". Or, from the perspective of the periphery, it is seen as a locally developed, more or less autonomous, egalitarian participation in art production, in reciprocal, transnational artistic exchange processes and a consequent diversification and, ultimately, enrichment of contemporary art as global art.

Without doubt, the growing transnationalization, above all since the end of the East-West confrontations in the year 1989, has led to a pluralization of the art world, a process which can be differentiated in terms of geographical area and content. The art field has not only expanded massively in volume; it has become noticeably more international in regard to the actors and the institutions involved and to contemporary visual art itself. We should not, however, overlook the fact that we are dealing with a very hierarchically structured sphere whose center of gravity is still to be found in the Western art centers, whereas in the peripheral areas only few regions have been included within the framework of globalization. In this connection the attention of Western actors is today drawn particularly to Asia, and especially to China, whose rapidly growing economic power has been accompanied for a decade by a strongly expanding art market.

A report published in May 2011 caused a great stir in the art world. The Swiss MCH Group, the organizer of probably the most important international art fair, the Art Basel, acquired 60 per cent of the shares in the Asian Art Fairs Ltd., the operator of the Hong Kong International Art Fair. Two years later, at the end of May 2013, the fair, now renamed Art Basel Hong Kong, took place for the first time under the management of the Art Basel with the Swiss big bank UBS as its main sponsor.

And thus a hitherto largely unknown white spot on the map of the art world suddenly stepped into the international limelight. On account of the special social, political and artistic conditions prevailing in the former British crown colony, it had in the past already become a central hub of the East Asian art market. But with the expansion of the Art Basel to Hong Kong, characterized by the management as "business as usual", the Chinese metropolis now presented itself as a new nodal point of the international art market and art field. "In Hong Kong, we want to create a fair that shows the different cultural influences. Geographic diversity has been one of our core values from the outset", the Art Basel director Marc Spiegel announced on the occasion of the takeover.

In the meantime Hong Kong has not only become one of the largest trading centers for art in the world alongside New York, London and Beijing but has also achieved the status of a central hub in the Asian region. The metropolis is, therefore, an ideal-typical setting for a case study in which the specific national and international conditions, structures and processes of the artistic field can be examined in an exemplary fashion. As a privileged location, at which Chinese and Western culture meet, the world city also offers an opportunity to describe and analyze mechanisms of transnationalization and regionalization in the art market and the transcultural interdependencies. This process has already been sketched and commented upon in part in the media and the relevant publications, but it has to date scarcely been the object of scientific studies and empirical analysis.

At the time the expansion of the Art Basel to the Asian area was made public our small research team was engaged in field research on the other two locations of the art fair in Basel and Miami Beach. We therefore wished to take the opportunity of examining the processes of transformation at this other central hub at close range by means of explorative field research, and in this way to attempt to identify and analyze the dynamics of globalization where the action was taking place. The study focused on the positions and perspectives of the actors of the art world on the spot, their view of what was going on, and the concrete practices of the local and regional art markets, art scene and art world in their specific socio-historical form as "being historically so and not otherwise" (Max Weber), and in their interweavement with the Western art world. How do the local actors depict their own art world, its institutions, rules and practices? What has changed in their opinion? How do they experience and interpret these changes?

This publication is based on the results of a research project which was funded by the Swiss National Science Foundation (SNSF). The basis of the methodologically multidimensional field study, which was carried out in the years 2013 and 2014, is provided by over 60 detailed interviews with important actors in the art world, predominantly gallerists, collectors, curators and artists. Excerpts from the talks, which have been authorized by the interview partners, make up the major part of the present book. The interviews are supplemented by two written questionnaires presented to gallerists and visitors to the Art Basel Hong Kong, which were evaluated with the help of multivariate procedures. In addition, explorative short interviews were carried out with visitors from the East Asian cultural area, which give an insight into the different ways of using and perceiving art. And although the present volume concentrates primarily on the presentation of the positions and perspectives expressed by selected actors in the in-depth interviews, insights gathered from the use of other methods of ethnographic field research also find their place in the study.

Of course the 16 interviews presented in the book cannot and do not claim to be representative. Nonetheless they reflect a variety of relevant and striking positions in the Asian art field and can therefore certainly claim exemplary status. In the choice of the excerpts preference was given to those actors who live and work in China and so perceive and can mediate the Chinese art world from a local point of view and from a bottom up perspective. An exception is consciously made for some representatives of the Western art world who can be considered to be important go betweens between the Eastern and Western spheres of art. We are dealing overall with reports by persons who stand in the center of the stage but have hitherto attracted little attention in discourse in the West.

The book is addressed less to the social scientific community than to the actors in the art field and to a wider public interested in art. It invites them to take part in a tour d'horizon and to reflect on the question as to how the narrations on the globalization of the art market and the art world widely and constantly recurring in many variations in the West are seen, experienced, interpreted and judged by the actors these narrations report on, although their voices are so seldom heard – as if there exist, as in the time of the colonial occupations, active participants in globalization on the one side and more or less passive observers of the process on the other.

We hope that we have thus made a small contribution to a better understanding of the processes of transformation subsumed under the phenomenon of globalization. Our thanks are due particularly to all the interview partners for their willingness to answer our questions in detail and so to make an active contribution to this study.

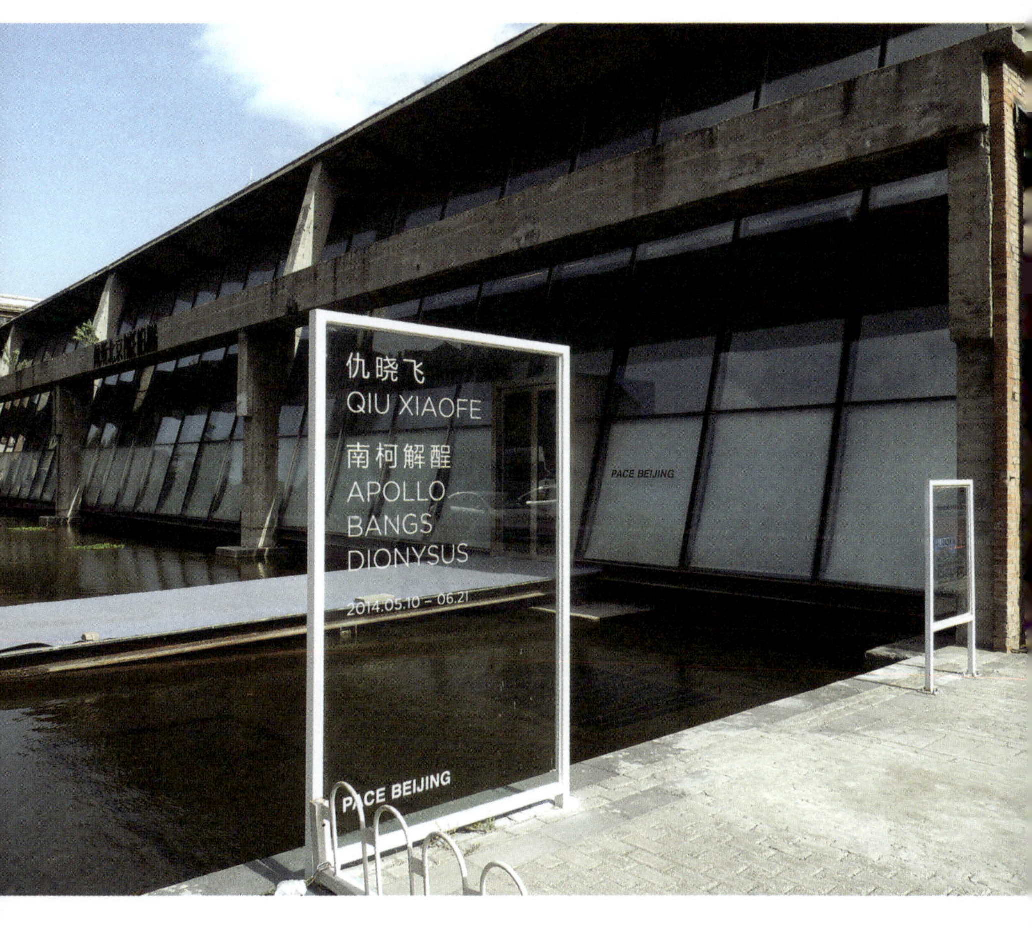
仇晓飞
QIU XIAOFE
南柯解醒
APOLLO
BANGS
DIONYSUS
2014.05.10 – 06.21
PACE BEIJING
PACE BEIJING

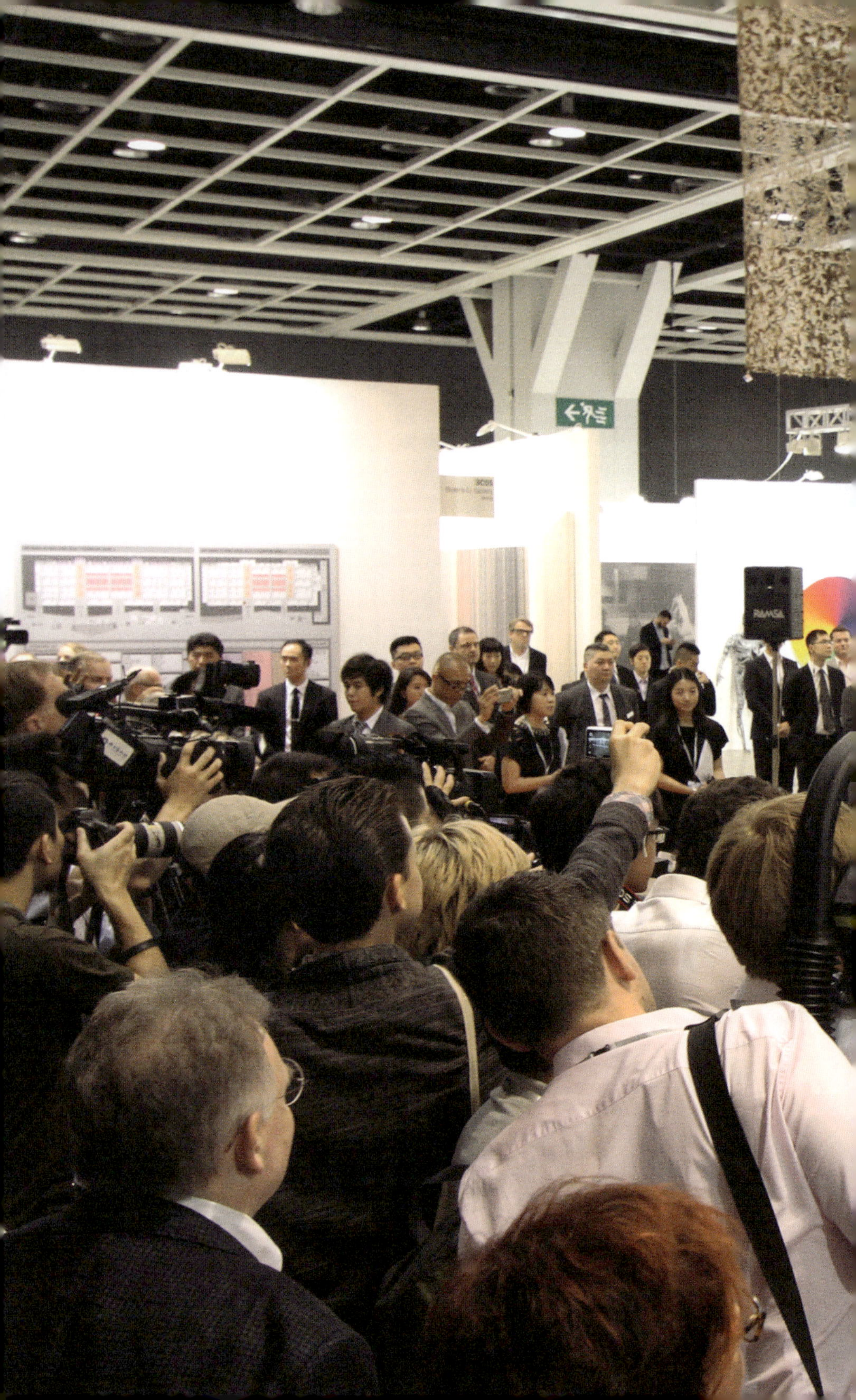

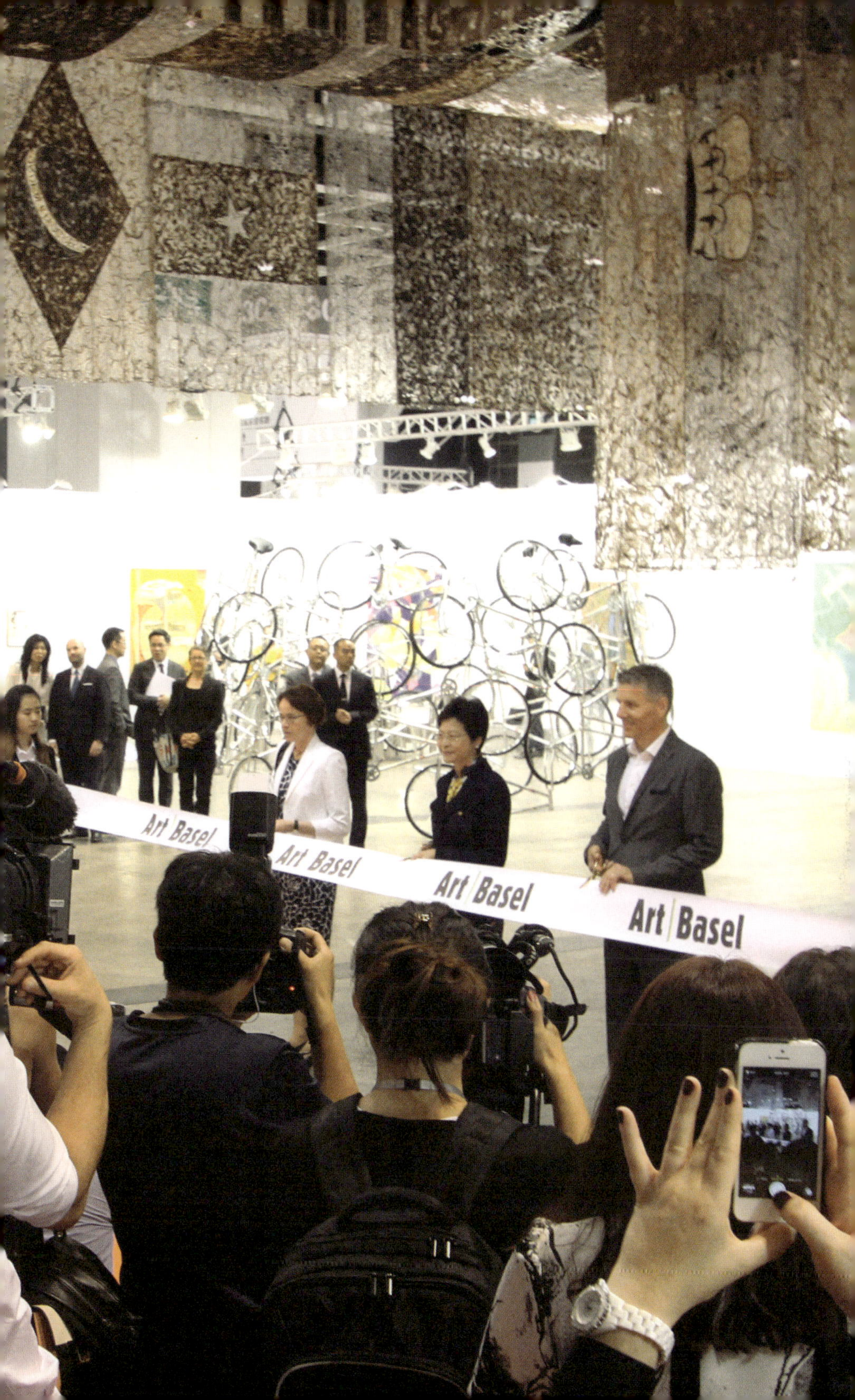
Art Basel
Art Basel
Art Basel
Art Basel

Introduction: Art unlimited?
The globalization of the art world and its limits

With the end of the Second World War the contours and the weighting of the continents and regions of the world map of art shifted massively. The division of Europe, the rise of the USA as a super power, the beginning of the Cold War and the world-wide triumph of Western capitalism did not fail to have an effect on the sphere of art. The rapid and lasting erosion of French hegemony in the art market and of the predominant role of Paris in the production, circulation and consecration of art after the war was accompanied by the equally swift rise of abstract expressionism and pop art, as a result of which New York developed into the leading art metropolis in the course of the 1960s. And to the present day it has maintained this position of power and monopoly, enabling it to determine the canon of what was now called contemporary art. Around the middle of the 1980s an opening of the art world took place which is frequently associated with the transition from the modern to the so-called post-modern age in art and with the dynamics of contemporary art itself. The appearance of young artists from post-colonial contexts at the Paris exhibition "Magiciens de la Terre" in 1989 is an exemplary, ever emblematic sign of the increased inclusion of non-Western actors in an art scene whose mapping had hitherto been almost exclusively restricted to North America and Europe.

The historical and paradigmatic upheaval symbolized by the year 1989 and characterized by the end of a bipolar world order is accompanied by an increasing and widely attested globalization. The art world, organized around the museums, galleries, fairs, auctions, biennials, the throngs of artists, collectors, curators, critics and a steadily growing public, did not remain untouched by this change. The transformations of the world of art have also lastingly influenced and changed its representations, discourses, institutions and artistic practices and positions.

The opening up and expansion of an art world largely restricted to the Western hemisphere can be seen, for example, in the current representations of art in the established art institutions such as the biennials or in art criticism, which have in the meantime opened their doors to artistic influences from all regions of the world and no longer represent only the centuries-long privileged and dominant Western art. This development is not least due to the diverse dynamics of interaction, cooperation and mobility unleashed in the course of globalization. The progressive globalization seems to have brought with it not only an increased cross-fertilization of various artistic traditions but also a growing transnationalization and internationalization of the art world in general and of the art market in particular, accompanied by the world-wide institutionalization of contemporary art and a visibly growing standardization of the presentation and exhibition of art from all and in all regions of the world. It is, nonetheless, still necessary to ask whether this undoubtedly existent intercultural and transnational diversity of the origins of artists and works of art does in fact reveal an all-round permeability of the former boundaries with their specific obstacles, filters and selection mechanisms in regard to the circulation of artistic goods. Could it not also be the case that the increasingly colorful international, pluri-ethnic and pluri-cultural exoticism of the contemporary art world may well exist at the level of the origin of the actors but not at the level of relevant structures and powers and processes of consecration, and that in these spheres the continued existence of powerful monopoly positions of a few Western art institutions and art centers in regard to the legitimate definition of art must be assumed?

The strong expansion of the art market in the past decades is above all taken as an indication of an increasing globalization. The rapid ascent of China to the role of global player on the art market and the high growth rates for trade in art in Brazil, India, Mexico, Russia or the Arab world – which are directly linked with the rise of a wealthy upper-class in these countries whose interest in art derives from a variety of motives – are proof of a territorial and structural transformation of the art world. On all continents, with the possible exception of Africa, a large number of public and, above all, private art institutions has arisen, which have contributed to the visibility and popularization of contemporary art. Biennials and art fairs have extended into the furthest corners of the world. Even in countries and regions which were still characterized as marginal a few years ago prestigious galleries and art dealers' shops, museums and exhibition projects have been established. Art has developed into a privileged medium of city branding: countries or metropolises consciously deploy this symbolic capital in the international competition for visibility and attractiveness, not least in order to remain competitive in the struggle to attract financially powerful populations in a time of increasing transnational mobility.

Art production has also clearly become more international than it was in the 1970s. The art scenes in the Asian, Pacific, Latin-American or Arab regions have in the meantime developed into more than mere exotic blossoms and side issues. In spite of the already mentioned continuance of the hegemonial influence of Western art metropolises, the art milieus in economically upward-moving art centers such as China follow their own laws of organization and cannot simply be subsumed under the concepts of Western art history or the Western art field. This is one of the most important developmental trends in the art field, whose consequences can as yet scarcely be estimated.

Artists from all corners of the earth are in the meantime exhibited around the globe and can be seen, above all, at the international big events such as the Biennale in Venice or the documenta in Kassel. In many states so-called art residencies and residential art programs count among the important instruments of the public and private promotion of artists and artistic exchange. Not only the creators of art themselves but also curators, organizers of exhibitions, art dealers and gallerists, collectors and art lovers have become hyper-mobile actors in the course of the globalization of the art scene, who jet around the world from one event to the next. The so called love of art, an attitude hitherto regarded as a distinctive and distinguishing cultural pattern of Western elites, is in the meantime shared by a part of the new bourgeoisie in the so-called threshold countries. Rich collectors from Asia, the Arab region, Russia and Latin America have established themselves on the global art market and compete with Western collectors at auctions and art fairs around the world for the acquisition of representative and correspondingly expensive works of art. And for the big auction houses like Sotheby's and Christie's and mega-galleries like Gagosian, Pace or White Cube with their world-wide network of branch offices the sun literally never sets in this "brave new world".

This development towards a "global salon", towards an apparently extensive dissociation from the regional context, which can be observed at the top of an increasingly internationalized art world and is seemingly characterized by ideals or pretentions of savoir vivre and urbanity, was promoted, above all by the growth of the art market and the crystallization of formats such as the international art fairs and art biennials. A throng of mega-galleries, powerful auction houses and mega-collectors moves in orbit from event to event around this nexus.

GLOBALIZATION AS A NARRATIVE OF THE ART WORLD

Globalization is a complex and multilayered concept defined and used very differently depending on the position and perspective adopted and is directly associated with the narration of the rise of the West.[1] With the upheaval at the end of the 1980s it came to be a leading category of various scientific disciplines and has since been used as a kind of signature for the expansion, concentration and acceleration of world-wide relationships. The term, which comprehends various economic, political and cultural processes, is, however, not undisputed and is controversially discussed. Globalization is not so much a historical phenomenon; it is rather the result of the interaction and reciprocal reinforcement of long-term processes such as the inter-relationships in the world economy, world-wide communication and networking or massive transnational migratory movements.[2] We use globalization less as a social scientific and economic

---

1 | The definition of the concept of the "West" is blurred and differs according to the context. From a geographical point of view it comprehends America and Europe, but sometimes – in distinction to the "East" – it can include Africa, the Arab world and Southern Asia. Furthermore, the concept refers to a "values community" based on the proclamation of human and citizens' rights and the legacy of the French and American revolutions. When we speak of the "West" we mean primarily that normative project of the modern age and modernism comprising the "achievements" of political enlightenment since the end of the 18th century.

2 | On the concept of "globalization and its scope" see Osterhammel, Jürgen/Petersson, Niels P. (2003): Geschichte der Globalisierung. Dimensionen, Prozesse, Epochen. Munich: C.H. Beck. The sociological globalization discourse is very heterogeneous and refers to networks (John Urry), network societies (Manuel Castells),

leitmotif and more as a contemporary diagnostic concept in order to describe specific structures and interactions in the art field.

And although the neo-liberal model of free trade is customarily cited as a prototype of global development, globalization cannot be reduced to an economic dimension. The idea of cultural globalization starts from increased contact and a mixture of heterogeneous cultures around the world, which were formerly isolated or only occasionally or peripherally linked with one another – a process of cultural reproduction which gives rise regionally and locally to new kinds of virtual neighborhood which are fragile and pervaded by breaks and contradictions.[3] This process involves a more or less paradox dynamics of contemporaneous and parallel cultural homogenization, whose results are often characterized as "glocalization" (Roland Robertson), "hybridization" (Homi K. Bhabha) or "creolization" (Stuart Hall), in which global and local elements are reciprocally transformed and reorganized and lead to a merging of differing cultural elements. It is created discursively and is mostly affected by relationships of dominance.

It is clear that the morphological and structural changes in the art field described above cannot fail to affect the distribution and weighting of the economic and symbolic factors. The map of the art field is being transformed. With the upheaval at the end of the 1980s not a few representatives of the art world saw the end of the Western monopoly looming on the horizon, not only in the art market but also in the status system of art and in regard to the power of definition over what art is and what can be included in an extended global canon founded on the history and science of art. Even the idea of the concept of art coined by Western modernism seems to have been overrun and challenged by the development.

Are we then on the way to a global art world without a center or a periphery? The readings and interpretations of these transformations differ substantially in this regard. Whereas some of the actors and observers expect a stronger interlacing of the institutions of the art world on the periphery with the established Western art field, others simply

transformation processes (David Held), "globality" as a new orientational framework and a new age (Martin Albrow) or "global cities" (Sakia Sassen) to name only a few examples.

3 | See Appadurai, Arjun (1996): Modernity at Large. Cultural Dimensions of Globalization. Minneapolis: University of Minnesota Press.

register a further expansion and reinforcement of Western positions at a global level. The massively extended global practice of art production and art distribution apparently challenges Western art as it has developed over the last 150 years along with the accompanying modern canon – not least because modernism itself, which has been directly associated with progressive European expansion, Eurocentrism, the ideology of progress, universalistic claims and modern capitalism since the age of colonization, has been disputed and questioned by a part of the world of art experts. In the art world the concept modern is scarcely ever used and instead the talk is mostly about contemporary art. This can be understood as an unmistakable sign of the transformation process, although a linear equation of global art and contemporary art as global contemporary seems highly questionable and problematic. This is so not only because, from an ethnographic point of view, it involves a disdaining narrative in which cultural circles are included which were and are remote from the Western topos of art. Contemporary art as a global universal concept of art which unites the practices and traditions of all places thus remains highly unspecific.

On taking a closer look the frequently postulated unlimited, so called flat and cosmopolitan art world quickly turns out, however, to be an illusion. It manifests itself only at the top of the hierarchically structured art field, where a global clientele of super-rich collectors buys contemporary art on an increasingly globalized and no longer nationally or culturally structured market. And the art they buy is produced by a relatively small circle of internationally renowned artists and marketed by equally select, transnationally operating galleries and auction houses. In business transactions in this top segment several borders are often crossed at one and the same time. It is, for example, standard practice that collectors from Western art metropolises acquire through galleries abroad the works of Latin American or Asian artists who themselves live and work in a Western art center. Or collectors from emerging countries might in the same way procure the works of Western artists. Whereas this top segment has in the meantime been largely deterritorialized, the great part of the art market continues to be enclosed within national and cultural borders. Here the artists, the art trade, the buyers and collectors belong for the greatest part to the same cultural circle.

The weak inclusivity can be explained, above all, by the strongly hierarchical structure of the art field. The three large economic areas of Europe, the USA and China also dominate the global art market; in

2013 the rest of the world had only a 6 per cent share in the market.[4] The distribution of the art market corresponds to the density of the institutions in the regions. Scarcely any museums, academies, galleries or art exhibitions can be found in many parts of Africa, Asia or Latin America. Even in China the numbers lag far behind those in the European states.[5] In these regions the process of the institutionalization of art, which first renders it visible, is still in its infancy; they have not gone through a historical development similar to that in the West. This indicates, in spite of all the internationalization effects, the continuing massive geographical disparities in the world of art. These processes of concentration or unequal distribution are often cited as evidence against the widely attested push towards globalization. Moreover, numerous empirical studies can be quoted against the established narrative of the globalization of the art field, which continue to point out the high level of hierarchization in the field, the low inclusivity and the maintenance of Western dominance on account of the strong incline between the center and the periphery.[6]

---

4 | See McAndrew, Clare (2014). TEFAF Art Market Report 2014. Helvoirt: European Fine Art Foundation, p. 22.

5 | The data bank of Artfacts lists world-wide around 31,500 institutions in the art field. The list is headed by the front-runners USA (5,746) and Germany (5,223), followed by France (2,444), Great Britain (2,033) and Italy (1,972). China (591) and Hong Kong (141) have just about as many art institutions as Belgium. Other Asian states such as India (170), Indonesia (61) or Thailand (43) are also on the bottom ranks. Only Japan (765) and South Korea (464) can more or less keep up with the level of West European states. And even in the so called BRICS states Brazil (284), Russia (203) or South Africa (144) art institutions are still not widespread (as of 22nd of October 2015).

6 | Buchholz, Larissa/Wuggenig, Ulf (2004): Cultural Globalization between Myth and Reality: The Case of the Contemporary Visual Arts. In: Art-e-Fact, 4. Bydler, Charlotte (2011): Global Contemporary? The Global Horizon of Art Events. In: Harris, Jonathan (ed.), Globalization and Contemporary Art. Malden: Wiley-Blackwell, 464-478. Baia Curioni, Stefano (2012): A Fairy Tale: The Art System, Globalization, and the Fair Movement. In: Lind, Maria/Velthuis, Olav (eds.), Contemporary Art and Its Commercial Markets: A Report on Current Conditions and Future Scenarios. Berlin: Sternberg, 115-151. Quemin, Alain (2012): The Internationalization of the Contemporary Art World and Market. The Role of Nationality and Territory in a sup-

CHINA'S RISE TO THE STATUS OF A GLOBAL PLAYER

A massive shift in the regional weightings and the zones of influence on the international art market can, nonetheless, be observed since the turn of the millennium. China suddenly appeared as if from nowhere on the map of the international art trade. Until recently the continuously growing art market was dominated unchallenged by the USA and the West European states. In the year 2013 the story of globalization acquired a new dimension and accentuation: China overtook the USA as the art trade center with the highest turnover in the world, if only for a time.

China's share in the global art market increased from 23 per cent in the year 2010 to 30 per cent in 2011, thus overtaking the USA, which had a share of 29 per cent. The Chinese auction market grew by 177 per cent in 2010 alone and by 64 per cent in 2011.[7] Among the five most successful artists on the auction market in 2011 there were three Chinese. The Chinese landscape painter Zhang Daquian even superseded Picasso, taking the top place as the artist with the highest turnover. The most expensive picture of the year sold at an auction was painted by Qi Baishi.[8]

However the boom quickly came to an end. In the years 2012 to 2014 China's share in the global art market fell back to 22 per cent.[9] The prices also sank considerably, illustrating how volatile the art market is precisely in the emergent regions. But in spite of the drop the "Middle Kingdom" remained the most important of all the new art markets in regard to both the market volume and to the importance of the buyers world-wide.[10]

This development brought numerous actors and institutions of the Western art world on to the scene, who began to expand their activities to

---

posedly 'globalized' sector. In: Lind, Maria/Velthuis, Olav (eds.), Contemporary Art and Its Commercial Markets: A Report on Current Conditions and Future Scenarios. Berlin: Sternberg, 53-83.

7 | The figures derive from: McAndrew, Clare (2012): The International Art Market in 2011. Observations on the Art Trade over 25 Years. Helvoirt: European Fine Art Foundation.

8 | See Artprice (2012): Art Market Trends 2011. Saint-Romain-au-Mont-d'Or.

9 | McAndrew, Clare (2015): TEFAF Art Market Report 2015. Helvoirt: European Fine Art Foundation.

10 | See McAndrew, Clare (2014): TEFAF Art Market Report 2014. Helvoirt: European Fine Art Foundation.

include this region of the world. The first art fairs were initiated, galleries from Europe and the USA opened branches in China, the big auction houses attempted to penetrate the growth market via Hong Kong. This strategy was accompanied by endeavors to school and refine Asian taste in art in order to make it accessible first of all for the import of Western art commodities.

How strong the temptations of the potential of such an emerging economy were for the actors of the Western art field is impressively demonstrated by the example of the Art Basel. As early as 2005 what is probably the most important art fair in the world arranged a panel on contemporary Chinese art and the future of museums in China. This was followed in 2006 by a first official appearance in China: at the National Art Museum of China a discussion meeting was held in the series "Art Basel Conversations" under the title "China: New Opportunities in the Global Art Arena" with the support of the Ministry of Culture of the Chinese People's Republic and the Swiss ambassador in Beijing. "Art Basel works to build a giant bridge between Chinese contemporary art and international contemporary art, and perhaps this is one more reason why it remains so influential", the director of the National Art Museum at the time, Fan Di'an, acknowledged at the opening.

Nonetheless, it took a lot of time until, in the summer of 2011, the starting pistol for expansion was fired. After its expansion to the USA in 2002 with its offshoot Art Basel Miami Beach, the Art Basel also entered the Asian market with the takeover of the Hong Kong International Art Fair, which was, according to Magnus Renfrew, the Art Basel director at the time, already "one of the must-see events on the global art calendar", at which numerous renowned galleries from the West were already represented. In May 2013 the fair took place for the first time under the management of the Art Basel. The art fair in Hong Kong thus finally discarded the status of a regional niche fair, which it had shared with other comparable events in the Chinese and South East Asian area since its foundation in 2007. And the Art Basel, now with three fairs on three continents, itself acquired the status of a global brand in the field of art.

HONG KONG AS A BRIDGEHEAD

As has been said above, China has in the meantime become a global player on the art market. The former British crown colony Hong Kong, since 1997 again a part of the Chinese People's Republic, is, together with Beijing and Shanghai, the center of the Chinese art trade. The city is now one of the four largest trading centers for art in the world. Although the city government has for a long time pursued a purposeful policy of promoting and financing cultural institutions which laid the cornerstone for the rise of a vibrant art market, the establishment of the city as the creative hub in the Asian-Pacific area, and the parallel assertion of the claim to be a global cultural metropolis, have only taken place in the last 10 years. Apart from the auction houses Christie's and Sotheby's, important galleries from North America and Europe such as Gagosian, White Cube, Perrotin or Pace have also set up branches in Hong Kong since 2008. The mixture of auction houses, galleries, artists, collectors and curators, the West Kowloon Cultural District, which was developed for 2.8 billion US dollars, and the Museum Plus (M+), to be opened in 2018, as its future core, have made Hong Kong an emerging center of the international art market and the art scene.

As already mentioned in the preface the metropolis of Hong Kong is an ideal territory for an exemplary case study examining the specific national and international conditions, structures and processes of the art world. As an Asian-European epicenter the city has, from a historical standpoint, also been a center for the transfer and migration of ideas and cultural goods. In this privileged location the mechanisms of transnationalization and regionalization involved in the art market and the processes of transcultural interdependence can be illuminated and evaluated in exemplary fashion.

The observable economic developments are, however, only of secondary importance in regard to the starting point of our study. Instead we are primarily interested in describing and analyzing globalization as both an economic and cultural phenomenon with the help of a methodically multidimensional approach. The initiation and acceleration of globalization of the art market in Hong Kong and China, indubitably the product of American-European hegemony in the art market, encounters a massively different socio-historical formation of cultural preconditions in the East Asian region. Consequently the "Middle Kingdom" and especially Hong

Kong as an epicenter can be utilized as a kind of laboratory of globalization from which knowledge of the structure, manner of functioning and dynamics of this special sphere of social production and reproduction can be gained. These processes are highly insightful precisely because the emergence and existence of the sphere of art is characterized by a highly culture-specific context which massively determines the nature of the market.

The particular significance of these processes results from the conjuncture of different factors which overlap and mutually reinforce one another in the object of our research. On the one hand we have the rapidly growing economic importance of the art market, which has not only developed into a privileged place for investment and speculation over the last 20 years but also reveals processes of transformation which affect the internal relationship of a quite specific market situation. On the other hand the object of study is for precisely this reason an interesting terrain for social scientific enquiry, and particularly for questions concerning the special characteristics of markets for symbolic goods or the functions they fulfill in regard to stabilization or transformation of cultural, social and normative hierarchies.

What happens in a country whose economic opening up after decades of isolation also leads to a cultural reorientation? What kind of productive misunderstandings arise here between the traditional understanding of art and Western structures of art mediation and evaluation? What happens when a world-famous art fair which functions as a kind of temporary gallery mall penetrates an emerging art market in which, in contrast to the West, galleries have hitherto played scarcely any part as gatekeepers and intermediaries between artists and buyers, collectors and a public interested in art? How are intercultural divergences and convergences constructed, enacted and symbolized? How is this order thematized and legitimated by its directors, the actors of the art world? And how is it perceived by the visitors and buyers who are interviewed? What transformations in the manners of perception and judgment can be ascertained?

The list of interesting questions can be extended at will without any reasonably satisfactory answer being found. The art field is not a self-contained sphere, but involves instead a contest of forces which is both internally and externally open. It presents a challenge not only to the knowledge of the "other" and the "far away" but also to the ideas, standards and practices of one's own cultural circle.

The interfaces between Chinese and Western culture are concerned not least with the clear socio-historical asynchrony, different concepts of authenticity and originality, cultural divergences and differences in mentality between a Western understanding of art developed historically step by step since the 19th century and the emergent field of art on its periphery. The encounter between this dominant socio-historical setting of the Western art field and the particular cultural characteristics of the emergent field, which involves no less than a so called cultural gap, is one of the frequently repeated themes of the actors in the Western art field in their contacts with "alien" forms of the appropriation of art. "The only way that they could really experience it was through photographing themselves in front of the piece", a gallerist explained in a discussion, "just hundreds of people around us doing the same [...] But no one ever spoke to us. There were no conversations, no engagement at all. They had no interest in having any conversations with you. Even collectors, but the audience also. They treated us as shop assistants. [...] I don't think they understood what a gallery did or anything like that. [...] It is totally a completely different place. I felt like I had gone back 40 years. I really don't think that they experience the work in the same way. I think there is a long way to go there."

It is not surprising, therefore, that the spellbound eyes of the art world are on the events in China. But what can one see with Western eyes in this geographically and culturally distant, even exotic region and how can one assess its assumed entry into in the contemporary world? What stories can be heard when one speaks with dozens of actors from the Western art field about this new El Dorado of the art market and records expert opinions of widely differing provenance – from gallerists, collectors, museum staff, representatives of auction houses or curators?

From the many-voiced Western choir of the art world, recorded at various locations in Europe and the USA, a colorful kaleidoscope of images of the "other world" emerges, which is nourished by sporadic encounters on journeys, educated middle-class knowledge, spectacular and spectacularizing media reports, culture-specific stereotypes and current myths and assessments underpinned by market analyses and statistical key data. Again and again such dialogues create the impression that this emerging region of the global art world presents a projection screen for partly promising, partly alarming scenarios rather than a terrain surveyed in accordance with rational viewpoints and empirically well-founded insights. Each dialogue partner provides a specific image of the dynamics of the expanded art market, whose perspective is determined by the position adopted and transports various combinations of economic, political, geographical, historical or sociological interpretative patterns. As the respondents are all without exception actors and connoisseurs of the art world, they usually possess a more or less distinctive insider knowledge of the structures and dynamics of their life world, which is, however, always nourished by current plausibility structures and supposedly self-evident assumptions and expectations of the Western tradition of modern art with its 150 years-long history and a resultant high degree of self-reference. This leads again and again to ethnocentric generalizations of the personal socio-historical background and the projection of habitualized patterns of perception and thinking onto unfamiliar realities.

In what follows we will first of all condense these insights and outlooks on the Far East from the perspective of Western actors of the art world to a kaleidoscope, which will, as a next step, be confronted with the insights gained on the spot from local actors. The confrontation with the appropriation of the "other" is subjected here to a critical revision. It turns out that the Western viewpoint adopted from an apparently privileged and superior position seems more and more questionable the closer one comes to the object of study. Like the Western public the majority of the actors from the Western centers of the art world continue to follow the familiar ethnic patterns.

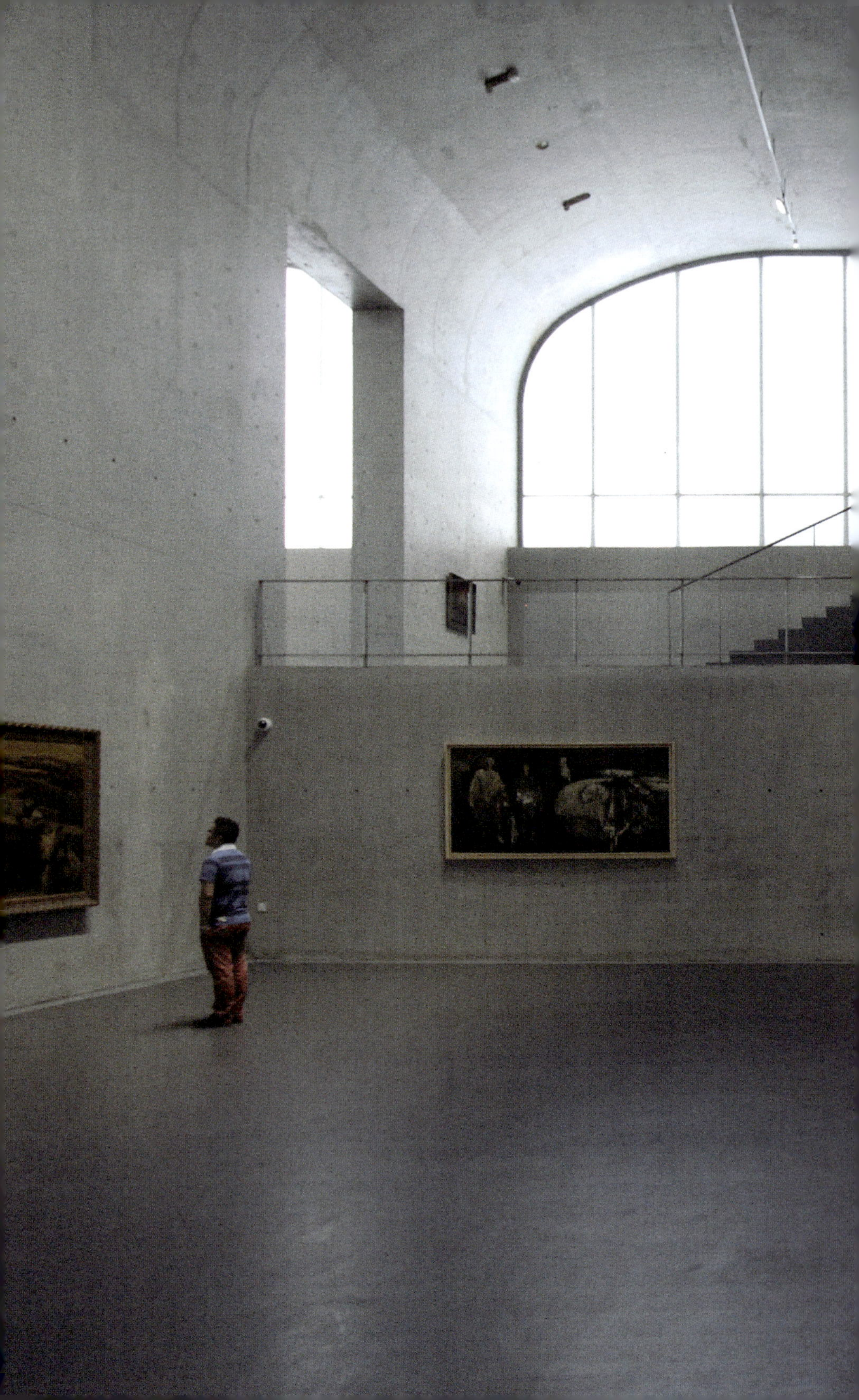

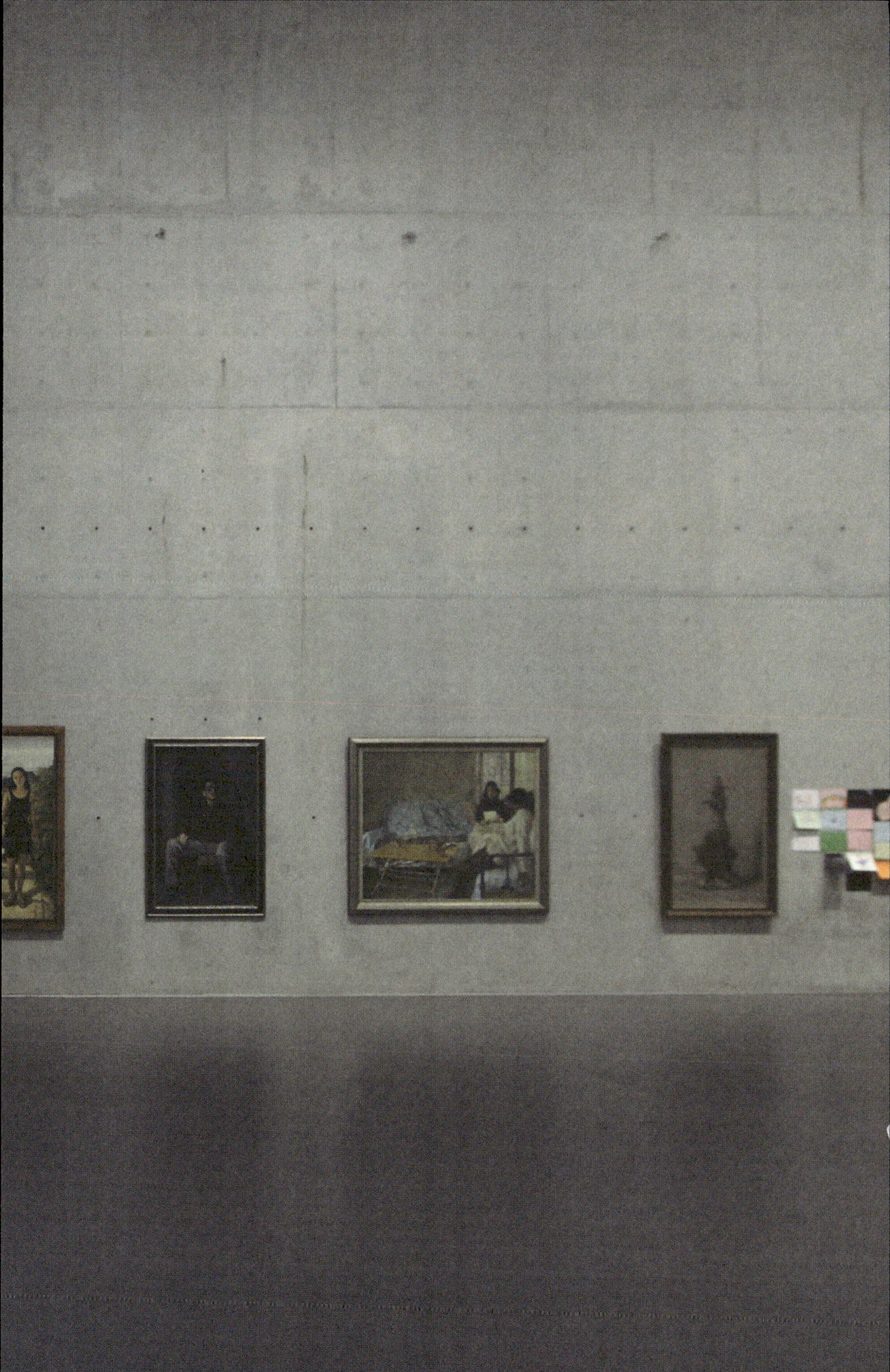

Prospective territorial occupations
Western perspectives on a "terra incognita" of the art world

In the course of the spectacular and steep economic rise of China the notion has spread rapidly among the general public of the developed industrial states that in the future the action will take place above all in the most heavily populated country in the world. The art world in the Western states has not remained untouched by this mood and looks, sometimes euphorically and sometimes anxiously, to the Far East in the belief that a flourishing art market will develop in Asia and particularly in China. For most of the actors China was endlessly remote, foreign and downright exotic. In 2011 at the latest the enticements and promises received fresh impetus from the news that the Chinese art market had overtaken the USA and Europe in its volume. A gold-rush mood spread widely, nourished by the sensationalism of the media reports. Scarcely anybody could resist the departure of the Western world for the Far East. "Going global" mutated into a slogan of the powerful actors on the markets of the international art trade who, attracted by the sheer wealth of the Asian world, opened up branches especially in Hong Kong, Shanghai, Beijing or Singapore. But the building up of corresponding market positions did not always run smoothly, not least because of misunderstandings arising from cultural differences. For the Western art world China remains a difficult terrain.

When it was publicly announced in the spring of 2011 that the Swiss MCH Group had acquired a majority share of the Hong Kong International Art Fair, the decision to position the Art Basel brand on the forward-looking location of Hong Kong was seen as a clever move by the experts and the media. At precisely this moment our research group was working on an ethnological field study on the Art

Basel.[1] As research instruments surveys were undertaken with gallerists and visitors and, in particular, in-depth interviews were carried out with all the groups active in the art world. In the run up to the ethnographic field research on the spot in Hong Kong, we collected at that time data on the assessments and expectations of these Western actors in regard to the emerging South East and East Asian art market and on the role the announced "occupation" of the territory by the Art Basel could play in the region. The following snapshot is based on the results of these empirical surveys, which sum up the perspectives prevailing at the time on the distant "terra incognita" of contemporary art and the art trade. We then shift the terrain of our research to the Far East in order to capture the autochthonous view of these relationships.

THE FAR EAST ON THE RADAR SCREEN OF THE WESTERN GALLERISTS

As was only to be expected, the supposedly lucrative siren call of the Chinese art market also stimulated the imagination of the Western art trade. Among the galleries represented in our survey at the Art Basel in Basel[2] globalization was already one of the dominant themes for the art dealers. We will now deal with some of the findings which seem relevant in this context.

The galleries take part in the Art Basel in Basel primarily for business reasons. The most frequent motives named in our Basel survey were "selling artworks" (95 per cent), "getting in contact with new clients" (88 per cent), and "presence of the main clients" (69 per cent). Only 15 per cent stated that the discovery of new artists or trends played a part. It is a well-known fact that art fairs have not only become an important sales channel for gallerists and art dealers; they also increase the renown and the reputation of the galleries. In the meantime a large part of their turnover is generated at art fairs. According to a study by the cultural economist

---

1 | Schultheis, Franz/Single, Erwin/Egger, Stephan/Mazzurana, Thomas, 2015: When Art meets Money. Encounters at the Art Basel. Cologne: Walther König.

2 | The survey of the galleries was carried out in 2012 during the Art 43 Basel by means of a written questionnaire. 96 gallerists took part in the survey, which amounts to about one third of the galleries represented at the fair.

Clare McAndrew it already amounted to 40 per cent in the year 2014.[3] All the interviewed galleries stated that they would reapply for admission to the Art Basel in Basel, three quarters (78 per cent) for the Art Basel Miami Beach, but only half (49 per cent) for the Art Basel in Hong Kong. The clear ranking of the relevance of the three locations demonstrates that for the entrepreneurial strategies the regional sub-markets do not have the same value. In addition, it is clear that in the expectations of these central actors of the art trade the new locations of the Art Basel on other continents are not of equal worth and cannot compete with the fair in Basel, which has been described as the "Olympics of Art" (New York Times). They are merely satellite positions occupied in the course of a globalization strategy of the Art Basel brand.

As far as the choice of the works presented by the interviewed galleries at the three different locations is concerned, three quarters made it dependent on the cultural environment and the expected public. For Basel as a chosen location the line taken is quite clear: "best possible works", "important works", "very strong pieces", "major 'museum-like' pieces", "international established artists", "artists with universal content", but also "high profile new works" and "new works/intellectually challenging" – that is to say: the "best of the best" for the "international clients" who travel in droves to this fair from all over the world. For the location at Miami Beach the emphasis is different, namely on art from the USA, but also "major South American art". The focus seems to be put more strongly on contemporary art and – as can be expected to some degree – on the stereotypes "colorful" or "colorful/big". In other words the hierarchical ranking of the three locations is also reflected in a more or less subtle differentiation of the symbolical capital representing "legitimate art". The competence and expertise of the public at the three fairs, which correlates with the length of time they have belonged to the elite of the art world and to the availability of symbolic capital is reflected here in an anticipatory diversification of the works exhibited in terms of their adequacy for the different publics.

As far as expectations in regard to the emerging art market in the Far East is concerned a relatively conventional mixture with Asiatic elements can be identified in the reactions of the interviewed gallerists.

---

3 | McAndrew, Clare (2015): Art Market Report 2015. Helvoirt: European Fine Art Foundation.

For the "Asian clients" and the "Asian market" they wish to present "local artists and modern art" which is less "conceptual" but rather "traditional" together with "brand names". The statement "nothing delicate or intricate" is already a clear indication that in Hong Kong – in comparison to the elitist Basel variant of the fair – the gallerists do not expect to encounter a public initiated in the spheres of a discerning and sophisticated love of art. Some gallerists also make no bones about the fact that the potential buyers belong to the category of new money instead of old culture. In other words a reserved and relativizing perspective of the Western actors in the art world is reflected here in regard to the transcultural contemporaneity of the love of art. This is reminiscent of the classical attitude of Western civilizations towards the economic, political and cultural developmental deficits of other regions of the world in comparison with their own one best way of occidental modernization and rationalization.

The exhibitors interviewed at the Art Basel participated to a high degree in other art fairs. Sixty five per cent of the galleries were represented with a booth at the Art Basel Miami Beach; the figures are somewhat lower for the direct competitors of the Art Basel: Frieze London (40 per cent), Frieze New York (34 per cent) and the Armory Show (32 per cent). The FIAC Paris also evidently plays a big role with a participation rate close to 40 per cent. But the greater the geographical distance to the traditional art fairs in Europe and the USA is, the lower the participation of the galleries represented at the Art Basel in the fairs. Only a few of the galleries interviewed have hitherto attended fairs in Latin America or Asia. One reason is that the majority of the galleries represented at the Art Basel come from Europe and the USA – in spite of the repeatedly proclaimed global character of the fair. In the year 2014 64 per cent of the galleries came from Europe, 28 per cent from North America and only 8 per cent from the rest of the world. Until its decision in 2011 to conquer the Asian market the Art Basel was committed only to a very modest extent to an East-West exchange. It seems instead to have been primarily interested in the marketing opportunities this financially strong region offered for the goods of the Western art trade.

Characteristically the gallerists and art dealers interviewed saw the factors which could influence the development of the art world mainly in the sphere of demand. In their opinion the future art market will be determined "very much" by new types of collectors (62 per cent) and new groups of buyers (59 per cent). To which geographical regions could this better apply than to South East and Eastern Asia? It is not, therefore, surprising that in the opinion of the interviewees the centers in the Far East would, above all, gain in importance in the global art market of the future, clearly led by Hong Kong (85 per cent), Shanghai (58 per cent) and Seoul (52 per cent). They also felt that the significance of Latin America would continue to increase, above all Sao Paulo (68 per cent) and Mexico City (46 per cent). Nevertheless, in the opinion of the gallerists interviewed, the hitherto predominant metropolises of the art world, New York, London and Paris will continue to be of extraordinary importance. The opinions expressed by the top gallerists represented at the Art Basel in Basel thus reveal a strikingly clear prognosis on future market developments, which clearly point to a shift in marketing opportunities from West to East.

The emerging geopolitical shifts in the world of art also directly affect contemporary art itself. The gallerists interviewed see the globalization of art as leading to an increasingly pluralistic notion of aesthetics (55 per cent) or expect a more powerful influence of aesthetics from the "emerging countries" (30 per cent). Only one in seven (14 per cent) of the interviewees believes in a continued dominance of Western aesthetics. This is also an eloquent testimony to the fact that the "big players" of the art market clearly expect fundamental cultural-aesthetical transformations as a result of the shifts in the market.

In the opinion of the gallerists interviewed these rapid and radical changes in the art world can also be seen as one of the central causes of the recent price increases for works of art. The dynamics behind the increases are regarded as being primarily driven by financial factors. "New groups of purchasers with high incomes" (49 per cent) and "capital investment and market speculation" bear "very much" responsibility. In addition the factor "the growing market power of auction houses" is frequently mentioned (39 per cent).

Significantly the interviewees, mostly US-American and European gallerists, emphasize that a high percentage of their customers do not attend art auctions. Here a purist feature of the "initiated" is evident, which sees a direct relationship between the collector and the galleries and artists: "gallery clients", "good" collectors "who only do primary market"; "many collectors only buy art on the primary market, 'clean art' that has come directly from the studio", "they prefer to buy at the gallery because they prefer to speak about what they purchase", they are "more involved, interested in both the artist and the work" and in addition they are "independently minded", "patient, knowledgeable & secure", all in all "serious!" and "uninterested in money games".

The ideal type of the gallery customer as a lover of art in the pure form depicted here contrasts sharply, however, with everything one could and should know from our survey of 2012 on collecting and purchasing behavior, the existence of art investment groups or art trusts and the blatantly commercial practices of the Chinese art market. After all the typology of the collector evoked by the questionnaire gives an absolutely clear picture of the polarities between "pure" love of art here and superficial appropriation of art and pure money matters over there: "art lovers, investors, prestige snobs". Although some of the ascriptions to types go into detail – for example contrast collectors who accompany an artist from the start, bank on upcoming artists or only invest in firmly established artists – the opposition between "commercially motivated" and "artistically motivated" remains all too clear. How far this dichotomy, be it implicit or explicit, can determine the assessment of the emerging Far Eastern market must for the moment remain an open question.

Another fundamental problem thematized in the survey of the gallerists in regard to this highly sensitive and atypical market for singular goods concerns the way in which the galleries assess the respectability of a new potential customer. Hints from professional art experts play the most important role in the answers given (48 per cent), old established customers are of similar importance (48 per cent) and other personalities from the art world are cited rather less frequently (41 per cent). Above all, however, the first and the second impression are decisive: "by having a personal conversation with the client", "from the seriousness of the conversation", "by intuitive confidence", or quite simply "if they have manners". So far, so good. But how do these strategies designed to create trust work in an alien cultural space, where "old established customers" can scarcely serve as references for largely unknown newcomers and a variety of problems – filters and barriers – set limits to intercultural communication involving intuition and empathy when business negotiations based on mutual trust are to be initiated?

To put it briefly: the picture arising from our representative survey of the top galleries represented at the Art Basel in Basel is highly ambivalent if not contradictory. As in the case of "territorial occupation" in distant continents by Western colonizers we are dealing with a mixture of very different and partly contrary sensitivities and motivational stances.

On the one hand we have the siren calls of the "treasures" and market opportunities waiting in the faraway world, which must be quickly seized upon, if the train into the future is to be caught on time. And on the other hand there are the uncertainties of an alien world, in which the customary rules of art encounter totally different cultural dispositions, so that, like Columbus, one is searching for India but must in reality be prepared to discover a different continent.

DIAGNOSES, PROGNOSES, PROPHECIES

What are the assessments and expectations with which the actors of the Western art world anticipate the future of the art market in the lands of the rising sun? Some answers can be found by looking in more detail at the statements made by the gallerists, collectors, curators and museum staff in the in-depth interviews when the conversation came round to the question of the situation of these emerging markets. In the talks held during the Art Basel in Basel in 2012 the topic of upheavals in the art market inevitably came up in view of the growing significance of the new markets, although the tone and the nuances of the contributions varied widely. All of the interviewees agreed that the Asiatic region would be a determining factor in the future global art market.

"THE MARKET OF THE FUTURE"

"That is the market of the future", the owner of a large Swiss gallery proclaimed. "There are figures which show how wealth will increase there or museums sprout out of the ground. The collectors guilds will grow and so it is absolutely necessary to go there. Absolutely! The art market has changed in the last five years. USA was in first place, Great Britain second. Ten years ago China's share in the global art market was around or under five per cent. Now, in 2011, China is the number one. Of the 10 biggest auction houses in the world seven are Chinese. And so it is only logical that Sotheby's and Christie's go to Hong Kong with their auctions."

On the increasingly apparent geo-political shifts in the art market the owner of a big German auction house states: "Ten years ago, I would say, 10 years ago London was the number one, the USA number two, and then for a long time there was nothing. Then came France. In the meantime the USA is number one and China is number two. Then there is nothing for a relatively long time. And then comes London. But we know that it is only a question of two or three years until Asia – I say roughly speaking Asia – is number one and New York is number two with a big drop after these two. If you observe these currents you have to react and I have to establish myself in Asia. But I don't believe that the Asians will let the Europeans or the Westerners take this market away from them."

Important players in the Western art market seem to be convinced that the big business in art commodities will definitively shift to Asia within a relatively short period of time. This also means that they will have to gain a foothold there in order to participate in the emerging market scene or they will have to abandon this business to the local actors. And so auction houses, gallerists and art dealers are going east, although the enthusiasm is subdued. "Now we are going to Hong Kong to the Art Hong Kong in two weeks time", a Swiss gallerist says. "This is a new field for us. So going global includes the Asian region. For us this is completely foreign territory. Up to now we have been oriented on the West and have built up a network here. I believe that a lot will now change. Everything will move a little bit more closely together."

A journalist and art critic distances himself from these sweeping interpretations and assesses the influence of these shifts in the market in a much more reserved way. "Of course there is a series of new collectors from the threshold countries. There have been collectors from China, Indonesia, South Korea, whereby everyone has actually said that the market is carried by the NATO states. If last year we had four Chinese instead of two, that is an increase of one hundred per cent, but that is still relatively few. And the markets are only in the process of developing. The Art Basel is now trying to offset this by setting up in Hong Kong from next year onwards. And from the NATO states there has certainly been a series of younger collectors. What made this year less strong, I believe, was the hedge-fund types who started investing in art on a large scale before the crisis of 2008 and then had to cope with consolidation. But I believe that at the moment art as a field of investment is still a bit too fluctuating for them. I have the impression that there are a lot of new collectors going around, but they are interested in building up collections and less in making short-term investments."

The statements of many interviewees express a kind of fatalistic acceptance of the apparently inevitable transformations, as in the case of a well-known London gallerist: "But, increasingly, the more adventurous collectors are coming over here and looking at Western art. You know there are 35 cities – I think it's probably changed now, this was a while back – with a population of over five million in China. And each of these cities in the next five to 10 years will have an art museum, I believe, a contemporary art museum. And when that happens it's natural."

"Luxury goods"

From the perspective of all the interviewees the future and already observable relocation of the global art market is a fait accompli and they are equally convinced that this process is and will continue to be accompanied by considerable ambivalence and contradictions. The interviewees provided differing accounts of the transfer difficulties involved in the import and export of symbolic goods across very divisive cultural borders. Many of the actors questioned pointed to the discrepancy between economic purchasing power and cultural competence in dealing with contemporary art, which they felt to be characteristic of this emerging market.

A big collector from Switzerland put it as follows: "Why has the interest in contemporary art become greater? Well my theory is, I believe but I don't know whether it is true, that in the last 15 years the number of big fortunes in the world has grown. But big fortunes have no tradition; the new ones that have arisen in the last 20 years have no tradition, but when these people have everything, car, dog, wife, house, bank account, ship, then at some time or other they want culture. Not perhaps because they are culturally interested, but because it is a status symbol, something that can be exhibited. And the easiest way for them to acquire culture is to buy a picture and to hang it on the wall at home. And it is a status symbol if the picture bears the name of an artist who is well-known. 'I have a Gerhard Richter. And you?' 'A John Currin, a Damian Hirst and Andy Warhol.' 'Wow, I have to buy it.' That's what happens and it happens worldwide, particularly through the auction houses. And because wealth has grown faster in the Asian Pacific region or is generally booming art from this region has suddenly become interesting. In the beginning it was the Europeans and Americans who exploited the situation. But now the main customers for Chinese, Indonesian and the other art are the local people, the rich people from the region."

The opinion of an Austrian museum director has a similar ring: "But of course these super-rich Asian and Chinese also want to fill their museums with the same classical modern works that fill the museums everywhere here in Europe and the USA. Filling the museums comes first." Here a well-known pattern of social distinction within the community of art lovers shines through, involving changing variations of the same theme of the opposition between "old money" and old cultural capital on the one hand and "new money" and social upward movement with cultural aspirations on the other – a pattern which is here converted into a West-East opposition within the global art world.

Typically the arguments are based on a kind of spontaneous social psychology of the class of the "nouveau riche", who attempt to underpin their claim to social status and legitimacy by demonstratively acquiring luxury goods, of which the most luxurious are works of art. Along these lines a London gallerist says: "You've seen how luxury goods can be acquired in every city in China now. There's a shopping mall, Louis Vuitton leading the way with a lot of other brands piggybacking on the back. Shopping malls have developed in every city, and all of these 35 cities have this focus on luxury goods. The natural next corollary with people of high net worth is to engage in looking at other ways to build up their assets, and contemporary art is certainly going to be an important asset field for Chinese investors in the future. I believe that they will naturally look to international art and not just their own."

This view, which is shared by other dialogue partners, seems to assume a kind of cultural evolutionary principle according to which it is only a question of time until the "nouveau riche" from the emerging countries who are searching to satisfy their desire for luxury goods "naturally" turn to the "higher" cultural goods of the art field – and "not only to their own" but also to internationally established art. A kind of transcultural or global model of elitist distinction is postulated, the one best way to become cultivated as practiced by the European upper classes, which will sooner or later be followed by all the other members of the transnational class of the economically privileged.

A Swiss art collector speaks in a similar fashion: "Formerly the big works disappeared to America and now they disappear to Asia. If I now think about India, for example, it will certainly take another decade until they enter the market. But these up and coming countries will certainly become important participants in the market. I'm convinced of that. Today the Chinese are buying luxury watches and in a few years it will be works of art. The art market is just as much affected by globalization as all the other markets, that is more than 100 per cent sure." In an analogous way an art critic analyzes the relationship between the new wealth and the awakening of a new love of art. "There is a new layer of very rich people who want art. Such a simple development always happens when someone begins to take an interest in art and this stage has been reached."

In other words the deficiency of a culture of collecting for the development of a primary market is deplored by many people. A Swiss gallerist puts it in a nutshell: "I have heard that Asian collectors at the moment either tend to buy Asian art or if they buy European, Western art they prefer blue chips, established artists with a reputation. They are less interested in wanting to discover very young artists."

"Asians love brands"

Again and again the Western actors we interviewed pointed out that their opposite numbers in the Asian region are at the moment still involved in a learning process which will enable them to catch up on a developmental deficit resulting from understandable specific socio-historical circumstances. "Of course they do not have the taste in art of our Western culture", a Swiss gallerist reports. "Where could it come from? The Chinese do not even have it in regard to their own culture. [...] Cultured people sometimes tend to show a certain degree of intellectual arrogance and of course it shows. [...] But if they want to do business they have to go there. And then they have to find out what the people there actually like, what they want to see. And they also have to offer them something."

In other words this gallerist advises his colleagues to "get off the high horse" of elitist Western cultural smugness and to show openness towards the developing competencies and needs of the newcomers in the Asian art market, as they did successfully three decades earlier with Japanese buyers. "There's a lot of money circulating, more people can afford art and more people have access to it, as the level of education is higher than in the past. One should not forget that all these upcoming countries do not possess European art. But they are now also entering the market. You can see this, for example, with the Japanese. They are willing to pay any price."

Another colleague, who also owns a well-known Swiss gallery, takes Turkey as an example for this process of catching up: "Perhaps I should add the following point: Why do you think the art market is now growing so rapidly in Turkey? Because the country is prospering; because there are rich people there, extremely rich people. And no museums, scarcely any museums. And the collectors dominate what happens there to an enormous degree. And they collect. And they inform themselves. They are very clever. They go to Europe and the USA and then art begins to take root in their own country. At first it is guided by Western norms but it develops further in a direction of its own. That can be ascertained very precisely." A Swiss collector explains the fledging collector culture in this region with the following words: "But it's fully clear that they are not in a position to judge a painting by Richter or somebody else from an artistic standpoint. [...] But they know that it is expensive. So there is a certain danger that the Asians will, how should I put it, buy art with a brand name. Because they want to be on the safe side."

"But with brands the case is clear: the Chinese or Asians love brands", another gallerist says. "They also enjoy just looking. But logically there are a few collectors who can afford it. There are more rich people there than anywhere else. That's true. I believe that when a gallery is active in this segment it's absolutely the right thing to do. They must take what they have with them. They deal in brands. And that is absolutely right. [...] There are other artists whose fame as a brand name exists outside our regions, for example Anselm Kiefer in Asia. That has to do with education. Artists see this Kiefer at a very early stage. Possibly they don't know anybody else to the left or right of him. He just happens to be a big hero right now. For example White Cube has organized a Kiefer exhibition. About 20 of his big paintings are hanging in the White Cube in Hong Kong. And around 10 of them deal with Mao. So Kiefer has actually rediscovered Mao. He had already produced several pictures in the 60s, 'Let a thousand flowers bloom' or something like that, and now he is taking it up again. It is quite a pitch for the market. I can't explain why nothing else occurred to someone like Kiefer. I simply can't explain it. Unless the White Cube suggested to him that this is the right choice. The Chinese will probably buy it. That's what I mean. There are a few brands, but they do not necessarily stand in the front row in our part of the world. If I wanted to get rich by investing in art here, I really wouldn't buy a Kiefer. There are also other brands. [...] The fact of the matter is that they like colorful stories. The further you penetrate into South East Asia, Indonesia and so on the art also becomes very colorful, very flowery and so on. It is then necessary to look for a Western artist who fits in with such a direction in taste."

In view of the lack of an autonomous culture of collecting, which has grown historically over a long period of time, and of the accompanying collector's habitus as an ensemble of aesthetic, intellectual and moral dispositions, the novices of contemporary art from the Far East must bank on safe values, that is to say values which have already found recognition in the market and in medial representations. As the newcomer does not possess a kind of gyro-compass enabling him to take his bearings autonomously with the help of his own competence, he is guided by a radar screen which captures and displays the relevancies and conventions predominant in the relevant social environment. He is not "inner directed" but "other-directed" as the American sociologist David Riesman would put it. It is interesting to note that such judgments are also made by interviewees from the West who themselves are not at all acquainted with the East Asian region in general or its art market in particular. Accordingly we are dealing with speculation and projections on the basis of the domestic context of current patterns of thought and interpretation. And we can assume that here the customary stereotypes about the type of collector termed "nouveau riche" deriving from the familiar local context and its competitive struggles as to what can be regarded as genuine collecting are simply converted into an ethnocentric blanket (pre-)judgment.

"Very much market oriented"

At the same time there are regular references in the dialogues to the fundamental contextual differences between the Western art field and its typical institutions and professional actors, which are the product of long-term historical growth, and the emerging, very much market oriented art world in the East. "I regard it as an operation system for art, that's the way I see it all" is the description of the art world given by one collector. "It consists of a network comprising the collector, the gallerist, the artist, the museum or the institution, the art critic, the auction house. I see the whole as an operating system. Here in the West it is highly developed and everyone plays his part. But in China, for example, this has only evolved in the last 15 years; it was totally rudimentary before that; there were only artists. Of course we are always speaking about contemporary art. There were two or three magazines with art critics, but there were no galleries and no institutions which showed contemporary art. Fundamental elements which define the system here did not exist. It was a system sui generis. It has of course developed further, but in contrast to the system in the West, which is perhaps halfway balanced out, in China it is very much market oriented and is dominated by auction catalogs and auction houses, because the balance we have is simply lacking, for example independent art criticism, and institutions which have exhibited contemporary art for a long time and have a certain tradition in this respect. On account of this the two markets are differently constituted."

In other words, according to the accounts of these Western collectors it is absolutely evident that in view of a massive socio-historical delay in the development of autonomous structures of the art field in these Asian regions and of the lack of a well-functioning network of relevant institutions they cannot be expected to catch up with the Western game of art and its rules within a very short period of time. This applies specifically to the aspect of the very weakly developed gallery culture, which is the core of the operating system in the occidental field of modern and contemporary art.

Asked for his judgment on the reason why a completely different importance is attributed to auction houses in China and why they enjoy more trust and credibility than galleries one collector answered: "This difficulty will disappear in the course of time as the galleries are visibly taking over a similar role to the one they have here. This role simply did not exist earlier, as the galleries could not do anything for the artists in China. For a long time the artists were not able to exhibit their works, on account of the censorship and so on. A gallery, if it had existed, would not have been able to organize exhibitions or publish catalogs; every catalog has a book number which can only be acquired officially. But this was simply impossible in the case of contemporary art. And so the artist said 'Why do I need a gallery at all, basically I have to do everything myself anyway'. And this has led the artists to sell their works themselves. I have bought 90 per cent of my collection directly from the artists themselves. This generation of the 80s and 90s, who are now perhaps around 50, are still accustomed to sell their works themselves, or now perhaps through a gallery or even several galleries, or themselves. [...] They still know the tradition of the times when the gallery only played a marginal role. Nowadays it can perhaps round off or increase purchases, but the artist still believes that he himself does it best. But the younger artists already cooperate increasingly with galleries. More and more galleries from the West are indeed introducing the Western custom of the exclusive contract, the anchoring in the market. In the course of time the systems will converge but the auction houses are still more important there than they are here, and the trust in the galleries is not the same as it is here. The Chinese buyer believes in the pricing of the auction houses, although he himself cheats most of all. He cheats the most. But he believes in publicly visible pricing. And vice versa he believes that the gallerist tells him one thing and me something completely different. That is why the tendency to do a lot of buying at auctions still exists. It is often the case that he only gathers information, further information from the catalogs. If the big museums haven't organized an exhibition, then they also haven't acquired a certain visibility. They then see it in the catalog, write a text about it and he reads it. That's why they carry particular weight, greater than here."

"Don't trust them"

Incidentally, the criticism expressed here about some of the business practices in the Asian region also applies to the behavior of some art buyers, as is shown by the account of a German auctioneer: "The problem is: don't trust them. That is always the case. The worst payers we have in the branch are the Chinese. It's very risky to do business with them. And the provisos and thumbscrews we use are in the meantime hard, very hard. They have to deposit a quarter of the estimated price in cash in advance. They have to submit two credit cards and the like. So it's very interesting to see the way the market there is changing and shifting."

A gallerist in Switzerland also sees the dominance of the auction houses in the Asian context of art collecting as a key explanation of the striking difference to developments in the West: "If we think about the Asian region, and above all as far as mainland China is concerned, we must realize that, from the perspective of the tradition and history of contemporary and even modern art as we understand it, a start was made only about 30 years ago. That was with the departure of Mao Zedong and the takeover by Deng Xiaoping, with the opening up; it was only then that contemporary art actually began slowly to reach Asia and China through various information channels. That means that there were no collectors of contemporary art; this was something completely new. There were probably people who were interested, on the margins. It is interesting that, in contrast to the Western world, the one or the other collector there whom we would describe as a collector came to be a collector through the auction market. He got his information and did his buying there and not in the galleries, but first of all through auctions. That has something to do with mentality. As people lacked the information they took their guidance from auctions; they felt safe there. It has nothing to do with prices, whether they say that's realistic, 100 or 15 is realistic. But they have seen people there, a lot of people, all of them make offers, and they have known one or the other. They have seen how a price comes about. It doesn't matter how high or unrealistic the price was, for them it was real. And they shied away from going to galleries, well, because they didn't know how the price came about or what it meant. But it was really fascinating to observe how many of today's collectors have come into the primary market."

Overall it seems as if such Western observers of the more recent developments in the Far East art market show a great deal of understanding for aspects which tend to fill art lovers and collectors of the old school with consternation and explain everything again and again according to the pattern of delayed development and catch-up learning processes. Some of the interview partners speak of already observable progress in the Asian collectors' community. As one collector from Switzerland explains: "Among themselves the collectors don't necessarily put their cards on the table. They're so very ambitious. Gradually they no longer only want to buy brands; they also buy for investment reasons, as it has at all events been drilled into them that art is a good investment. But now they want to start differentiating; slowly they have reached the point here they don't want to have the same collection as other multi-millionaires. The differentiation is now setting in."

One aspect of the frequently demanded tolerance towards newcomers to the market is the acceptance of the eclecticism regarded as typical of the Chinese approach to contemporary art. As a museum director from Austria observes: "Of course it is in part extremely eclectic, particularly for Chinese art. But of course this eclecticism also produces something completely new. Whether we as Europeans are interested or not in this is a completely different matter."

In the opinion of one auctioneer such eclecticism typically comes into play in the Chinese context in the interaction of two different co-existing types of collector and motives for collecting: "This market in the Far East has developed over the last 12 to 15 years. The situation is the same with the nouveau riche in China, in South Korea, in Indonesia; they all want to be served on their own doorstep. So the gallerists take a specific program with them when they go to Hong Kong. Of course this other tradition exists there, which is much more calligraphic in character, pays much more attention to craftsmanship. Here one of the driving forces was to destroy, and to eliminate tradition, to set oneself apart. But it's just the other way round in Asia. There imitation is quite important. This produces a different mentality, another way of looking at art. But now, since the end of the 80s in China, a completely new generation has arisen which is well informed about what is happening in the West and uses this knowledge to formulate its own interests. So there are many different layers. It is said that in China a large part of the market is still traditionally orientated and that a large part of Chinese art is bought by foreigners. But this is changing with the younger generation which is now earning money. In Korea and India similar processes are taking place. The Western orientation has perhaps gone furthest in Korea."

A collector from Switzerland observes: "This means that the artists know the strategies developed in the West in order to create art, but combine them with their own tradition and attempt to formulate their own interests." And he continues: "But it is absolutely clear, of course, that contemporary art went through a phase in China when it had to be set in motion. Of course it copied, of course it looked at what was being done in the West. On the other hand perhaps the third generation of Chinese artists is in the meantime working, and they are working very differently; they are people who produce really excellent works. And, of course, as is the case everywhere else, 80 per cent of Chinese art is total rubbish. Fifteen per cent is far too expensive and 5 per cent is good. But it's the same here too. But here in the West the process of selecting starts a little earlier. And that is the problem."

A big Western collector goes on about the emerging young collectors' community in the East as follows: "Japan, Korea and Taiwan have been collecting for a long time; they have knowledge, are sophisticated. And then there are the new countries, Indonesia, China, above all, and also Hong Kong and Singapore. They have collectors as well, but only a small number, who formerly collected traditional works and perhaps some contemporary art. But most of these collectors are not sophisticated; they have only become active very recently. The collector I regard as the biggest collector in Asia didn't even know what art is six years ago. And within six years he has spent hundreds of millions. [...] There are only a few well-known collectors in Japan who have some understanding of art. The same is true of South Korea where there are a couple who have been involved for a long time. In Taiwan there are very sophisticated collectors who go about it differently. They collect in the same way as we do, gather information, hold lots of conversations and then finally decide. Whereas the others take advice from gallerists and so on. There are also some who are resistant to advice and simply buy out of a gut feeling. The behaviour is different from here. And new money behaves differently from old money, rather flashy so the visitor sees and immediately knows that's a Warhol. But when I buy something which I like but which nobody takes any notice of, then I've defeated the purpose of it all. Status is very important in Asia, appearances are of central importance, much more so than here."

"THE ASIAN HAS NEVER LEFT HOME"

These statements are a mixture of seemingly sociological explanations of the delayed developments in collecting practices in the Far East based on the argument of the late appearance of Western cultural patterns on the Eastern scene and cultural stereotypes postulating collective characteristic features and ethno-psychological properties. These include the notion of a long period of splendid isolation in Chinese art history, which a Swiss gallerist describes in the following words: "It's always been like this. It has something to do with exchange, which has a long history here in the West, I would say. It always sounds a bit stupid when we say, 'Here in the West'. I mean the centuries old habit of going out into the world to look for something; the Chinese have never done that. The Asian has never left home. He was never anywhere else, has never colonized the other side of the world, never, never. He has never gone out. But if you never go out or get any information, then you are stuck with, I would say that I am stuck with my present knowledge. And if nothing exceptional occurs, no inspiration or information comes, then I always stay, probably always, where I am."

But over and beyond the generally admitted historical delay in development, it is possible to consider the path taken by Asia into the world of contemporary art as a kind of special route with an kind of accelerated dynamics which paradoxically modernizes the global art market, as a Swiss gallerist explains in an interview, taking India as an example: "Well I have a very good friend who owns the second or third largest auction house in India. India has never experienced an entire epoch of the art market – the so-called market for contemporary art. And this is similar to the situation when China entered the communications market 10 years ago. They didn't have to install copper cables or telegraphs or the like. They skipped over entire developmental epochs and jumped directly into the mobile market. There is no in-between any more. You skip over entire stages. You don't buy any old weaving looms; instead you buy modern, computer-controlled production machinery. In a new country, or on a continent in which this kind of art is new, the path taken is rather similar. The entire artist-buyer relationship and the invitations to bid and this and that and being interested all disappears. And it is increasingly the case that an investor is looking for an equity. And there is an artist who has a 100 works that are good, but has sold none or only very few. And the investor says, 'I'll buy'. The artist also knows, because he is also participating in this race, that when this gallery or this promoter buys up his current stock, then it will be for a very low price. So I buy a hundred pictures for 50,000 Swiss francs and sell them for two million. I have made a big profit, conducted a huge promotional campaign, promoted the artist, and when he has reached the top, sold his works. At the next encounter the artists' starting price is much higher. So one doesn't pay 50,000 Swiss francs for the next hundred works; they go for three million francs. That is probably the future."

This narrative casts an interesting light on radical processes of change in the entire art field and its rules which may possibly have the emerging regions of the global art market as their starting point. Because these regions entered the world of modern art at a late stage, remained largely uninfluenced by its more than a hundred years-long history and did not have to overcome the burden of historically evolved obstacles and barriers standing in the way of the assertion of pure marketing principles and commercialization in the field of art, they were in a position to practice the buying and selling of art unashamedly as business just like any other business. And in view of the enormous market power of these players on the field of contemporary art, the rules of the entire game are changing: business as unusual is now obviously possible and has even become the order of the day.

"THERE IS ONLY ONE SINGLE PLACE"

Beyond all possible divergencies and nuances in the ongoing or prospective development of art in these economically so very important regions all the actors of the Western art field interviewed in 2012 agreed that with the establishment of the Art Basel in this area optimal conditions will be created for its connection with the global art market.

On being asked how the establishment of the Art Basel in Hong Kong should be assessed a Swiss gallerist, for example, answered: "That's the most important thing. They are now the Gagosian of the art fairs. There's only one place in Asia where you can organize a fair and that is Hong Kong. It has the bureaucratic infrastructure. It has the freedom, the artistic freedom. Although it is not a democracy it is one somehow. It is under the rule of law. In all other cities you can forget that. It's not even the case in Singapore. Singapore can react very allergically if something false is depicted or presented. People always forget that. I mean, it's quite nice to have a fair in Abu Dhabi. But I couldn't bring half of my pictures there. That's a joke! And then it's closed because the Sultan happens to be visiting the fair. I mean, anyone who wants to should take part. But it is certainly right to go into the Asian region."

"It's the centre", a colleague from London adds, "it's the focal point of the hub of art dealing in that whole region around, when one looks at Taiwan, Indonesia, Korea, and mainland China. I'd love to be in mainland China as well. And at some point we may venture into mainland China, but it's very prohibitive to be there because of the protectionist tax regime that they have there for importation of artwork. I think Hong Kong has a wonderful trading history; so it's a great place to do business. It's pretty much a tax-free zone. It's accessibility to these other regions and territories make it very attractive. Personally, also, it used to be a British colony; I lived there for a little bit, I know Hong Kong. I feel very engaged by the place, and so for personal reasons I thought it would be interesting to be there. But, obviously, the professional reasons override that. But it's clear to me that mainland China is going to be a huge marketplace in probably five to 10 years' time."

Nobody makes the point that Hong Kong is also significant as a site of artistic production or that there are other good reasons for implanting a future metropolis of the global art world here apart from purely commercial ones, for example, the existence of the framework conditions necessary for the smooth functioning of market activities.

For a Swiss big collector only economic reasons apparently count: "First of all Hong Kong is extremely well suited logistically for this Asian-Pacific region. Secondly it is a free port. Thirdly the control over taxes, import and turnover taxes et cetera et cetera is not so strict, at least not at the moment. And that is the future market. There are after all figures showing how greatly wealth will increase there, how museums are sprouting up out of the earth. The collectors' guilds will also grow and that's why one has to go there. One simply has to!"

In various interviews the actors were concerned that the blatantly commercial orientation of an art fair which presents itself in Europe as the Grand Old Dame of the art market and claims to be a high culture event might put off some of their usual customers. When asked what she thought of the new art branches in Miami Beach and now in Hong Kong a gallerist from Central Switzerland answered: "To be honest, I don't really have an opinion about them. I move around too little and don't know enough about this market. Honestly, I don't find Miami so fantastic. But my perspective just happens to be different. Perhaps it's necessary in order to remain the leader in Basel. But to me it sounds a bit like Guggenheim or McDonald's, whom you can find everywhere. Personally I don't think it is so good."

Her colleague from Vienna is even more critical: "I'm not at all familiar with the Asian region. I seldom travel there because I have the feeling I am an imperialist and a colonist when I travel there, because I haven't a clue about these countries, so why should I travel to them? I understand nothing and then I attend some fair or other there. What's the use of that? If I went somewhere I would have to stay for weeks and decide whether the culture interests me or not, think about what it produces, what it does and how it does it. But I don't have the time because there are simply so many other fields that interest me. There are specialists in this area who can do it and I admire them and find it super, but I believe that you can't have too many irons in the fire. So I must say that I'm a little bit out of my depth with this globalization."

A Swiss big collector answered the same question as follows: "It's clear to me that I don't have to go to an Indian fair yet. I don't understand it all. I take a look and what I see are extremely colorful pictures. But I would never say, 'That is rubbish'. But I'm too far away. In order to understand things here and to cope with them takes up a good part of my time, attempts to understand and comprehend them. So how should I do that in India?"

MIND MAPS: THE NEW WORLD MAP OF ART IN THE MINDS OF WESTERN ACTORS

So much on this mixture of different statements on the shifts in the map of the art market towards the East. All of the interviewees agreed unisono that in the future there will be a considerable and long-lasting shift of the market scene in the trade with art from the current metropolises in North America and Europe towards Asia, and particularly to the emerging hubs of the Chinese art market like Hong Kong. All of the interview partners are looking expectantly, either hopefully or skeptically, at the new world map of art, which, after the expansion and shift from Europe to the USA after the Second World War, now indicates an equally profound drift towards the emerging market in the East. There is also substantial agreement on the causes of this dynamics, as interview partners from all spheres of the Western art field point again and again to the factor new money or the existence of new groups of buyers. All speak of the drawing power or pull effect of this growth potential for the Western art trade and its big players. And it is invariably pointed out that they have already won a foothold in the region or are in the starting blocks and want to, or even must, take advantage of all the marketing opportunities there, if they are not to abandon them to the actors in the Far East and particularly to the local auction houses.

At the same time there was a broad consensus on the assessment of the specific features of the booming Chinese art market, which is animated by potential customers with little experience but all the more financial power. This is accompanied by the equally widespread opinion that there is a certain vacuum in this flourishing market place for art in regard to institutions and to actors who decisively determined the history of modern art in the West. In comparison to the Western metropolises the Eastern markets are characterized by a notable absence of galleries, curators, art critics or museums.

Here the picture emerges of a region which is only slightly developed, if not even under-developed, in regard to contemporary art, whereby one the one hand, a rapid catching up process can be observed (with frequent reference to the booming development of private museums in mainland China) but, on the other hand, a completely different dynamics of art reception and art collection arises on account of the asynchrony between an art market with a high turnover and the weakly developed structures of the field of art mediating institutions.

From the point of view of our interview partners this is expressed in a stronger market orientation of the buyers and the priority of auctions as a result of the hitherto weak development of a gallery system. However, for Western observers the asynchrony scarcely seems to present a problem, as the majority see the region as an open terrain for the actors in the art market established in the West, a terrain full of attractive marketing opportunities which cannot be taken advantage of without the corresponding pioneer spirit. In none of the statements we recorded on developments in the East was there any expression of expectations or hope in regard to meeting artists or their art there or of finding the traces of a foreign culture and aesthetics. There was no mention of curiosity or the chance to discover unknown forms of artistic expression, not even in connection with the planned Art Basel in Hong Kong, at which, according to the organizers, half of the galleries would come from countries in Asia ranging from Turkey to Australia. No mention was made of the possibility that this interface at the future hub in Hong Kong could facilitate the exchange between two cultural spheres and lead to a reciprocal import-export of art. Nor did any of the interview partners see an opportunity to revitalize the domestic market with the fresh blood of young contemporary Asian artists or to win marketing chances for them among collectors in the West. The insights gathered in the interviews on the standpoints of the Western actors of the art world confirmed the impression that a territorial occupation of faraway continents was being undertaken as in the times of classical colonization. And its primary purpose was to be the conquest of sales markets.

The scenarios projected in 2012 in regard to the Art Basel in Hong Kong are similar to the model of the current luxury goods market in which the fetishes reflecting the distinguished and approved taste of social elites in the West are offered to the upcoming new moneyed class of this distant region as proven signs of the social branding of privileged classes.

In times of a generalizing narration about global art and the contemporaneity of the creators of art in all countries and cultures it is all the more astounding that so little interest is expressed here in the new opportunities for artistic and cultural exchange and that there is no awareness of the chances the emerging market for art in the East opens up for emerging fields of art production and the supply of symbolic goods in an East-West transfer. We conclude our survey of the perspectives of Western actors in the art world on the proclaimed expansion of the market with these impressions of a rather one-sided conception of exchange and change the perspective by presenting the views of their Eastern counterparts in order to comprehend their view of the ongoing transformation of the art world. As stated at the beginning of this chapter, the following quotations derive from interviews carried out locally in Hong Kong, Beijing and Shanghai in the context of our research project.

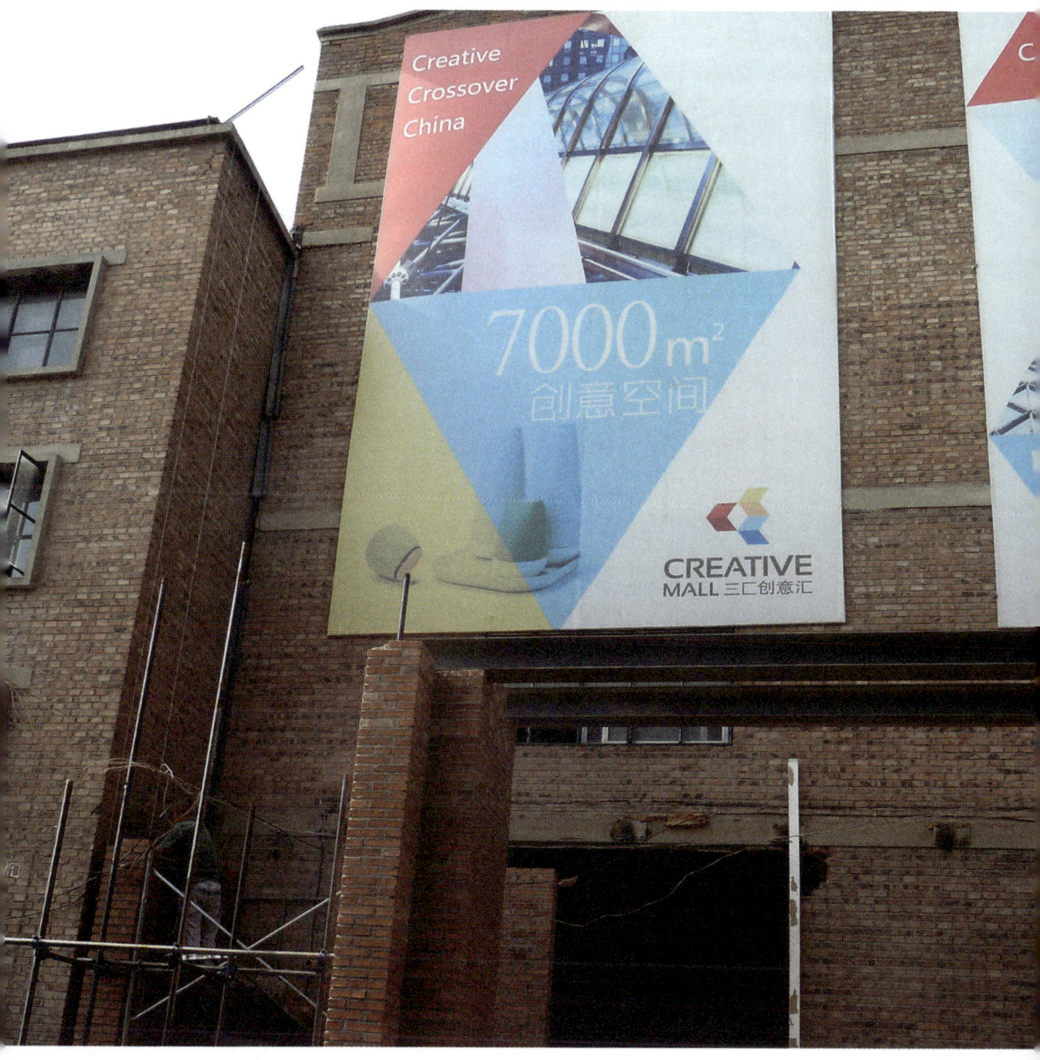

Creative
Crossover
China
7000 m²
创意空间
CREATIVE
MALL 三仁创意汇

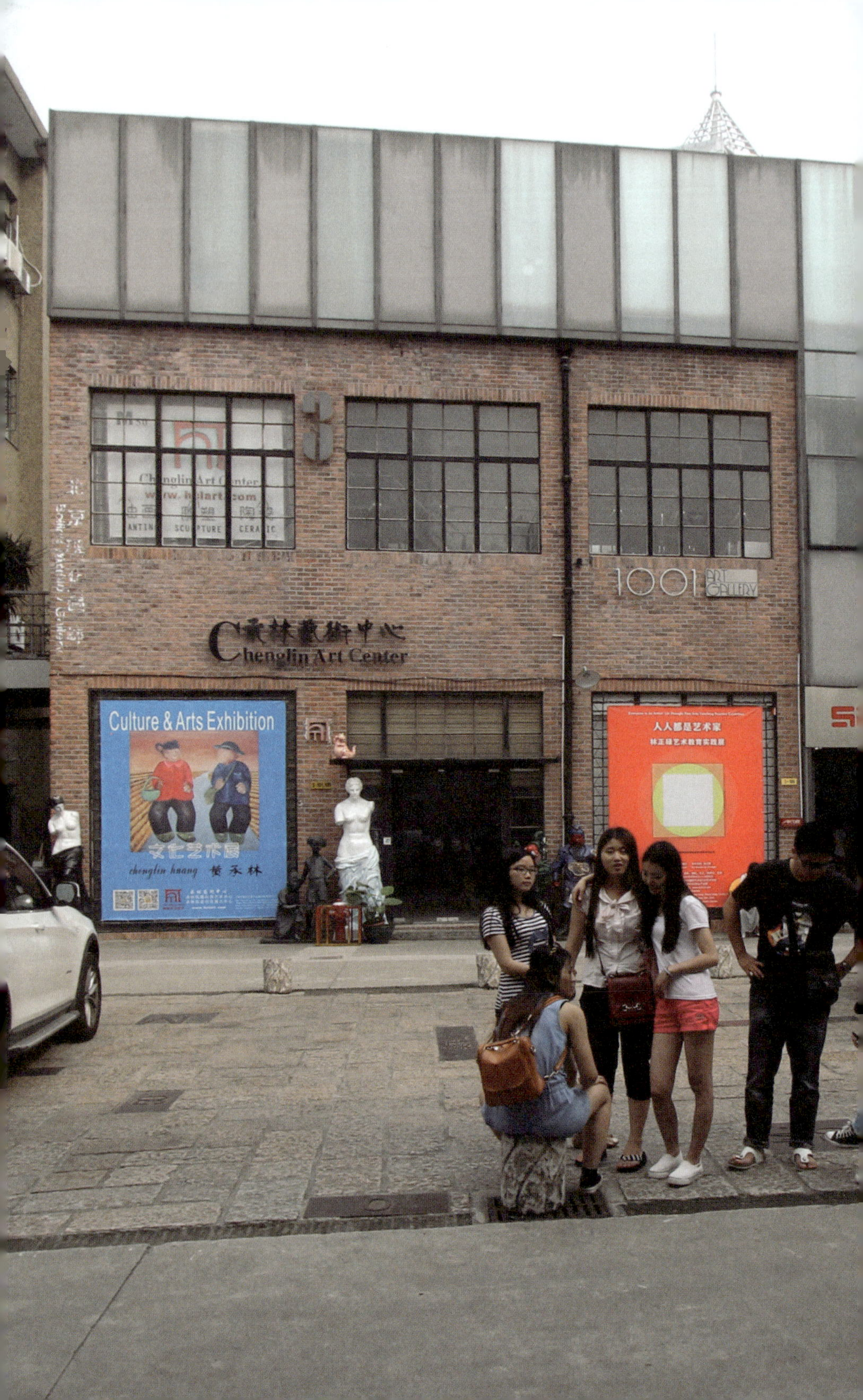
Chenglin Art Center
www.hslart.com
Chenglin Art Center
Culture & Arts Exhibition
chenglin huang
1001
人人都是艺术家
林正禄艺术教育实践展

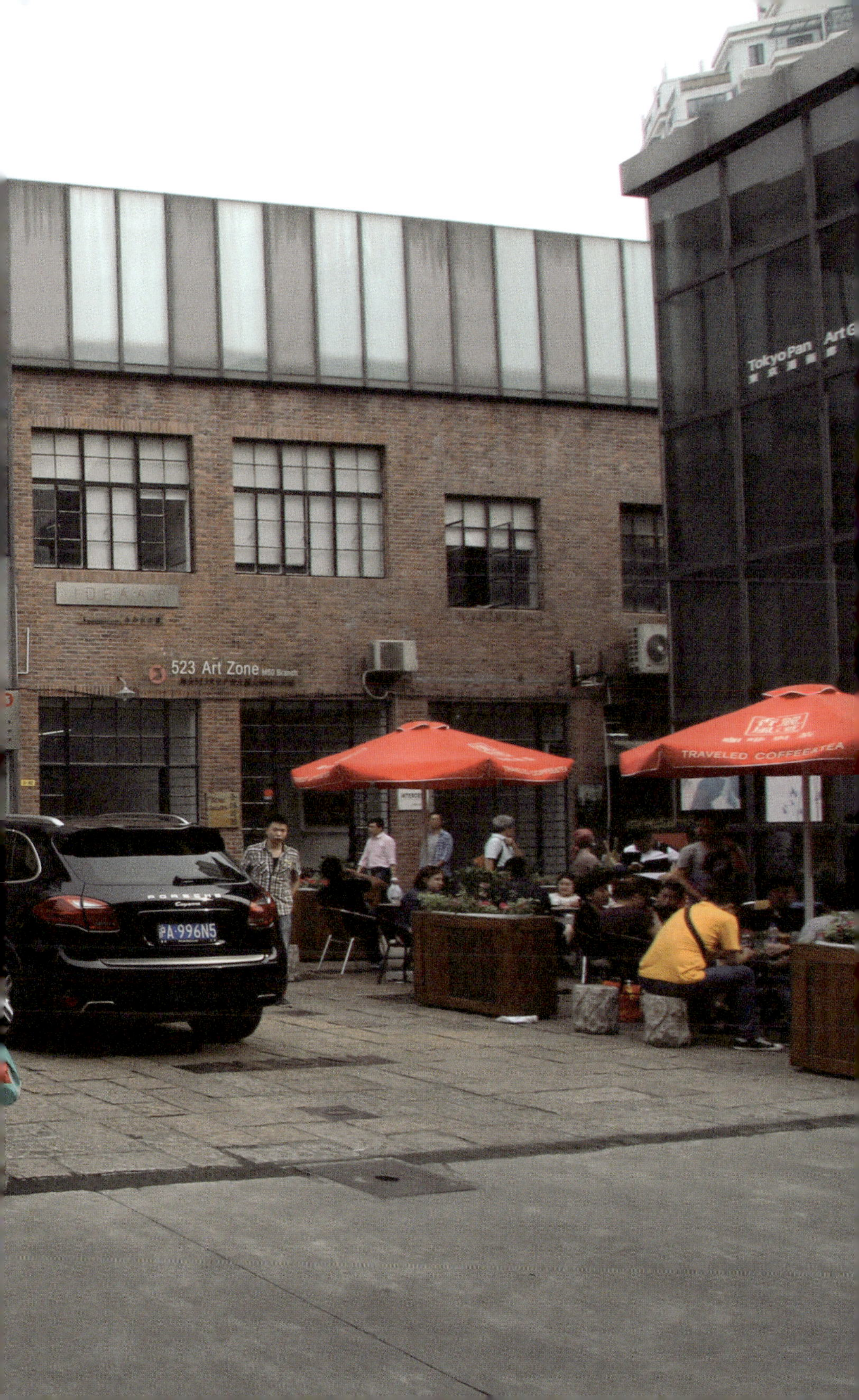

523 Art Zone M50 Branch
TRAVELED COFFEE&TEA
PORSCHE
Cayenne
A·996N5
Tokyo Pan Art

Voices from an emerging art field

"Too much of an emphasis on the commercial"

A talk with Ming Ming
Gallerist/Collector, Shanghai

Ming Ming represents a young generation of gallerists and collectors in China at the time of the opening up of the country to the outside world and the accompanying rapid economic, social and cultural changes. The Around Space Gallery is one of the most influential galleries in Shanghai. It was founded in 2006 by Ming Ming together with her long-time partner Jeff Zou, an important collector of contemporary Chinese art who lives in the USA. For more than 10 years the couple has concentrated on the promotion and collection of Chinese contemporary art. Their first group exhibition, which included well-known artists such as Mao Yan, was already a big success.

Whoever visits the gallery is impressed. The rooms are on the fourth floor of a mansion built in the 1930s for a bank, which has been converted into a representative office building. It is situated in a road intersecting the Bund. They had resided before in Moganshan Road, the well-known M50 art district of Shanghai. When Around Space opened there was virtually no market for contemporary Chinese art in China. As with many other things in China, this has radically changed.

The gallery focuses primarily on artists of Ming Ming's generation, the third generation after "Chairman Mao's" Cultural Revolution, who were born after 1980. There are numerous innovative and versatile artists among them, for whom galleries such as the Around Space Gallery are a reason for optimism. Their works differ distinctly from the majority of the colorful, sometimes garish and cartoon-inspired exhibits of their colleagues in other galleries, who have shaped the image of Chinese contemporary art among the general public. Their works are "more peaceful and plain" as Ming Ming puts it, but partly also avant-gardist in the classical sense. In the early years Around Space presented, above all, experimental artists and video art – art which can otherwise seldom be seen in China. Today emerging and more established artists are predominant.

Ming Ming was born in Nanjing and studied graphic design at the Nanjing Art Institute. In 2003 she moved to Shanghai. She worked for several years for English media companies before she founded Around Space. For her a gallery is not a supermarket, as are many galleries in China, which she compares with stores which are only interested in a flourishing business. "I don't want to change my standard or follow something just because of these kinds of reasons."

She is primarily interested in promoting contemporary Chinese art, thereby redefining and reinterpreting traditional Chinese aesthetics. She is especially interested in supporting "art without boundaries" which encourages young artists to eliminate the difference of national identities while they are creating art. Most of these artists of the "third generation" studied in the USA or Europe and then returned to China. Their works no longer have a purely Chinese identity. Ming Ming and Jeff Zou endeavor to combine them with European artists of the same age, not last in order to bring them closer together.

According to Ming Ming, rapid changes in the art field in China are visible everywhere. The Chinese art scene has become clearly more international. Ming Ming complains, however, about the poor quality of many artists and their work. For collectors like herself and her partner it has become more difficult to find suitable works. For this reason she began a few years ago to add to her collection the works of artists who were not exclusively Chinese. The prices for contemporary Chinese art have also risen sharply. But after years of unexampled growth the Chinese art market is now in a corrective phase. "We've been buying art with our ears, not with our eyes", Ming Ming sums up, "there has been too much of an emphasis on the commercial."

*What is the program and
the philosophy of your gallery?*

Our gallery is almost eight years old now. The first two to three years we focused on quite experimental art, video art installation, and when we moved to the Bund area, our artists changed a little bit. Now we focus more on emerging, as well as more established artists. That is our change in the past eight years. I have a partner, who used to live in Los Angeles. He is also Chinese and started collecting Chinese contemporary art in 1999, actually for the last 10 to 15 years he has collected almost all the famous names in China. Around 2000, there was almost no market in China for Chinese contemporary art. His family has a big collection of works from China and Western fine arts. Also at that time, Chinese art pieces were worth just a few thousands of dollars; this is also why he bought so many pieces. During these 15 years, he didn't sell any piece in auctions. He still keeps all his collection, even now when the prices are very high. In 2006, we started working together on the space of this gallery. Why I mention that is because the first show of this gallery was actually his collection. Also at the beginning we asked ourselves, what is the standard. And the first standard is that all the artists, their works, their insight must be related to Chinese tradition, philosophy and culture. Because we did Chinese contemporary art. We still keep our collection, we still buy a lot of things, even for every artist I represent; I already collected their art before. It helps me to talk to collectors, because I also really appreciate this artist. We keep the collection, people ask what is the standard of the collection, now the standard is time.

*What are the characteristics
of Chinese contemporary art?*

Chinese contemporary art has a very short history compared to Western contemporary art; it is only about 30 years. And in the first 10 years, most Chinese contemporary artists got deep influences from Western art pieces. Concept is quiet important for contemporary art. But this part in China is not so strong and not good enough to compare with international artists. What is much more valuable and unique for me is the Chinese philosophy. How they express our philosophy in our own language could be the most important reason to collect Chinese contemporary art. Each collection is dependent on the influence of the collectors' generation. Our society has changed a lot in the past 15 years. I am not sure when your first trip to China was because I am 35 now, and when I grew up, it was a totally different place. Even 10 to 15 years ago it was very different. You can't imagine how big the changes are. In the first generation of Chinese contemporary art, as you can find it as part of the collection at the Long Museum here in Shanghai, the pieces are related to political themes. People couldn't get their rights and were in very poor living conditions. So they tried to fight against the government in their way. So the pieces are more storytellers. And the second generation is artists who were born in the 1970s, so their works are more concerned about the human being, the common society and reality, maybe it is just my opinion. And the third generation is the 1980's or 1990's generation and their works are more related with the digitalization and technology. You will see more pieces that are similar to the work of Western young artists.

Now the gallery focuses on the second generation and also a little bit on the third generation. The second generation is quite stable, they don't have experience of the Cultural Revolution so they don't really love Chairman Mao, while they don't really hate Chairman Mao either. They don't have this kind of experience. And also the older artists, most of them, just like me, when we were very young, we studied calligraphy, I studied calligraphy for more than 15 years, people of a similar age to me, they all studied it; it is just like

a tradition, your grandfather teaching you this. Everybody has the traditional part in their blood, even though you cannot see it directly from the visual part but underneath it is more peaceful, closer to Zen, this philosophy is still in those artists' minds. That is the standard by which we choose most of our artists, not visually strong, not really colorful. A lot of Chinese visitors come to my gallery and tell me that my gallery is more peaceful and plain, not about a lot of color. Because if you visit other galleries, I think they are different from this. And the second standard is that we focus more on the so called no border artist, to connect with the third generation. Most of the third generation has studied abroad. They had their education in Europe or in America and then they come back and become teachers or professors, as Europeans do, so their works have no Chinese identity, but the two standards are mixed.

What was the motivation for you and your partner to collect art or contemporary art?

Actually we feel less excited about Chinese contemporary art. It is true. A few years ago, we started collecting not only Chinese art for our own collection but Japanese and Indian too. There are only a few creative and unique Chinese pieces of very high quality. So for our gallery this year I only did four exhibitions. To be honest, I want to present only the good part of Chinese contemporary art. I try my best to compare with similar-aged European artists, I mean a similar generation. After many years I think there are many artists who have no identity or language, and are without any background. Based on this standard there are not so many good pieces that you can find in most galleries. We have a saying in Chinese: "Same people always go to the same room", so you might find someone to communicate with. When I want to work with an artist I will watch him or her for at least one or two years. And also I will collect his or her work, then we do the exhibition. In China everything is changing so fast. My sister lives in New York. She interviewed Marian Goodman and all these Chelsea galleries. Marian Goodman's owner told her that when they prepare for the artist the plan is 10 to 15 years. But in China the artists just want to have an exhibition, want to be rich and get fame without any patience. In China my plan is three to five years for a young artist, I cannot make sure for 10 to 15 years later because it is changing so fast and you must balance the speed. Another concern is the price. To be honest, Chinese young artists' prices are much higher than those of young Japanese or young Indians. There is also another thing to think about. For example, for one piece by a Chinese artist I could buy two or three Indian pieces. Or even Vietnamese or Thai. We already collaborated with a gallery in Kyoto because our cultures in these thousand years were really close. And also in Kyoto people don't consider a number of artists such as Yayoi Kusama as really Japanese artists. They think they are Western, Western standard, so they also really want to keep their traditional culture, which is not very contemporary. But now what I am thinking about art is that after many years there is just a small part that could touch you and you could remember. I know contemporary art could not be put together with traditional art. Sometimes they even have conflicts, maybe contemporary art sometimes is not even an art piece. But we really like to put contemporary pieces with classical pieces and to see the dialogue between them. Maybe for this gallery, because we also have our own collection, for the gallery the standard is mostly contemporary art but then for the inside, it is closer to the culture and the philosophy. I think this is what people could remember even after 100 years.

How do your collectors respond to this philosophy? What kind of collectors do you have?

Just as I said, that Chinese saying, that the same people will find the same people. I always say it depends only on how unique one person is. At the beginning, not a lot of people appreciated it or understood it. I have a very good collector from Basel, actually he is Austrian but born in Switzerland. His job is not really close to art. He never bought Chinese contemporary art and his first piece is from here. And also we have one client from the German Consulate and others from the Spanish and Swiss Consulate. From my experience all these kinds of people, they have quite an open mind and a high education level and focus on culture and philosophy, so this part will be easy to communicate. Also they have been in China for a couple of years. They won't take these colorful dragons home from China. They will buy a kind of tea, it is a white tea, you may think it is not typically Chinese. Most Europeans or Americans, they have an image about China from Chinatowns, such as red lamps, or the Great Wall from a certain movie, but it is not the real China.

For example, some collectors, after checking a piece, will always decide to think about it. Sometime I will wait for a year for their decision to finally buy it. In my experience, if I can remember a piece for some months or one year, for me that would be very important. Also, I tell my collectors that they don't need to make a decision now. If they really love that piece, next year they will come back. Sometimes their friends come to their home and ask where the piece is from, they say from China and they are very surprised with the good quality and price. This is my business philosophy. Some galleries just make the price too high. I think different galleries have different styles to do their business.

So art fairs are not the best form for your business?

Yes, but you have to do this. In Chicago, in Los Angeles and New York, the last two to three years, a few galleries closed down; very good galleries with more than 30 years of history. Because now more than 60 or 70 per cent of the sales are done at the fair and not in the gallery. These kinds of old-fashioned galleries prefer to communicate with the collectors in the gallery space on a personal level, not at art fairs, which are like big marketing.

What was your experience at Art Basel Hong Kong?

I heard a joke, maybe it is not true. Our First Lady, she loves abstract works so this time Art Basel Hong Kong brought abstract paintings. I am not sure if it is true or not. I think

Art Basel Hong Kong is of a really high standard in this system. But for the high standard in art, the good part is that you must reach this level in order to be in this system. But the important part for me is that art should be free on creativity; if you set up a standard you will miss some really nice things sometimes. Last year I saw the Discoveries part for the young artists and was disappointed actually. I also think that Art Basel in Hong Kong is quite different than in Switzerland because it is more about the Asian market. We also make a joke, the first in line gallery brings the first in line artists with their third level pieces to the Asian market. Because Asian collectors mostly buy pieces based on what people told them, not on what they really see. They just follow the big names. Unfortunately some galleries were not really successful last year with the big names. I was talking to the director of one gallery from New York, which brought Lucien Freud, really nice paintings, worth about four million dollars, just this small size. But they couldn't sell them. People think that local Asian collectors are really rich, but they won't buy a modern piece worth a few million dollars; they still need to think about it, to do research. But they will buy Picasso, Monet.

Somehow Art Basel Hong Kong for Chinese people is like a big party. Everybody is there, everybody from the art business. Maybe it is a good thing for the future but I don't know. I feel like I still have to prepare enough quality and also the price level, to compare, or to match this art fair. You couldn't just bring young emerging artists, I don't think it would make sense. But if not, nobody will pay attention to you. The cost is very high for a young gallery, and if you just do it for one year nobody will remember you. You need to do it for three or five years, every year, then people will remember you. I would like to join the art fair but I didn't prepare enough yet.

If you can give an outlook on the Chinese art market or art field, what is the direction in which it is going? You said it is rapidly changing.

Yes, it is changing and for Chinese contemporary art to be more international, one way is to invite more international artists to come to China. When I did that, nobody bought the idea, just a Swiss consulate bought a small piece; it cost a lot of money to do that installation. It is for the communication and education of the local artists and local visitors. But people do need to do this, even our government needs to support it. So if the Chinese art or Chinese market were to be more international, we would need more internationals to come in. Japan is a really good example. I visited 10 private museums in Japan. 90 per cent of the museums show foreign art pieces. That is really important. Another thing, Chinese people should go out on to the international stage, not only to auctions. I hope that more foreign curators will come to China. Foreign curators at the beginning chose Chinese artists to go to the Venice Biennale and the Kassel documenta; it is still done in accordance with their own understanding and personal standard of Chinese art. Then later they changed a little bit. I just hope that they can really understand our culture, our philosophy, then they can really choose well. Some time ago the Metropolitan Museum in New York had a big Chinese ink group show. Even this exhibition chooses all the artists from 10 years ago. They also choose some young artists but the topic is about Chinese ink; but for us it is not really Chinese ink; they just chose this title. You know what I mean, I am happy they realized that Chinese culture is not only about Chairman Mao, that we also have Chinese ink. But what goes further deeply inside is what I hope will be understood. If this could be successful, because now it is all about earning money or being happy. There are still a lot of foreigners coming to China buying the pieces with a budget of a maximum of 5,000 dollars. The price for a good art piece will never be the same as 10 years ago. It takes massive time and knowledge for people to understand. These are intangible assets that people will finally realize.

I always respect discovering another culture and the contrary. Respect to me is when you could find positive and negative, either love or hate. China's society is in the socialist system. After 30 years of high speed developing, we are becoming more open to Western society and life style. I hope more and more people could break this system to know more about our culture in reality. If you stay in China for a week you could write a book about the people, the life story, the experiences in fresh feeling; if you stay here for a decade, you will have a totally different version telling about the culture, the social life, the mindset of Chinese people, in a much deeper and broader way.

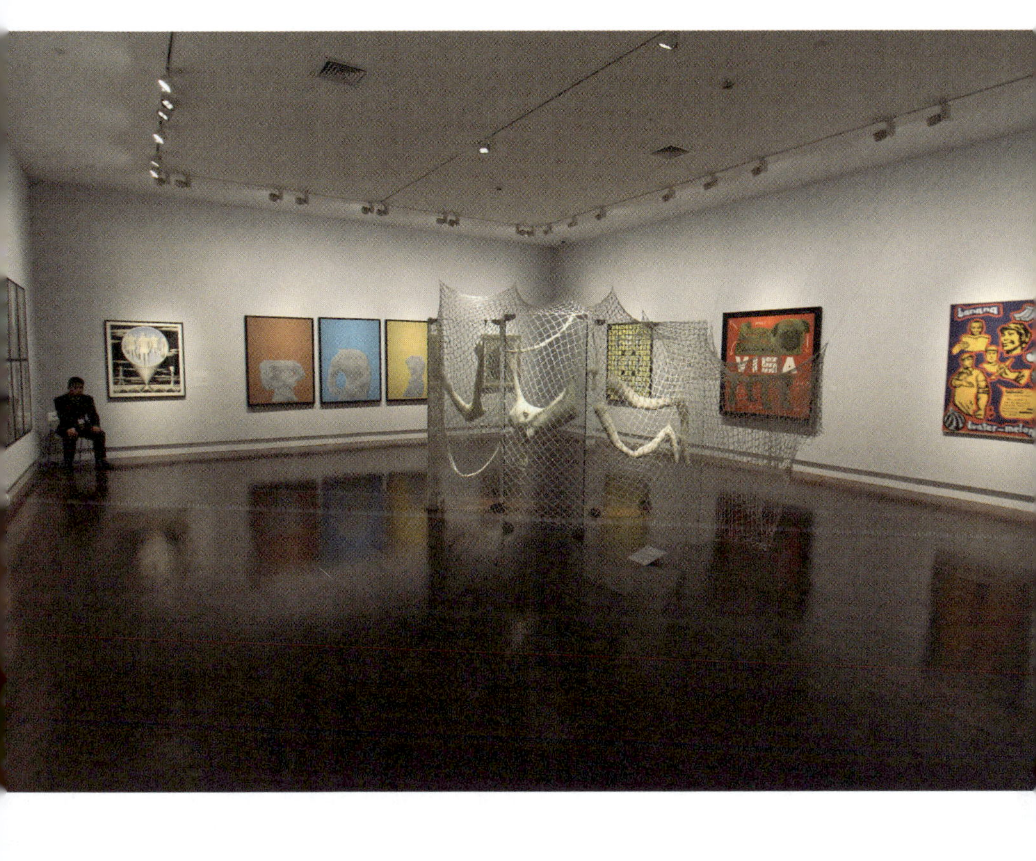

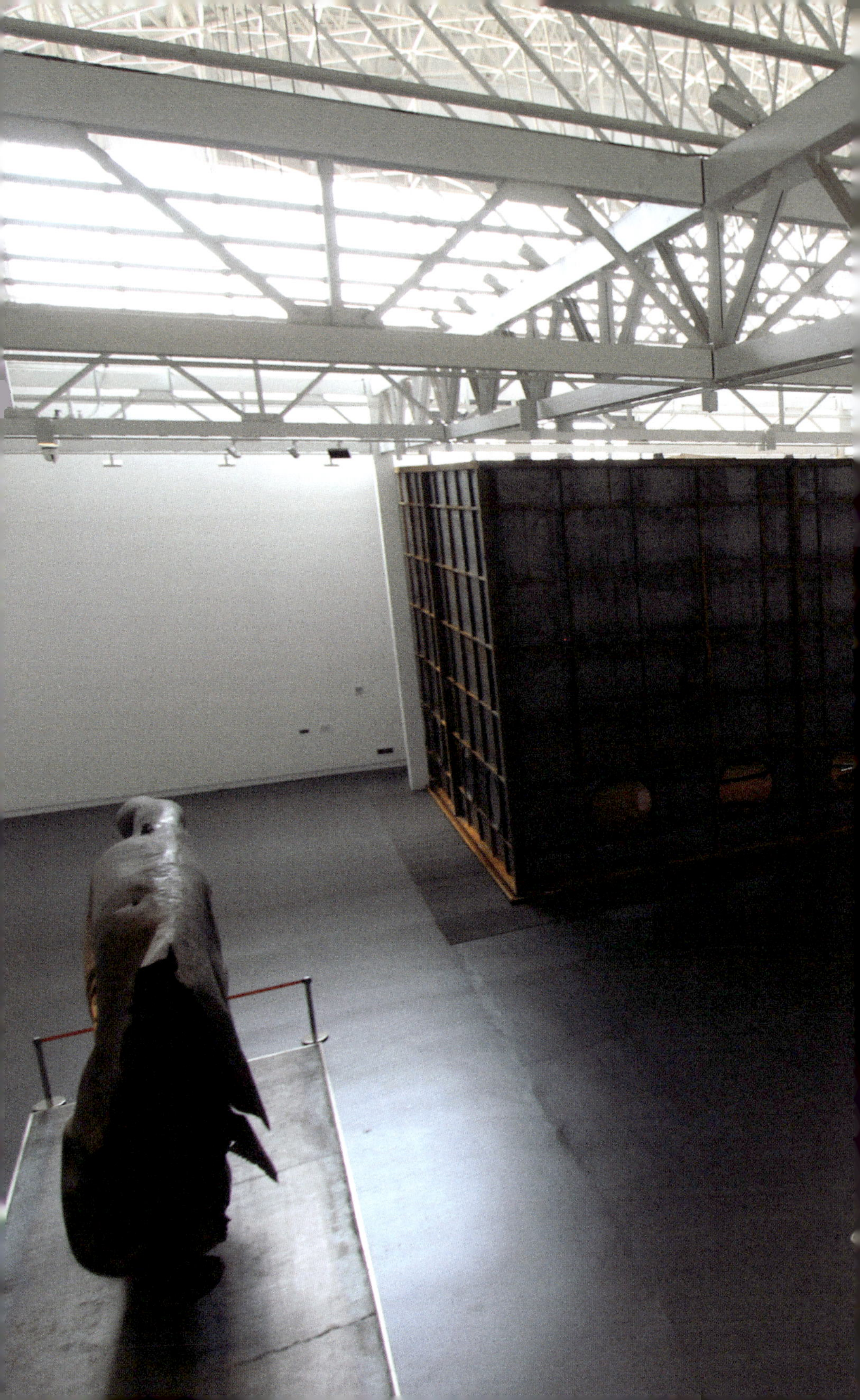

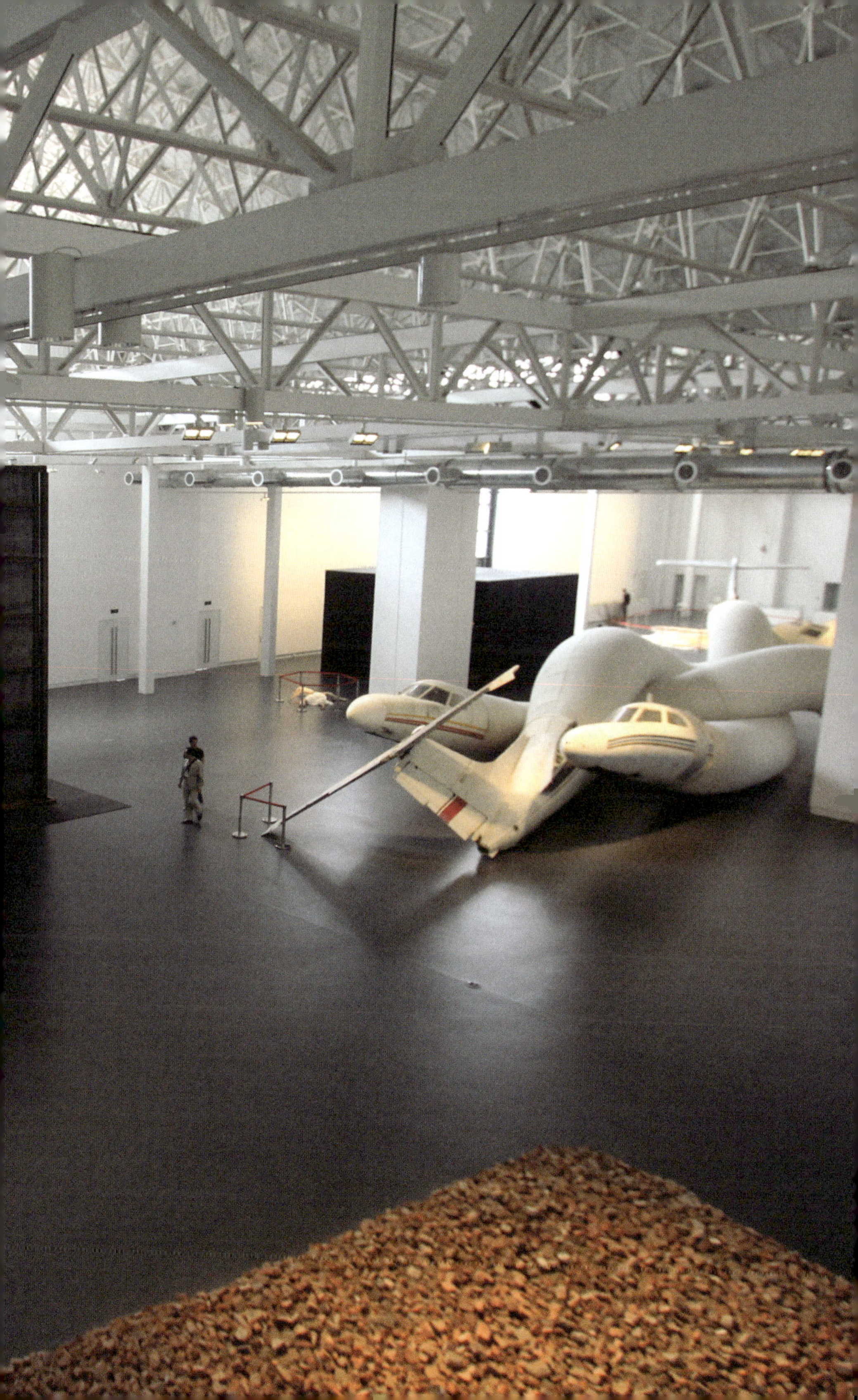

"Now that value is largely financial"

A talk with Karen Smith
Art historian/Curator, Beijing

Karen Smith is a British art historian who lives and works in Beijing. Since 2012 she has also been the director of the OCT Contemporary Art Terminal (OCAT) Xi'an. Only a year after graduating from the Wimbledon Art School in 1987 she travelled to Asia. In 1992 she moved definitively to China, where she devoted herself to the Chinese art scene and the "emergence of Chinese art", which were largely unknown beyond the borders of China. In her role as author, critic and curator both in China and in the Western art world she is in the meantime regarded as one of the most eminent experts on contemporary Chinese art. She is the author of "Nine Lives: The Birth of Avant-Garde in New China", one of the first systematic studies of the Chinese avant-garde to be undertaken by a foreign art critic.

Karen Smith's experiences during a stay of over 20 years in China provide an extremely complex but at the same time highly differentiated picture of the Chinese art world in which the individual aspects can only be separated from one another with great difficulty. She once described her own impressions and feelings as follows: "China's will to modernize has a tendency to co-opt the experience of those dwelling in its midst; today, details of the past are disputed by everything the present throws at the mind's eye". This was the hour of birth of cynical realism and political pop but also of an art largely invisible to the general public, which was acted out in artists' circles. This art is today the backbone of conceptual art practice in China.

What, then, has changed in the last two decades? Since China has opened itself up to the world its artists and other actors have quickly learned to adapt themselves to the conditions of international art production and art practice. Although China's new art was at first scarcely visible, the galleries in Hong Kong in particular, where Karen Smith first lived, began shortly after the Tiananmen Square protests of 1989 to present an astounding selection of artistic works which stood in no relation to one another in regard to style. An art scene also developed in China, which was simply waiting for a suitable space for exhibitions, even if it was only a garage – a practice which continues to the present and is reflected not only in the emergence of select art zones but also in the institutions and museums authorized by the state. Karen Smith concludes from her experience that the situation in China is certainly much more differentiated than is revealed in the mediated impressions which have asserted themselves abroad. Chinese art is grasped in the terms of Western narratives and, conversely, the West needs these narratives in order to understand Chinese art at all.

In Smith's opinion the rapid social development of high-speed China also has consequences for Chinese art and the Chinese art world. Many changes nowadays are played out under the "umbrella of capitalism and materialism". The speed of art production has fallen into line with the general speed of change; it allows not only the artists but also the other actors such as curators, art critics, collectors or the public interested in art scarcely any pauses for thought and reflection; they can mostly only react to the accelerated developments in order to keep in step with the changes. This analysis is shared by other actors such as the Shanghai gallerist and collector Ming Ming. China's contemporary art scene is generally seen as being shaped by those active and self-assertive artists who have raised a post-modern "anything goes" attitude to the standard of their artistic practice and usually pursue an aesthetics of "everything that is permitted and possible". In contrast, the positive energy of the "anything goes" can be seen in the efforts of many unknown Chinese artists to overcome conventions.

China has apparently caught up with the international art world. However, the country owes its visibility in the global art world primarily to the high prices and the growing art market. But scarcely any notice is taken to this day of contemporary art in China from an artistic point of view. In the opinion of Karen Smith contemporary Chinese art has little to do with art history, and particularly with the art history from a Western perspective. There are no museums which offer an overview of modern and contemporary art in China. Even the few books on the contemporary development of art forms in China do not pursue the goal of seeking for a scientifically well-founded art historical consensus.

Can you tell us a little bit about your experience? What has changed in the last 20 years since you have been here?

The major way that China has changed is economically. In the art world, the impact of economic change has had a demonstrable impact on the way that art is made, perceived and also traded. In terms of ideology, of freedom of expression, of other things that come under this umbrella, the rate of change cannot compare with that engendered by the economics of materialism. This has wrought a lot of cosmetic change: we have a lot of new buildings, artists now have big studios, and there is a general difference in living standards in urban environments. In terms of socio-political structures, the main arteries that feed the system are largely the same. There is, however, a discernible psychological shift in the outlook of younger generations, born in the era of opening and reform post-1978, who have had more exposure to the outside world and have grown up in a period of relative economic stability. They have a very different mindset to the older generations which grew up in an era of tremendous political instability, in the absence of economic growth and the freedom that offers.

Artists born in the 1990s or later?

Generally speaking artists born after '79. The majority of Chinese born after 1980 are also single children – or more likely to be single children. The big change really comes after 2001 when China joins the WTO. Prior to that there wasn't very much of an economic, or commercial, relationship with America. The increase in business and trade created a fertile environment for cultural growth, especially in the visual arts. Europeans tend to be more modest in their approach to purchasing art. They become more invested in the artists, getting to know them and personally researching works for their collection. In my experience, the American approach often involves an appointed advisor, who is involved with a museum – where collectors are donating patrons of the museum. The inflow of capital to which this gave rise was significant.

What about the development of the art scene here in China? Who are the most important actors and which are the most important institutions?

In China, institutions do not really exist in the way the term is used in the West. There is still an official system which is rather conservative, closed. The evolution of contemporary art has occurred in opposition to this official world, and remains largely outside its parameters. Yet I wouldn't call it non-official or unofficial exactly. These days it does not have the confrontational dynamics it had for a period in the 1990s. It has a relationship that is both complex and simple, something like the 798 Art District in Beijing which is an example of the system outside the system where artists went to have studios and then young curators began using empty spaces for exhibitions and now it is a government-sanctioned area for creative industries run by a state-owned enterprise. The problems faced now are more of a commercial nature than a political one, but with the direct connection to the state in the form of the enterprise that manages it, all that happens in any one of those spaces is closely observed.

The Central Academy of Fine Arts in Beijing is an official organization but is an example of how change in the unofficial field of contemporary culture is propagating change within the official one: CAFA is just one example of an educational institution that is establishing progressive new departments, all within the last 10 years. These offer courses in new media, experimental arts, arts management, curatorial programs and theory, as well as slowly being able to allow for some kind of contemporary art history as a possible course of study. In the 1990s this would have been unthinkable.

What about the art production and the younger artists? Is there a difference to the older artists in art production?

Not in practical terms, and not among the leading artists of each generation. There is a different mindset, different impulses and interests underscoring the work, but in technical and practical terms, the differences are not marked. If there is a difference it lies in the perception of what status artists may claim socially. For the older generation, most professional artists were artisans, viewed collectively as a powerful tool of society but not for individual merit or expression. Paradoxically, for the younger generation, whilst they take a certain degree of individuality for granted, few believe that art has any meaningful social or political power today. Now that value is largely financial. A lot of art produced in China today is vacuous. It is well executed, and may look pleasing but it doesn't really say anything. This is in part the result of the official teaching system. The emphasis is placed on technical proficiency, so students graduate with incredible skill but without having their imagination fired up, or having been accorded confidence to challenge the status quo through their own invention.

Are they more influenced
by something called global art
or the global art scene?

It is not as simple as that question makes it sound. On the one hand, of course they are. The whole impetus right through the 80s to the 90s was propelled by an idea that came, first from Mao, that China would catch up with the rest of the world, would catch up with America, having overtaken Britain. So there was an underlying determination that China would once again become a great civilization. For artists who emerged in the 80s, this was the big dream. It was a highly idealistic age. But then in the 90s after the June 4th incident, many of these artists were obviously disillusioned about the potential for realizing this idea. Some artists took themselves abroad in the 1990s, and tried to integrate themselves into an adopted cultural framework, which was not easy. The majority would return in the surge of opening up that took place post-2001.

Some who remained evolved a form of slightly political art, which was political primarily in terms of the Chinese arena but, significantly, was understood as being political in terms of the Western narrative concerning China, and China post-June 4th. For a period of time, largely prior to 2001, this placed an emphatic accent on a certain type of art, and was a cause for frustration among the community in general. It was unfortunate, too, for creating a certain type of image of China's contemporary art practice abroad. Looking back from now, we can see it was part of the complicated global shifts that were taking place at the end of the Cold War. The desire on both sides, East and West, to embrace the new, to engage with China now and put its recent past to bed, resulted in some of those political artists of the 1990s being somewhat side-lined in the last decade.

The maintaining of social stability is central to political policy in China. Many young artists have little idea about the complex political issues that underscored China's 20th century, and vis-a-vis its international relations. They engage with a global world just like any curious young person would. They listen to whatever music is current, whatever box office hit films are being shown. That is a part of the global culture. What is still missing though, and little discussed, is that usually when people travel from their own cultural framework to participate in some aspect of this global culture, like an artist invited to participate in a biennale, they carry a strong sense of personal identity, even if they are not necessarily aware of it before they leave. That sort of identity is less established for individuals in China. Perhaps it is merely a question of self-confidence, but it is also in awareness of the individual as an independent entity with rights to opinions, attitudes and actions. The Chinese have great personalities and ideas, but how these are marshaled and conveyed is impeded by psychological limitations that exist in the absence of the knowledge of one's own freedom to own them. It can make them vulnerable when they join the global party: if you don't know clearly who you are it is easy to lose yourself. We saw this happen in the 1990s when Beijing emerged as a center of art and artists from all over the country began migrating to Beijing. Before that there were many dynamic communities across the country, each quite different. Once they converged to Beijing you would see some individual artists start to falter. They found they were constantly comparing their progress to others, and became not exactly competitive, but in the dense communities of artists, they became intensely conscious of how they were doing vis-a-vis others. When curators would come to visit the community and no one knocked on your door, self doubt would set in. Artists adopted other strategies or adapted their art to what they thought was the prevailing trend. That's when everything started to fall apart.

Today, it seems artists are making a return to the provinces. Vibrant communities have begun to emerge again in some of the second and third tier cities. That is a phenomenon that will contribute to affirming the sense of self and confidence. It is not about being Chinese or doing something that looks Chinese but it is just about knowing what your values are and why you bring those values to whatever you express in art. The big picture is not that clear right now. New collectors are emerging but the extraordinary prices of recent years are leveling out. Private/corporate institutions are expanding, maturing, but galleries are struggling. Perhaps once we get through this current anticorruption campaign something new will emerge but so many things are contradictory that it is hard to say.

Let's talk about distribution, back to the institutions. What's the difference between the gallery system here in China and the auction houses? The market is dominated by the auctions houses, we think.

That's purely for pragmatic reasons. You could say that Chinese people don't easily trust each other and auctions seem to be public, transparent. The other thing is that few of the galleries have been established for a long time. If you are a new collector, especially if you are newly rich, you have a clear idea of how that money came to you, how hard it was to achieve this wealth. Maybe it is easy money, but however you got it, you are not going to part with it in an unthinking manner. So if a gallerist or an artist asks you to pay a million dollars for a painting, it would be natural to ask 'Why?' You would want to be sure that the work is worth its price tag. In the mind of many Chinese buyers auction houses are transparent because they appear to be public. Of course, we know how auctions are open to manipulation, as some in China have also learned, but at least auctions provide a public record of price so that in future when the collectors needs to prove it, say for insuring the work, they have clear evidence of the price paid.

The other thing is that it is not easy for galleries here to incorporate as a company because the regulations for Chinese companies and corporations are complicated and taxes are high. The official tax for artworks is almost 30 per cent, which wipes out most of the margin a gallery makes on selling art. By the time you have given the client a discount and covered your overheads, including paying the artist, you have little in the way of profit. There are now a number of galleries, probably between five to 10, that have been around for almost 10 years and are very solid. Many function more like institutions than pure galleries. They have been extremely supportive of artists, particularly early on when they began and when they would invest in helping artists produce works. Now this is more complicated. The cost of participating in art fairs is challenging. But if you are not participating in Basel or Frieze, then opportunities for brand recognition and building client relations are missed. There is a relatively small pool of artists and a lot of competition from international galleries. Artists perhaps still think international galleries can do more for them, although it depends how old the artist is. To be part of the global world, at a certain point an artist may be thinking that a gallery like Pace is going to be better for their career than a local gallery in a China with limited institutional collections/collectors. But Pace might not be the best choice, because with so many artists, the volume of promotional work a gallery can do for an individual artist is limited. You may be better off with a gallery which knows you, speaks your language and would be willing to work for you.

Do you think that contemporary Chinese art will be more recognized in the global art world?

It will eventually. There is already a marked difference from 2012 to 2014 with certain events like the Armory Show New York in March 2014 and the 2014 autumn Asian Art Week in New York. But artists have to keep making great new work. Without that no artists can sustain interest no matter who they are. In some ways it is already there in terms of how people view this idea of the market and China's museum-building program. But from an art critical point of view, China's art has a long way to go. Frieze Magazine has occasional reviews, as does Artforum. But there is a big gap to close there and some of these issues are to do with the outside world's understanding of China and the ability to engage in what Chinese artists have been talking about. It is also a process of people's getting to know each other. There is a lot of strong art here in China that doesn't get seen abroad. Sometimes when certain works do get taken abroad, they do feel different. They look different. The context is a really interesting element of how we experience artworks.

Can you give us an outlook on the Chinese contemporary art scene?

It is always quite hard to make predictions. Even though there has now been 30 years of development in contemporary art thought and practice

and things have changed, in a big picture sense, I believe it is the next 20 years that will be crucial. To date, the art world has flip-flopped from one extreme to the other. The 80s was pervaded by a kind of freedom; the 1990s was very political. Suddenly, the first decade of the 21st century was all about economics. This second decade feels rather flat. Perhaps, it is needed as a period to reflect and put everything in perspective. Out of that, some new, stronger contemporary cultural identity will emerge for the 2020s, which will be tied to what will happen in China as China's position in geopolitics becomes ever more clearly defined. In the next 10 years that's going to be a determining factor. If China does catch up with America, it is likely a lot of artists will be less interested in the outside world and more focused on what's happening here. If China begins directing the conversation, they will want to have their say in that. That's quite a possibility.

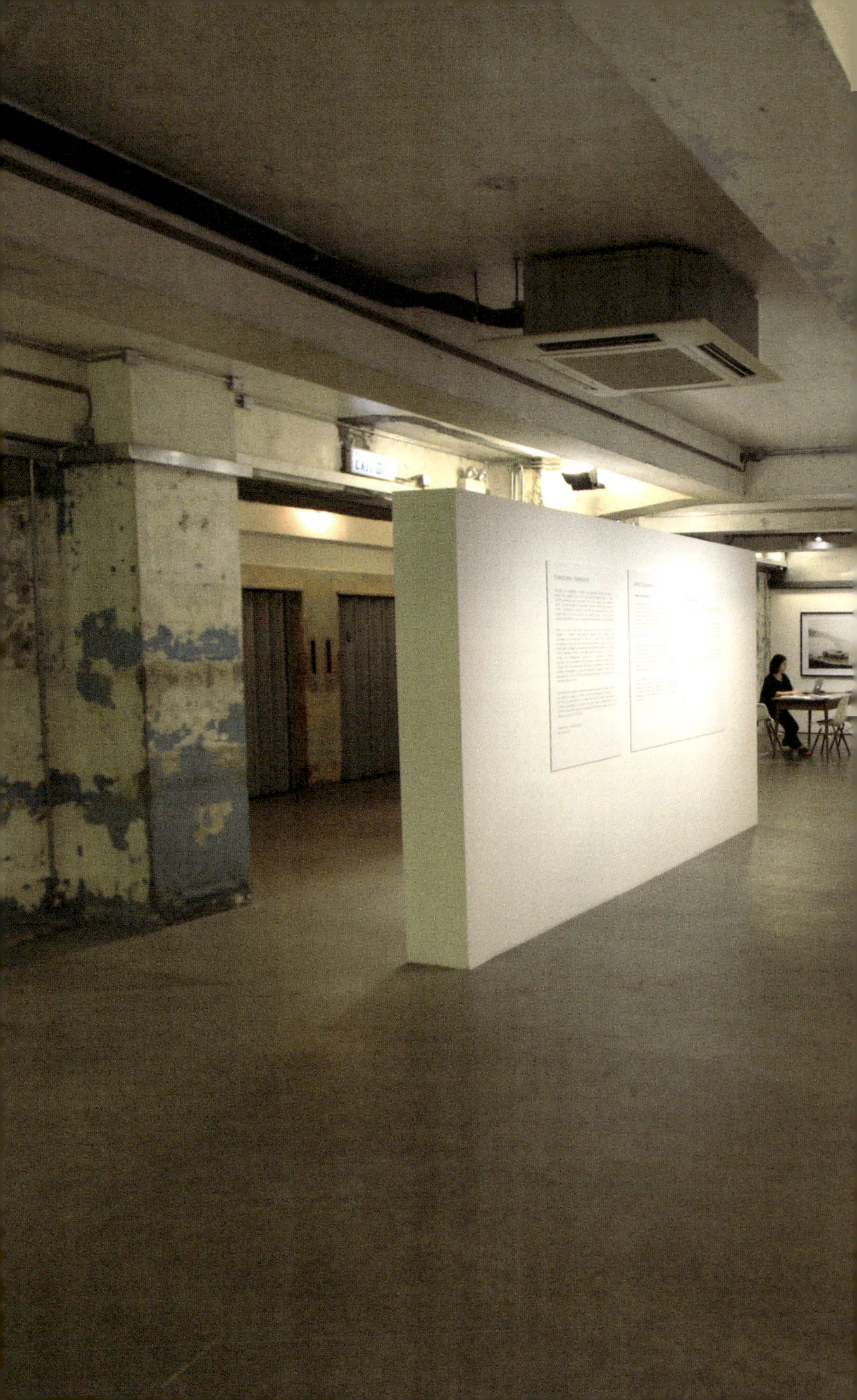

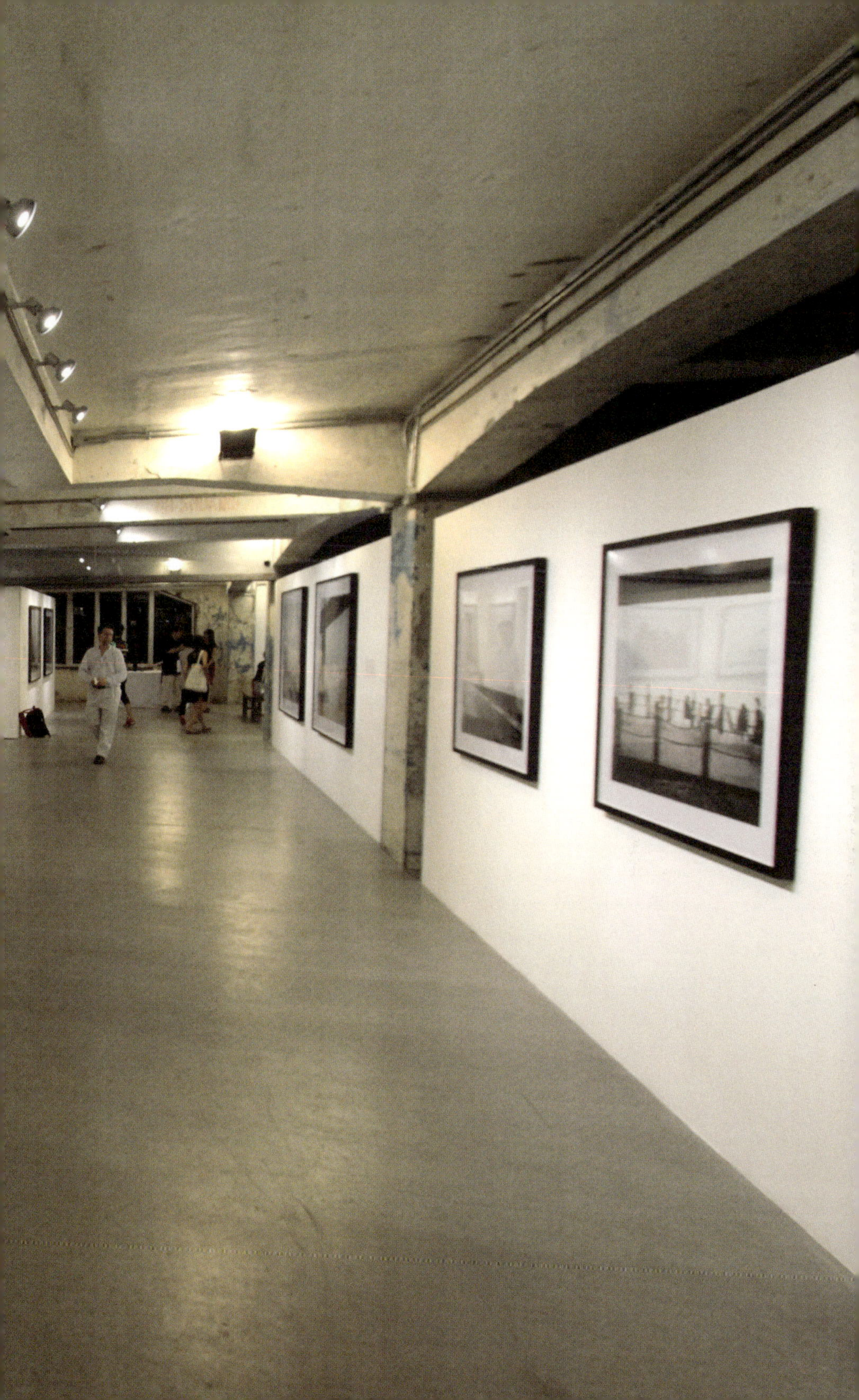

"Hong Kong art has its own character"

A talk with William Lim
Collector, Hong Kong

Our dialogue partner is involved in many ways in the Hong Kong cultural scene and the local art world. As a renowned architect and designer he is active in leading functions in diverse public institutions. In addition William Lim himself carries out research on the Hong Kong art scene, has been a committed art collector for many years and works together with a large number of actors in the local and the international art world.

He assists our team as an expert, but he also gives us detailed information on his personal love of art and the path that led him to it during the talk. He seems to have discovered his love of objects of art in early years, even though he has remained eclectic in his taste and would only describe himself as a collector since the year 2003.

At this point he began to make and cultivate contacts with Chinese artists and this was – whether by chance or not – precisely the time at which, according to his own statements, the art market in China experienced a boom. A few years later he then began to concentrate definitively and explicitly on contemporary Hong Kong artists and the collection of their works on a systematic basis. And so our source of information is part of a collective trend, carries it and is carried by it. Following the still existing preference of many of his fellow countrymen Lim at first attended auctions in order to acquire works of art until his growing interest in artists who until recently were not represented in auction houses led him to the galleries and then directly to the artists and their ateliers in the search for discoveries. In the talk he explicitly emphasizes his intellectual curiosity in regard to the special character of local art and associates it with the special path taken by Hong Kong in the modern period, its chequered historical development from being a part of China, then of the British colonial empire and then of the Chinese People's Republic, which in his opinion resulted in a particular cultural mix he regards as unique. In addition, until quite recently, there was no noteworthy demand for the works of Hong Kong artists and in Lim's opinion this protected them against the dangers of commercialization. According to Lim, this special path of the Hong Kong art scene was accompanied by an ensemble of aesthetic specifica. It is particularly congenial to him on account of its characteristic inner emotionality and he positively underlines the broad range of genres and media of artistic expression which characterizes its sensitivities.

Nonetheless, he is thoroughly positive about the new dynamics manifested in the Hong Kong art field as a result of the arrival of the big players on the global art market. At the Art Basel, for example, he meets many interesting collectors and gallerists and their strong local presence also motivated him to make a start on a book about the Hong Kong art world called "The No Colors: Living Collection in Hong Kong". In his opinion a growing interest in local art, strengthened by an increasing international visibility, and accompanied by an increasing presence of this art abroad, can be ascertained. According to his self-understanding as a collector of this art what matters is not the simple accumulation of individual pieces but the creation of a collection which is more than the sum of its parts and he hopes that the collection which bears his signature will meet with future approval. In this desire to be seen as the composer of a coherent aesthetic collection Lim is a contemporary of those Western collector colleagues who typically wish to see their collecting practice as a terrain of creative self-fulfillment.

In Lim's view of the Hong Kong art world the global and local levels are thoroughly compatible and, in contrast to other voices heard in this field, he does not feel that they give rise to any noteworthy contradictions or dissonances.

How did you enter the field of collectors?

For me, I always liked art objects even when I was small. Also, I always feel that every piece of art tells a story of the place and the culture and I think that's why it is interesting. Even when I was quite young, I started buying artwork when I travelled, but not in a very systematic way. And then I just accumulated a lot of things. Then I came back to work here in 1987.

So you bought art works before, but you didn't say that you were a collector. It is different.

Right. I think it was about 2003, around that time, that I started to think about maybe not just getting everything, but focusing in one area, so I was looking more into Chinese contemporary art. I got to meet some artists and they started to introduce me to, to talk about their work, and I thought that's very interesting, so you can come into close contact with the artists. I think that was around the time when the art market started to pick up in China. After a few years, I started to learn more about Hong Kong artists, and that was around 2006 and 2007, that's when I really started to be very systematic about collecting. I think that's probably when I considered myself as becoming a collector.

The first art works you bought, were they directly from the artists or from galleries? Or did you also go to auction houses?

At the beginning, it was actually through auction houses. At the beginning, before contemporary art, I was also very interested in Chinese antiques, and with Chinese antiques I got to visit a lot of auction houses, more auction houses than shops in a way. At the time, the auction houses started to do features of contemporary Chinese artists. That's when I started to realize that these are very interesting. The first couple of pieces are both from galleries and also from auction houses. The auction houses didn't start working with Hong Kong artists until two or three years ago. So for the Hong Kong work, at the beginning, it was definitely with galleries. It wasn't that common to go to an artist's studio back then. The first few works I got from galleries. Then I started to realize, because Hong Kong artworks were not very commercial, some artists are working with galleries, but some actually don't have galleries to represent them, so I started to learn more about these artists. For those artists, I went to their studios and started collecting directly from them.

What kind of artworks were you collecting? Paintings principally, or installations, videos?

Actually, all kinds. I think that for me what is more interesting is not just getting one painting here and there about an artist, but to really follow the career of an artist. There are a few artists that I am very interested in, so that I want to get their work at different parts of their careers. Actually, a lot of Hong Kong artists don't just deal with one medium, they deal with multiple media. Some would, like Leung Chi Wo, he would deal with photography and videos, and sometimes small sculpture pieces. For somebody like that, I feel that you need to look at their work in different media. There are many artists like that in Hong Kong.

Do you know other collectors?

I know other collectors. There are not too many for contemporary art, especially people that are focusing on Hong Kong artists. A lot of them just do it to support certain charity organizations and that's when you get one or two pieces of Hong Kong artists. I do like to talk to them just about collecting in general, but I think as a collector, I tend to also get quite subjective with what I think. And a lot of the time, it's really more impulse than having to talk with somebody. I do like to read up on different things, and look at what activities the artists have done. Also, Hong Kong people travel a lot, so it's not like we get together all the time. But sometimes we would see each other during an art opening and definitely during the art fair.

Do you visit art fairs?

Not intentionally, but if I happen to be in a place and with time, I would visit them.

Have you been to Art Basel?
Last year?

Not in Basel, no. Here, yes, this year and also Miami.

What do you think about it?

I think it's great that we have a major art fair in Hong Kong. I think it's very interesting, because not only do you go there and buy an art work, but you also meet other people. You meet other very good galleries, and become good friends with some gallery owners, because they came here for the exhibition. There are also a lot of other collectors. Sometimes I open up my studio for other collectors to visit. There is a lot of exchange and that's why I am doing my book. I feel that there are enough people interested in Hong Kong artists.

Do you have all your artworks in one place?

No, they're in different places. A lot of them are in storage.

Did you think about having them in private museums one day or how often do you now...

I think in Europe, it's common. But in Hong Kong, it's very difficult. Space is a problem. I haven't really thought that far, but I do feel that what I'm collecting is a good documentation of what people are doing in Hong Kong. And a lot of the time that is reflected through the artists' work. I don't look at artworks as individual items, but I think as a collection they become more interesting. I don't know what to do with it, but I hope that people would appreciate art and the collection that I'm putting together.

And your family? They are doing the same or only you?

My wife helps out. She is not as crazy as I am. My two sons, they are also interested. They are young, they are in their twenties, but they are starting to be interested in collecting and visiting artist studios.

It seems that collecting art has started only recently in Hong Kong? It has a long tradition in Europe and the States.

I think people have been collecting, but not contemporary art. People collect traditional ink art. There are some very good collectors. They definitely collect antiques, but for contemporary art, it's very new area for Hong Kong.

You have the impression that it is now thriving? More and more people...

I think there's a lot more people interested in contemporary art. They might not be just people living here, but they are maybe people visiting here or people in the region. I think it's getting more and more popular.

They're also interested in Hong Kong contemporary artists?

There's definitely a lot more interest in Hong Kong artists. I'm starting to see Hong Kong artists in other parts of the world, in New York and different places. I think there's definitely a growing interest.

And the museum M+? What about that?

I think M+ is great. Right now they have a show in Hong Kong on their collection of architecture. I think it is great because it is very inspiring. It inspires people to look at art as an important thing and also it inspires professionals. If you are an artist, they would encourage you to make better works because if you see how the works are in a collection, even if you were an architect, you would want to do better work because you have the chance of having your work collected by museums. I think something like that is very important and encouraging for Hong Kong.

*Do you have artworks that may
be shown in M+?*

I have one piece of work at the show right now. It is my own architecture work. I haven't really donated other things to M+.

Have you looked at the Sigg Collection? What do you think about it?

Yes. I think it's wonderful. I think Uli's collection is probably one of the most important and comprehensive for mainland Chinese artists. He is really systematic in his collection. I think it's great to be able to see a collection work like that. It's great that it is under one museum because it really tells the whole story about Chinese art.

*Do you know if he also collects some
art in Hong Kong?*

Yes, he does. I think some of the art is in his collection, in the M+ collection. Also I think the other collector is Sylvain Lévy, from Paris, France. He has this DSL collection. It's a collection in the internet. He also has very important mainland Chinese artists. He's starting to look at Hong Kong artists as well.

*What's the signature of Hong Kong
art for you? Is there specificity?*

Yes, I think that Hong Kong art has its own character, and actually that's what my book will be about. I feel that Hong Kong has a very different history from a lot of these other places. It was China and then it was a colony, and now it is back to China. So it really has a mixture of Chinese and Western influence. I think it is quite unique. Also, because contemporary art was not really important to people here, a lot of artists who did contemporary art don't really do it for the commercialism. A lot of them almost look at it as something that you can't really making a living out of. They produce work for a lot of the time for exhibitions, so the materials they use are quite temporary and quite grass-roots. I think it is very different from mainland Chinese contemporary artists. They have a lot of oil-based work, whereas in Hong Kong you see a lot less of that. A lot of work is on plywood, or with pencil or biro pen. The medium is very different. The mentality is very different. There is less of a concern for certain kinds of symbolism or creating iconic elements so that it is a lot more intangible in a way. A lot of the art work is about inner emotions of artists. To me, that's why I feel Hong Kong art is more interesting now because it is not something you look at and you see 'oh, this is… whoever the artist may be'. It is a lot more subtle.

So it is quite different from what we can find for example in Singapore. Seen from Europe, these cities seem to be rather similar. When you look at the art produced over there, you would say, no, Hong Kong artists are doing other artworks.

I am not that familiar with Singapore contemporary artists. I know a few, like Ming Wong, who does definitely very unique work, and it's very different. I don't think any Hong Kong artists would do work like his. I know Heman Chong. I think each place has its own different types of artists. I went to see the Singaporean Biennale. To me, they really have this concern over regionalism, that type of identity, and definitely Hong Kong is not included in that region. I think definitely there is an intention to differentiate.

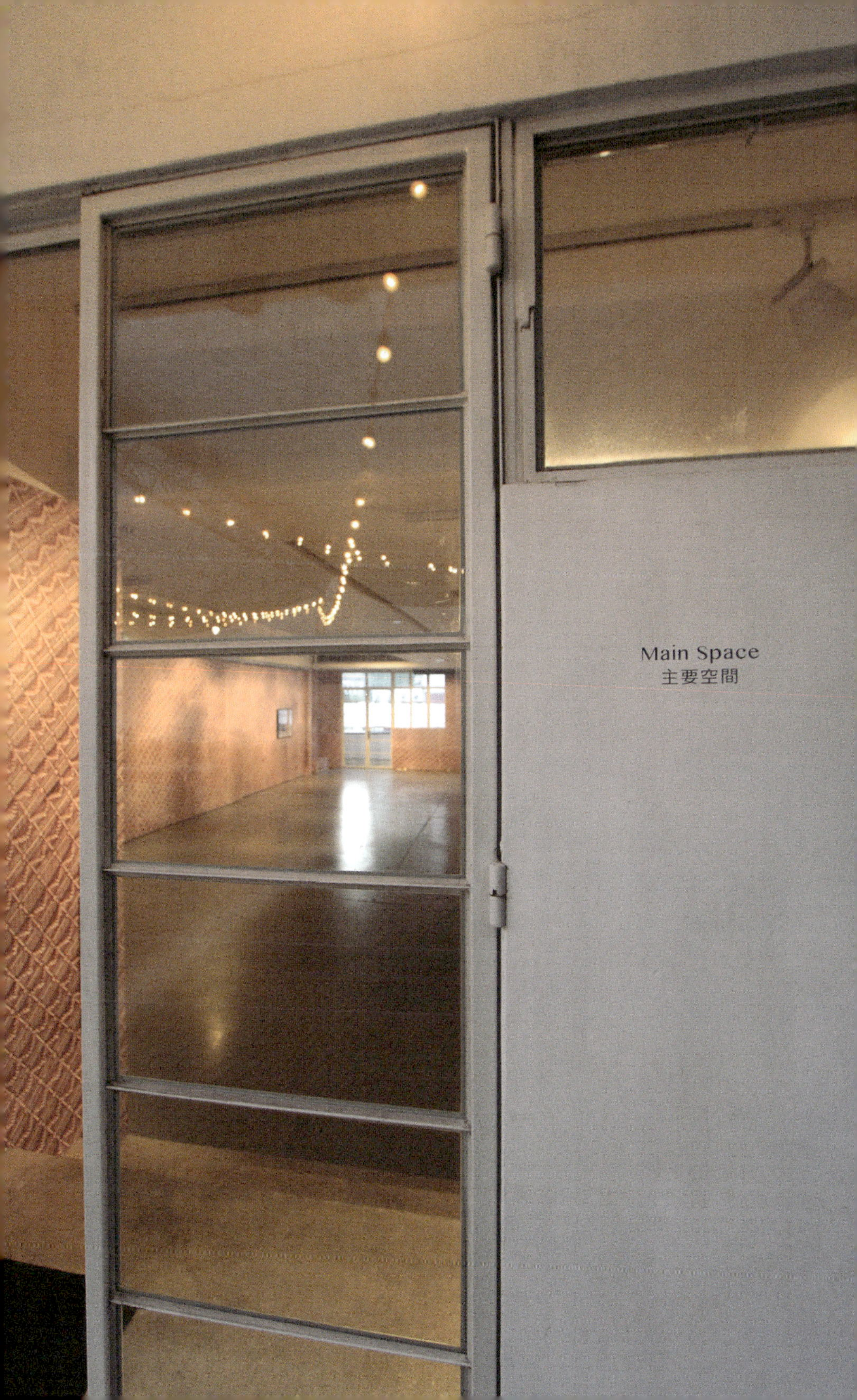

Main Space
主要空間

"Auctions are the worst place
for contemporary work"

A talk with Fabio Rossi
Gallerist, Hong Kong

In the following talk with a British gallerist with his seat in Hong Kong he presents us with his view of the structures – actors, institutions and mechanisms – of the Asian art market. It is a perspective dependent upon his position, which, although it is critical, reflective and highly expert in its skepticism towards the arch-enemy of the gallerists – the auction houses – nonetheless clearly represents the corporate interests of his own estate, when, for example, he declares that auctions are the "worst place" for "contemporary art, especially of a young artist". Our dialogue partner very sensitively depicts the specific attraction that the marketing procedures at an auction have, particularly for newcomers in the field of art collection, namely the – supposed – transparency of a public competition for symbolic goods carried out in front of a selected and select public, from which reputational effects can be expected. There is also the hope of acquiring art more cheaply than from a gallerist and the idea of enjoying a low-threshold access to this segment of the market. According to the critical judgment of our expert, this involves a fair degree of naivety and lack of experience, which he regards as teething troubles of an art world which is still in the process of creation, and which the as yet unpracticed collectors will leave behind them in the course of time. Revealingly, in the depictions he addresses to his visitors from a Swiss University, our dialogue partner puts some of the current myths and stereotypes he believes to be typical of the West into perspective, in particular those which see the Asian market as a gold mine. He explains that the number of relevant collectors is much more modest than it seems from the distance and that, in view of the enormous historical need to catch up in regard to the development of an understanding of art and of marketing competence in dealing with the goods and the institutions of the art field, a genuine culture of collecting will only emerge step by step.

The view presented on the Asian art market in general and Hong Kong in particular makes it clear how great the danger is for Western observers to fall victim to ethnocentric misunderstandings and prejudices. What is here understood by the terms "public" and "private" in regard to the status of museums is not identical with our customary categories and boundaries, and even the usual distinction between the museum here and commercial spaces there cannot be clearly drawn in the Asian region. Our dialogue partner expressly emphasizes the weight of local socio-cultural mentalities which render widespread current concepts in the West, such as art patronage, irrelevant. At the same time he warns the visitor from the West against overlooking observable local structural changes in the art field, for example in regard to the strength of auction houses in competition with galleries or to social motives for collecting beyond the actual love of art, such as a craving for recognition and reputation.

The picture painted here of a still young field of contemporary art turns upon a processual logic of collective learning in which, step for step, the region searches for and probably also finds a way of catching up on the long-term historical development of the cultural patterns of art production and the social uses of art in the West, even though this does not take place in accordance with a unilinear model of the one best way but as a dialectic of assimilation and accommodation in a process of catch-up modernization. How far this is a calculatedly optimistic picture of globalization from an actor who has found a clear business model for the import and export of cultural goods will be revealed in the future development of the field.

When we are looking at collectors in mainland China, it is an emergent field and they have started collecting contemporary art very recently. What do you think are the main motivations for collecting art?

Well, it is an interesting question. Generally speaking, in mainland China I mostly know collectors of classi-cal art, who have been very active in the past 10 years buying both Chinese classical but also more and more what I do, which is classical Himalayan Art from Tibet, Mongolia, Nepal and northern India. They are very keen on this material. My personal feeling is that – and I have been involved in the art world since I was 10 or 11 years old – I have met a lot of collectors in my life, some amazing collectors and legendary collectors, there aren't many of these yet in China. We have seen that things are moving very fast, not just pricewise. However, for example, the prices of certain works such as Chinese contemporary art or Chinese porcelain have gone through the roof. I don't think this is only limited to China with contemporary art, there is a lot of trophy buying throughout the world. People are spending insane amounts of money and you don't know why, just because they have it and end up buying trophies. For example, not so recently, a work by Francis Bacon was sold for 150 million dollars. It is monopoly money. It is a great painting, I love Francis Bacon but it doesn't make sense to me. I think there are various motivations, I think it could be prestige, fame, something that everybody is aware of, sometimes things can be bought because there is a lot of money involved and money needs to be put somewhere and art becomes a disposable asset which can be easily moved. It is also something that you give away as a gift. There is a term in China called 'guanxi', which stands for relationships, connections etc. and it is very important there. I don't want to sound too negative but I think there is an idea in the West that China is like El Dorado, but the reality is that there are not so many great collectors. There are, however, some very real passionate collectors. I have met some collectors that do not associate art with the money but have true love of art and want to build something special and meaningful. I think those are very few at the moment. They will develop and grow and find their own way to be collectors. If you look at the tradition of Chinese collecting, it goes back for centuries. It was always a very sophisticated tradition of intellectuals, scholars and emperors collecting. There is no reason that this won't happen again. But I think we are still at the very beginning of that. My experience is mostly with classical art and I have seen that there is an emergence of people who have more knowledge and passion, are learning fast and becoming more sophisticated. I will give you a small example. The early bronzes tend to be more aesthetically refined and more beautiful than the later bronzes. The later bronzes are more flashy, there is more gilt, they are more 'in your face'. With new collectors, there is always more interest in these gilt bronzes. But lately collectors come to me asking, for example, if I have any 12th Century Indian Pala bronzes which are much more subtle. This has been a very interesting trend to me; however, it is still at an early stage. The first time I went to China was in 1986 to 87 and I know people who went there in the 70s already. The transformation of the country has been incredible. But you can't expect that after the Cultural Revolution and after what has happened the generation of collectors will burst into the scene with tremendous sophistication. The collectors that I think are truly sophisticated are the Taiwanese and, secondly, Hong Kong collectors. The collectors in Taipei are the ones that have been collecting for longer; of course they have not lived through the trauma of the Cultural Revolution and they also have wonderful and comprehensive collections even in contemporary art.

Are there also collectors who are constructing private museums? Such as in Europe or in the United States.

Yes, there is a lot of that going on. This idea of a museum is something that has become more and more prominent in the West but also in China. I think it is a little too early to judge where these museums are going and how good they are going to be. Some of them will probably be vanity projects, like some in the West. The boundary between what is a museum and what is a commercial space gets very confused. Even in Beijing, the Capital Museum is a national museum, but you can still hire it to have an exhibition, and who knows maybe you can sell there as well. I think we have to wait a little bit to judge these institutions. Definitely there are obviously a great deal of museums being built in China whether public or private. If you build a museum you have to put something in it. And that is why there has been a demand for classical and contemporary art. It has been bought at auctions, dealers, everywhere in the world, because these new buildings need to be filled. Recently I heard that mainland Chinese collectors were donating works to M+ in Hong Kong. Again, it sends a message to collectors in this part of the world that you can do things like that, actually donate or partly donate your collection. This idea of philanthropy is not so widespread in Asia in general, whether it is India or China. We talk about philanthropy, they don't talk about philanthropy. They have other ways of being generous. I think this actually sends a message that such acts of philanthropy can be done and I think it's a very important message.

Some say that Chinese people have more trust in auction houses than in galleries concerning transparency of the market and the price development. When they go to an auction house they see how the others are reacting. How do you see this?

Again, I think it's a wonderful question, very complex. Sometimes we tend to focus on Asia. In fact, the relationship between auction houses, galleries and collectors has changed throughout the world, not just in

Asia. A bigger number of new collectors, or maybe let's call them new buyers, who want to enter the market these days often go to the auction first. Not just because I own a gallery, but I think as a collector you should go to the galleries first. The reality is that people around the world tend to go to the auction more and more, and the auction is very aggressively getting onto the turf of the contemporary world whether in Asia, America or Europe. There is the feeling at an auction that somebody else is bidding against me; he or she must like this piece so it must be good. You gain confidence in the piece. The other thing is that some people want to spend money very privately while others want to spend money very publicly, for whatever reason. Maybe they want to buy a piece to, then, gift it to somebody, so they can go back and show that they have paid one million dollars. It's an auction record, so nobody can dispute it. If they come to me and they buy something for one million dollars, I can give them an invoice, but it is not public, it is just a price on a piece of paper. There is a bit of inexperience, a bit of naivety in thinking the auction knows best. The reality is that the best work rarely goes on auction in any field, contemporary, classical, modern. Occasionally yes and more and more in certain areas. Very often, the best work is actually sold privately because exper-

tise and knowledge remain greater with the gallerists. The people who work at auction houses very rarely are truly knowledgeable. There are people who get shifted from one department to another department and are just there to make money for the auction house and to develop their career. It's unfortunate. For example, I work with several contemporary artists, not Chinese artists, as I mentioned. I make sure as much as I can that the work of my artists doesn't go at auction. They're young artists, most of them emerging, a few in their midcareer. Generally speaking, I think auctions are the worst place for contemporary work, especially of a young artist, because there is no track record to sustain it. You have to build up a track record. You have to place the work in museums, biennials, serious collections, etc. It's very discouraging when you open an auction catalog, it's March 2014, for example, and I'm seeing a lot of work dated in 2014, just out of the studio. This is not the way I was brought up. The system works well, not because it's not transparent, on the contrary, the system works well because the galleries work very hard to support and nurture artists. They support them when they sell and they support them when they don't sell. The auction houses, when you don't sell, what do they do? They dump the artist, because it's about numbers. As

I said, people are a little bit focused on Asia. I don't think that's just an Asian issue. The first artist to do a oneman auction was Damien Hirst. All his works went straight from the studio into the auction. He is leading the way, and he is certainly not Asian. It's a complex issue. I think the collectors that are really serious, even if they start at the auction, they will eventually find their way to the galleries because that's the natural progression. I speak with a lot of very good collectors who sometimes buy at auctions. They say that the auctions are where they fill gaps in their collection, but the galleries are where they go to look at art, learn about art and to understand it.

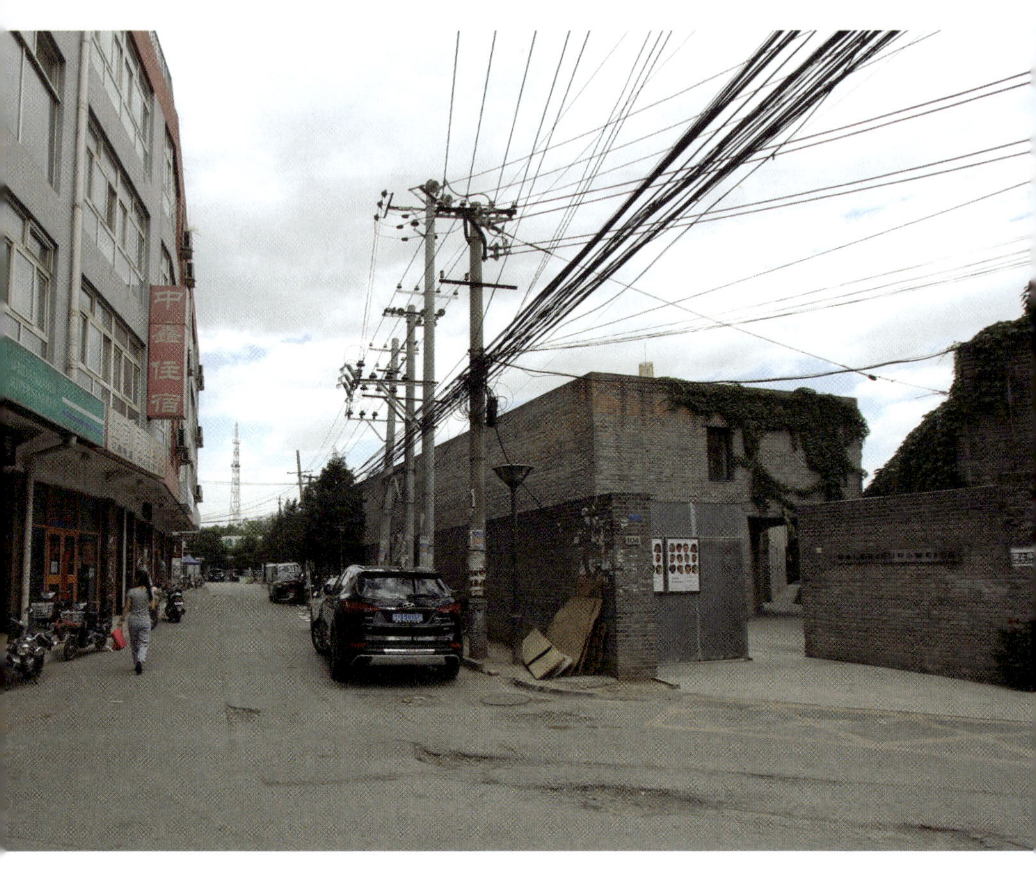

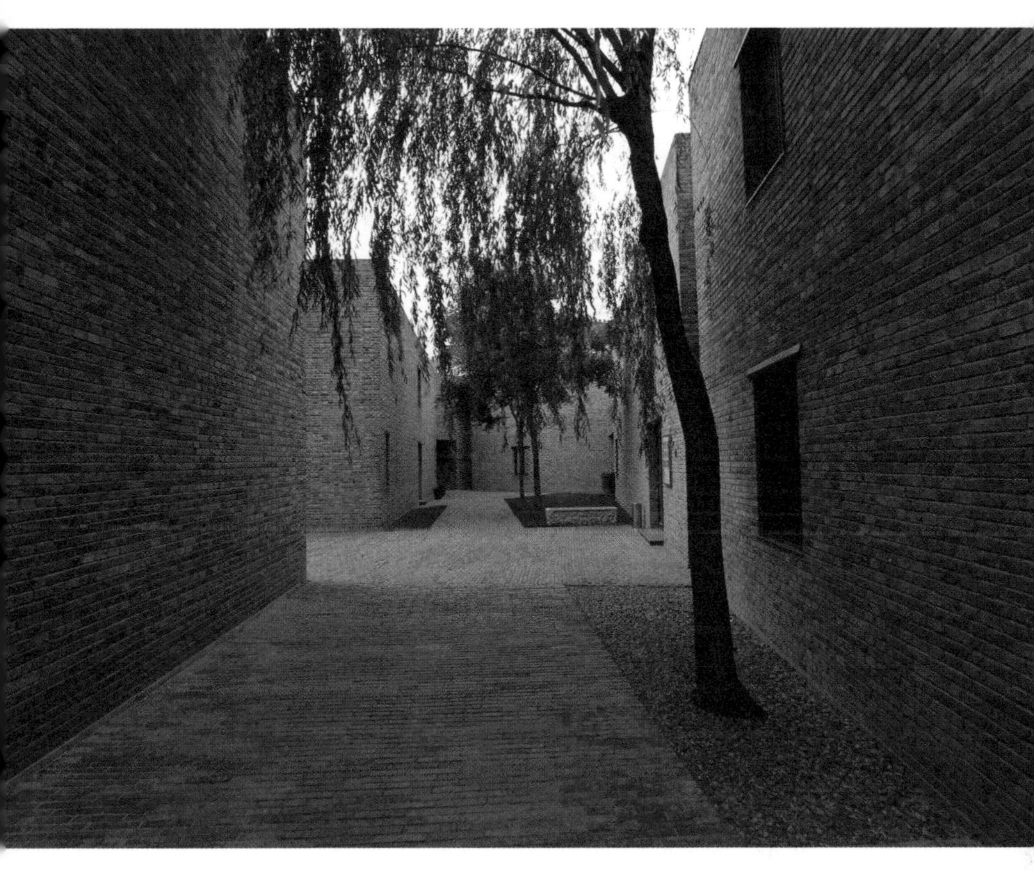

"We are all here 20 years too early"

A talk with Meg Maggio
Gallerist, Beijing/Hong Kong

Meg Maggio awaits her visitors in her gallery in Beijing. She has just opened another gallery in Hong Kong and is preparing for her participation in the Art Basel in Hong Kong. In a long talk lasting almost two hours she offers us a tour d'horizon of the most varied aspects and facets of the Asian art world, with which she has been intimately acquainted for a good two decades. The basic tone of her presentation is a composure which calls to mind the Buddhist virtue of serenity and a both historical and inter-culturally relativizing form of critical reflexivity. This concerns not least the all too evident tendency of Western people to overestimate their own role and importance in this geographically, demographically and culturally so important region, whose rapid and dizzy rise to the status of a global economic power of the first category still stuns Western observers. The leap of the tiger into contemporaneity is reflected not only in the process of catching up with the productive forces and market logic unleashed in the capitalist West during the last two decades, but also and not least in a rapid modernization of cultural codes and life styles, particularly among the upper and middle classes which have come to the fore in the recent decades. Like their Western counterparts almost a century earlier they too now emphatically seek an emblematic expression of their social status as a ruling class in modern or now contemporary art. Meg Maggio regards this development with the critical eye of an art lover, who sees in the often blind and unconditional fascination especially of the younger generation of Asian artists for Western consumer culture an obstacle to the further development of their own cultural and artistic traditions. She pleads, however, for an acceptance of these "teething troubles" as an almost inevitable and transient phase in the development of the Chinese art world.

It seems important to her, above all, that the Western, all too ethnocentric, distorted and narrow view of this region should be widened to permit an insight into its enormous cultural diversity. In this huge geographical space ranging from Korea and Japan to India, from Indonesia to Hong Kong, a multiplicity of economic and cultural traditions and activities can be found, which in her opinion offer the local artists better opportunities to achieve visibility and to establish themselves in the art field and can emancipate them from the still existing fixation on the long-lasting hegemony of the Western art field. At the same time Meg Maggio reconstructs in an understandable way the specific socio-historical features of the Asian art world, namely the lack of all institutional structures typical of the "operational system" of art in the West – museums, galleries etc. – and the accompanying power and decisive influence of the auction houses, which have filled the vacuum and become a central driving force in the emergence and further development of the Asian art market. This line of argument clearly relativizes the critically negative view of Western observers on the key role of the auction houses in Asia.

Can you talk a little bit about Chinese contemporary art? When did it take off?

I would say it started in 1979, the stars movement, post-Cultural Revolution. You can say, post-Cultural Revolution is slowly, then crescendo would be between 1993 and 2000, probably 2000. '93 is still quiet, still too much influence of the foreigners. By 2000, it really became indigenous. How would I mark that day? It's because 2000 was the first international attempt at an international biennale in China, and that was in Shanghai. Of course, what would they do? They invited an overseas Chinese, Hou Hanru, to be the curator. There's always been this kind

of inflated value here, post-1949 inflated value, over-estimation of the merits of an overseas education.

Some say that the first generation who entered the field of contemporary art in China also did a lot of importing of Western aesthetics and later on we could see the arrival of a more autonomous Chinese art.

I think the autonomous, indigenous Chinese art is less influenced by Western contemporary art. The influence is tiny. For Urs Meile and myself – he's a good friend, we have been doing this for over 20 years – it seems like a long time. For sometimes we forget that it's still the very early stages, super early stages. This tsunami of Western influence that is coming to China is going to take a while. The younger generation is still very much in love with the Western consumer culture. Sadly, it's going to take a while to sort that problem out. You complain about Hollywood, you complain about Gucci and Prada, you complain about whoever you want, but the reality is, there's a love of all that we call the bling-bling. You know, more is more, and that's going to take a while. I think the thing that happens, like, is all this influence coming in here, and I'm talking now about even the young artists; in many ways the young artists are the worst, the most influenced, possibly because they are young.

Would you say that the process of globalization of art is a kind of one way road coming from the West to the East?

No, not at all. It's two-way. And I don't think you can talk about, say, this is my problem, I don't think you can talk about China. I think China is the elephant in the room, but what's happening here is also happening all over Asia. I don't think you can talk about isolating China. The same thing is happening in Indonesia, Philippines, Korea, Japan, Taiwan, Thailand, Malaysia. Of course with local idiosyncratic characteristics, but this phenomenon of globalization has swept over all of Asia. These artists are getting drowned in all this Western consumer culture stuff. It's going to take time to digest and figure out what is useful and what is not useful, what is meaningful and what is not. It's still going to take some time. Another friend and I, we joked, we said we are all here 20 years too early.

In most studies in Europe, people say that it's quite difficult to install galleries in the Chinese world, because they prefer auction houses and they have another relationship to galleries.

I don't agree, no. Give me the example. Look in Zurich, look in Geneva, look in Basel, tell me how many foreign galleries you see. Zero! Maybe one. Zero! It's always difficult to run a business like a retail operation in a country that is not your own. Language barrier, cultural barrier, economic system, and taxation barrier, everywhere. I think Beijing, for many historical reasons, is peculiarly cosmopolitan. You look at this town, you have galleries that are operating with local partners or all autonomously from so many countries: Korea, Indonesia, Taiwan, Singapore, Thailand, Japan, Germany, Holland, the United States, the U.K, Switzerland, Russia. Just imagine, where do you have that anywhere else? It's very odd. In a way it's idiosyncratic. Beijing is a strangely and oddly cosmopolitan city. I often compare Beijing to Berlin. There are a lot of similarities, from the concentration of universities, the concentration of intellectual talents, and the concentration of galleries from all around the world. The fact is that you can go there and set up a business relatively easily. I think we get frustrated because we somehow had this unrealistic expectation that China should somehow conform to our foreign business needs. To me, it is a little bit post-colonial. The problem of why the hell should they do things our way or my way. Why? There is continuous frustration because China can be very charming in its ability to attract foreign investment and foreign business. But the complaint might be about the support and the infrastructure. The attraction is very strong. The sales pitch is very strong. Come in do business! Cost of operating is not so high, tax incentive, whatever. But then people think, I came in, I set up my business and no one seems to care. Of course no one cares. 1.3 billion people! Why should they care about you silly little foreigner with your little art gallery business. What's your annual turnover? Nothing. We're trying to build a steel plant and sell it to Iraq. Why do we care about your little business? Let's be realistic. Our little art business is small potatoes. I think with the auction houses, I don't believe the problem is unique to China. As far as the strength and power of the auction houses is concerned, it's really a worldwide phenomenon. The difference in China is that because of the Cultural Revolution, and there are post-Cultural Revolution events, the museum world was not very, putting it mildly, the museum world was not supportive of contemporary art. Of course, in the rest of the world, we have four legs on the table: the museum world, the gallery world, the auction world, the collector/fair world. You need all those things to make a mature system, a self-functioning system. In China, contemporary art took off without the museum, with little to some museum support, but it was erratic and less than ideal. It wasn't zero, but we couldn't really depend on it, it came and went, was there one minute and gone the next. They were very suspicious of the control by the Ministry of Culture, very suspicious of the contemporary art world, as if it was some kind of Trojan horse for subversive activity. So they said why should we support you guys? We don't trust you guys. You are just going to make trouble like in '89. Why should we trust you? So you're going to use the museums to barbarize. So it doesn't make sense. There weren't not only enough venues, but not enough critical affirmation of artistic value. You would normally look to the museums, the art historians and the art museum curators to affirm the value of why is this cup good art? Here someone fills that vacuum, and the people who fill that vacuum are mainly the auction houses. In a way, it's pragmatism. We can't wait for the museums to show up, we have to get on with things. So now the museums are more important. Today the museums are much more important, and now you have a very strange situation because everything here... we joke, we say this, something happens in China, and it's interesting and exciting, some phenomenon, or some market phenomenon, or some social phenomenon, so we say let's just hold on, and then sadly China floods the market, and it's a mess, and we've seen it, with antique furniture, with this, with manufacturing, with everything. Now we have too many platforms, too many museums, both state and private, too many galleries and none of content. This is an interesting recent phenomenon. It's going to be interesting for the next few years. You've got artists who are not necessarily in a way... it's back to localization, because they are not necessarily looking for the show abroad. They can run around all the provinces because every province is building a museum, and they don't have language problems, and they don't have

cultural problems. It's economically more feasible. They don't want money. Honestly, they really don't want money in Swiss Francs or US dollars. They want money in Renminbi. No language barrier. Of course, everyone wants recognition in their home country, and now this is a terrific opportunity for them to get that recognition. There's really a swing back to the local, and artists coming back here and artists who believe they were good artists. I always think, my personal opinion is, everyone underestimates geography, as far as the way it shapes national culture is concerned. People forget that China has such an active and busy presence in Asia. It is very much the same with the artists. If you ask most of the artists 'Where you are going to exhibit this year? Where have you exhibited the last five years?', the answer is 'Every Asian country.' They've been everywhere: India, Indonesia, Singapore, Malaysia, Korea, Taiwan, Japan. We sometimes mistakenly made this East West dichotomy. Do not discount the regional activity. It is super important.

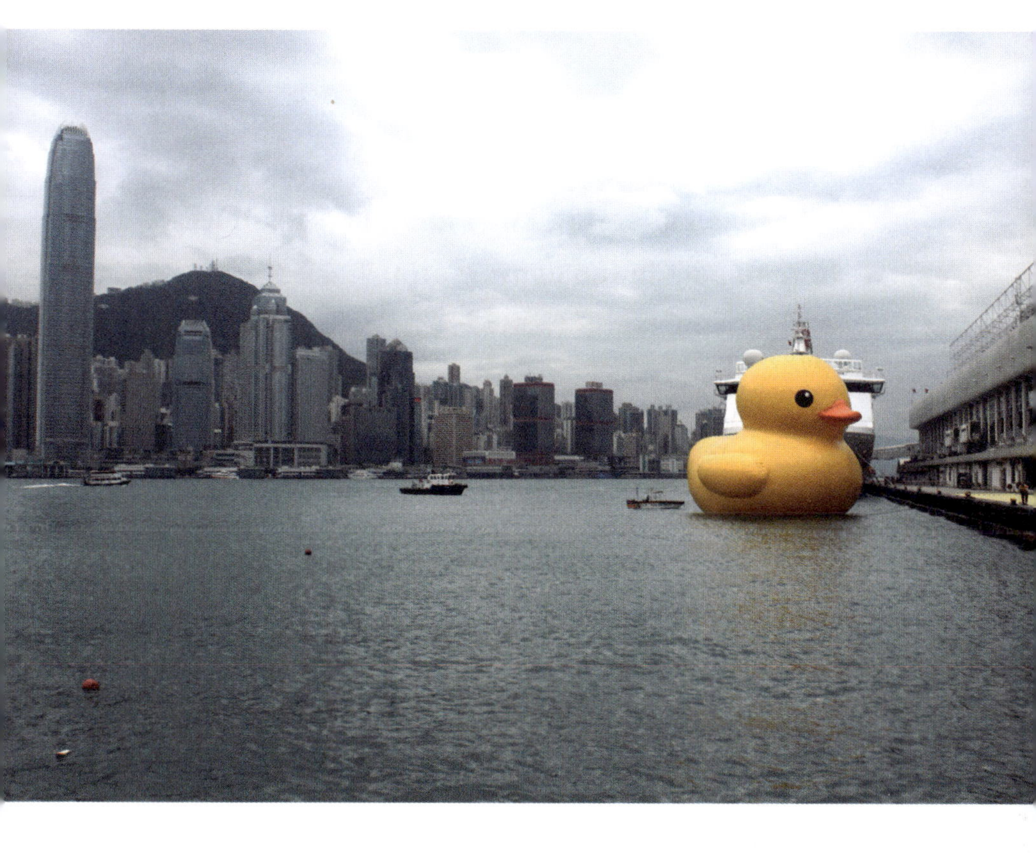

"Through collecting I was able, in a small way, to take part in the conversation"

A talk with Alan Lo
Collector, Hong Kong

In Alan Lo we meet a young art collector who occupies an important position in the art field in Hong Kong, who is excellently networked. He is the Chairman of the Hong Kong Ambassadors of Design with its seat in the Hong Kong Arts Council and was a member of the advisory group of the Hong Kong International Art Fair, the predecessor of the Art Basel in Hong Kong. As a businessman he is the co-founder and director of the Press Room Group, which runs restaurants in Hong Kong that specialize in the enjoyment of art. They present varying exhibitions on their premises which are curated by artists such as Ai Weiwei or Danh Vö among others.

As in other accounts, Lo also indicates how young the Hong Kong art field is in the sphere of contemporary art. In 2007, when he began collecting art, there were only a few small galleries which, according to Lo, did not offer any qualitatively high-class works. The market at the time was dominated by the auctions which took place in spring and fall. Although Hong Kong has a long tradition in the collecting of art this is concerned, as he says, with pre-modern Chinese art, with furniture and ceramics. His father belongs to the older generation, who live out their passion for collecting privately and do not share it with the public.

Lo, however, belongs to a generation which is closely connected with the emerging art field of Hong Kong, which has profoundly influenced their passion for collecting. In the way they go about collecting they can be clearly distinguished from the generation of their predecessors. Lo collects contemporary art by local and international artists, meets his peers at vernissages, and through various networks he attempts to improve the visibility of art, and hence his own position, in the city. Linking Hong Kong with the global art field is advantageous for him, as the international galleries and the Art Basel are allies in the process of achieving a view of art nurtured by contemporary and global aesthetics. He himself has become a master of this view.

In the city Lo plays a visible role, not only as a collector but also as a multiplicator. By global standards, however, he is in the same peripheral position as the local artists. He is not, for example, in a position to acquire the works of "museum-quality blue chip artists". He lacks not only the economic resources but also the reputation necessary in the art world.

How did you start working in the art field and what exactly are you doing?

I have never been professionally involved in art. My father has collected since the late 70s. His focus has always been on 20th century modern Chinese Art. More precisely paper works. That's the kind of the environment I experienced when growing up: going to galleries, museums, auctions with him. But I never studied art. I painted, obviously I painted. I did art when I was a student and I did potentially progress into architectural work when I was in college. But I never professionally practiced architecture. It was 2008 when Art HK started up. Before that I was even invited to be one of the advisory group members. And I don't know what kind of added values I can bring, but I am happy to support them. We had a fair, back in the 90s called Art Asia; I remember it was in early 92 and 93. Which also awakens memories of seeing a very

well executed fair. But I think timing wise, it wasn't ready. The city wasn't quite ready for it. So after a couple of years the fair went bankrupt. I think it was in late 2009, early 2010, that the HK Arts Development Council, which is the government's principle arts-related funding body, appointed me as a member of the council. That was when I started to get involved with kind of the public side of things and meanwhile I continued to collect casually, I guess. For lack of a better description I can't say I am a serious collector, as I think you need a lot of money to be collecting seriously.

Do you collect with a goal in mind?

I think it is more impromptu, and obviously in the preliminary phase. I started in 2007. That was before we had all these international galleries. It was the time when the scene was still very much dominated by auctions and simply because we didn't have a thriving gallery scene like we see today. I shouldn't say that. We did have galleries, but they were domestic small-scale galleries most of which were not very influential and did not play the role of educating, building the audience or developing the artists. They were simply the galleries that sell arts. I think auctioning actually very much sets the tone for what you see, what people buy, what is the status quo. That was the landscape we had: spring auctions and autumn auctions. And some not so nice or rather small galleries in town that dealt with all sort of things from the not so great, sort of BCD grade art to more quality things. I think it was very much China, China contemporary, contemporary Asia. I think there was really not that much else to see. So, you looked at the auction catalogues and you thought that whatever was in there was a great investment or had a certain validation. Because these artists were serious enough. But obviously you are soon to find out that this is not the case. So it is kind of a process that every emerging market goes through. I think it was actually very nice to see an art fair, because you meet quality, professional galleries and dealers and kind of learn about what is happening in the West. For example, in terms of how you develop a relationship with artists, or the importance of growing with the artist, placing the works in the right collections and institutions and going to the right places. That's just something we don't see very much in Hong Kong or in China. Everyone only talks about auction records, so it's quite different. It's very different. It's a good learning experience I guess to get to know about what's going on in the world and also to get to see a lot more than just what's in Hong Kong, China or Asia. The scope suddenly becomes completely international and a million times more interesting, especially in the contemporary context. Artists that are dealing with issues that are not just local but global issues. So, it's nice to see how that interacts with what other people are doing and with different ways to express ideas. The whole business of going beyond your traditional medium, going into performance and into videos and all these things, obviously in the earlier stages of collecting it feels very foreign and almost even irrelevant, because it is so out there, so beyond what my understanding is.

What is your motivation to collect art? What is your collection about? What has changed since you started?

I was buying from the auctions mainly contemporary Chinese art because that's mainly what the discussion is about. Obviously, with Art Hong Kong coming to the city, it exposed me to many other things and I became curious and started looking into other Asian areas like Korea, Japan and Southeast Asia. In 2011, that was when I started, that was when I bought the first Western contemporary piece of art. I have been doing that since then. It diversifies and is a kind of mix. To me, it becomes a lot more interesting.

I think I was very excited by what was happening here in Hong Kong in terms of the art scene, in terms of Hong Kong slowly becoming a part of this international dialogue. That's one of the reasons why. Through collecting, I was able, in a small way, to take part in the conversation. Obviously, this space I started a year ago takes my role to a wholly different spectrum. We use it as a platform to invite curators, to do free shows each year; we do talks, we do a lot of different things and we get to meet really interesting people. I guess with the museum, M+, this will be happening in a few years' time as well as now, with even Hong Kong art, Hong Kong artists becoming a part of that conversation; it's all becoming very exciting. Also, I love to travel. I think art often takes me to very interesting places and I meet really interesting people. I still think that I'm an amateur. I'm still learning.

Do you collect mostly contemporary art?

Yes. With a small percentage of things that are 20th century modern from Asian. But Western will be mainly contemporary, all contemporary, in fact.

Are there more unknown artists or more well-known artists in your collection?

I think it's a mixture. You would find interesting artists that are emerging artists who are becoming quite prominent or perhaps about to become very prominent. I suppose it becomes quite interesting when you start looking anywhere between the 20,000 and 50,000 US dollars area. In terms of good contemporary living artists, there is a lot. I try very much to zoom in and look at what I can manage. Obviously, I am not a professional curator.

No blue chips.

Obviously, for me, it would be very difficult to buy, I wouldn't be able to afford or have access to museum-quality blue chip artists. So I have to come down to what I can afford, to buy something meaningful. It wouldn't be meaningful if I were to go for a C-grade. It would be quite meaningless. Even if one takes an investment standpoint, it's not even a good idea.

Do you buy your art all over the world or do you have particular galleries here that you value the most?

There are galleries here that we have relationships with which bring good artists that I like. We would buy locally. But at the same time, I also try to go to fairs. I also try to work closely with Hong Kong-based art advisors who would also sometimes show us things that otherwise we wouldn't notice. Maybe some people do work with an advisor because they can get better discounts or because they have access to certain things. That's all important. But at the same time, they also help you in some ways to shape the collection. My advisor and I are very good friends too. He understands me. He understands what I am interested in. It's about also helping build personality in the collection as well.

Are you interested in the global art scene or in global art production? What's the reason? Travelling for example?

Why I am collecting beyond Asia, right? I feel that it's important to understand that the present generation or the present time issues that artists deal with are no longer restricted by their physicality. A lot of artists and the concepts and the body of work... it's becoming this cross-border situa-tion, added to the fact that there are so many amazing interesting Asian artists who are practicing abroad, in a way that I would collect. As you do that, you also start to see very interesting European and American artists who do things that resonate with Asian counterparts. Hence, it became apparent that the collection needs to become... I am not saying that... I think it's still a small collection.

How many pieces do you have?

There are 70 pieces in the collection, but I think eventually it would be a prominent part of the collection, the Western part. It's very interesting for me, for someone from Asia to be looking at this situation.

From your point of view, is there a difference between Western taste and Eastern taste in global contemporary art?

I think yes. But I think it's easy to generalize. I think a lot of galleries want to... I think they understand that. They say, 'I am going to this fair in Asia. Let's bring some works that are red in color because red is a prosperous color.' Someone actually said to me the other day, 'Is that true?' I said, 'Yes, but thanks.' I think sophisticated collectors or institutions must look beyond that because that's not very sophisticated. I believe the best collectors shouldn't be... It will be very unfortunate to stereotype to that extent.

Can you tell us something about the collector scene in Hong Kong or in China?

I can tell you about Hong Kong. China I am not so familiar with. Hong Kong has a long collecting history, longer than most... when you think beyond the contemporary context. We have some of the greatest collectors of old Chinese furniture; we have collectors of snuff bottles; we have ceramics; we have classic pre-20th century Chinese paintings, some of the best collections. It's just that that generation of collectors in Hong Kong tends to be very low profile. They tend to be almost a little secretive. That's the Chinese culture, you don't show off collections. It's to be looked at by the collector himself, his family, or his very close friends, or his close circle of collector friends he trusts. Obviously, the attitude is changing. Collectors have become a little bit more public in terms of taking part in things like that.

A young generation like yours?

Yes. There are collectors over there. It's still a very small scene. We always end up seeing the same 10 or 20 people in different galleries, in the openings. But it's growing. Peo-

ple are really open-minded now. In the past, the Western context was quite foreign to them. Now I think it's becoming much more... I suppose it was an education process over the last few years, a lot more people have become interested. They may not be big collectors. They are definitely willing to take risks. They buy challenging works. It's interesting. It's not just the most clearly commercial things. You see collectors that actually have unique thinking and they have a vision.

How important is the value of art for you or for your colleagues? Do you see art as an investment or is it only for the love of art?

We'd love to say it's just for the love, but no, value is very important. I'm putting a lot of my savings into it. I like to think that at some point the art will still be worth something. Who knows? Who knows what's going to happen? Maybe one day I'll need money. We are not looking at it in a speculative manner, but from a wealth preservation standpoint, it is important to look at it... We are not trying to make short-term money.

Is price an indicator for quality?

Is price an indication for quality? Definitely no. There are so many good artists who are relatively affordable simply because the market is not mature enough for their kind of work. I could name so many amazing Japanese artists who have exhibited in major institutions, whose works are probably less than 20,000 US dollars, but they are such good artists. It's just that the market is not seeing the kind of activity one needs.

*How would you define quality
in art production?*

I think there are a few ways to look at it. If you look at works that are traditional, in terms of workmanship and techniques, obviously that's one thing. But in the contemporary context concepts seem to be… In fact, it took me so long to understand in the contemporary context. It's not just about composition. It's not just about the way you apply the medium and all that, which is very much the case if you look at the pre-contemporary context; it is very much technique.

*So you are more interested
in the concepts of art?*

No. I am actually interested in both. For example, we look at an artist, like Zhang Dali, who is a great Chinese painter. It's interesting. For two decades, contemporary China was very much about revolution. It was very much about political gesture. It was very much about the propaganda. And then, you start to see a new generation of painters who are going back to being painters, which to me is quite refreshing, the fact that it's not just about Chairman Mao, this sort of thing that generalizes what contemporary Chinese meant for a while. It's hard to say I go for concept or I go for… It's hard to say.

*How would you describe Hong Kong
today as an art field, what kind of
characteristics does Hong Kong have
and how is it different to other places
that you know?*

Well I certainly think it has developed itself into the international art hub in Asia. I think progressively, in terms of the collecting scene here. I also think of the effect it has in terms of creating a lot more interest among new collectors, the younger collectors getting into it and with more people in the picture. There is you know M+; we see a lot more activities now, even though we don't have a museum yet. With the museum starting to acquire works and with the international competition for architecture, the momentum is building. And also what's nice to see is that Hong Kong artists are gaining a lot more recognition than before. Even though we are talking about just a handful. But at least it is a good message to the whole art community; obviously, there are no problems in the overall situation. In my opinion there is still a heavy imbalance in the whole ecology here, because there is a lot going on on the trading side of things, there is a lot going on with kind of more established and top artists and galleries and dealers. There is a lot going on, a lot of activities, but then if you take a bottom up approach, Hong Kong is still looking for that one home grown gallery, the true Hong Kong gallery that will have a program of regional international artists. One day, if we see something like that, it will be so amazing. Now you have local galleries and you have international galleries who come and open a branch in Hong Kong. I think there's something in-between that is missing. The regional international players need to take a more active role in engaging the local community, even if it's going to be only 2 per cent of your program and even if you take only one Hong Kong artist. I think it's essential not just to say, 'Okay we will do another Damien show, okay we will do another Richard Prince show'. Yes, for commercial reasons that makes sense, but I think a community, a city can't just be so skewed towards the business trade side of things. I think art is much more than that. It is not a commodity. There is the academic side of things, there is the sort of human side of things. A city where it's only

trade but no kind of active participation and interaction with the artistic community just feels very empty and lacks substance.

*Do you think the art community
also has to appeal to the masses?
I mean now it looks as if art is only
for a certain type of people,
it is really small.*

The audience is very limited at the moment, even though it is growing but it is still very small.

*Do you think that is also an aim of the
art community, or should it be its aim,
to also start to engage more people?
And how can or should they do that?
Or to get a bigger audience?*

I think also the fact that we still don't have an institution, like a major museum or a private museum or a non-profit foundation, big enough to attract, to generate interest from the general public, I think that's part of the... You know I don't want to put all the blame on the commercial players, because I understand they are here to do business so at the end of the day it's not a charity.

I think especially in Hong Kong, space could serve as a catalyst, I think part of the problem now is space and also the whole kind of building community. I mean if you look at 798 in Beijing, it all started with space, with some cheap space that was made available. This is how you start a community. And as much as Hong Kong is so difficult with space, we still have space. We were just talking about all these abandoned public schools in Hong Kong, schools that were previously not well run, that do not have enough students, the government has this policy of shutting them down, so basically there are a lot of these empty schools waiting to be redeveloped or waiting, in terms of the whole bureaucratic process, to become something else. And that was one of the things we talked about, we said if we could take it, we could be anywhere because Hong Kong is so small; even if it is a 30 minute drive outside of Central, you can build something really meaningful and these schools are pretty big and places where you can start to engage a variety of different kinds of players. You can work with commercial players, who pay a higher rent, will still bring in quality content. You could be working with a foundation like the Ullens, or maybe the Burgers, to do programs and support young artists, you could bring in some kind of a lifestyle element where you start to sell limited edition design. So there are a lot of things to do if you have space.

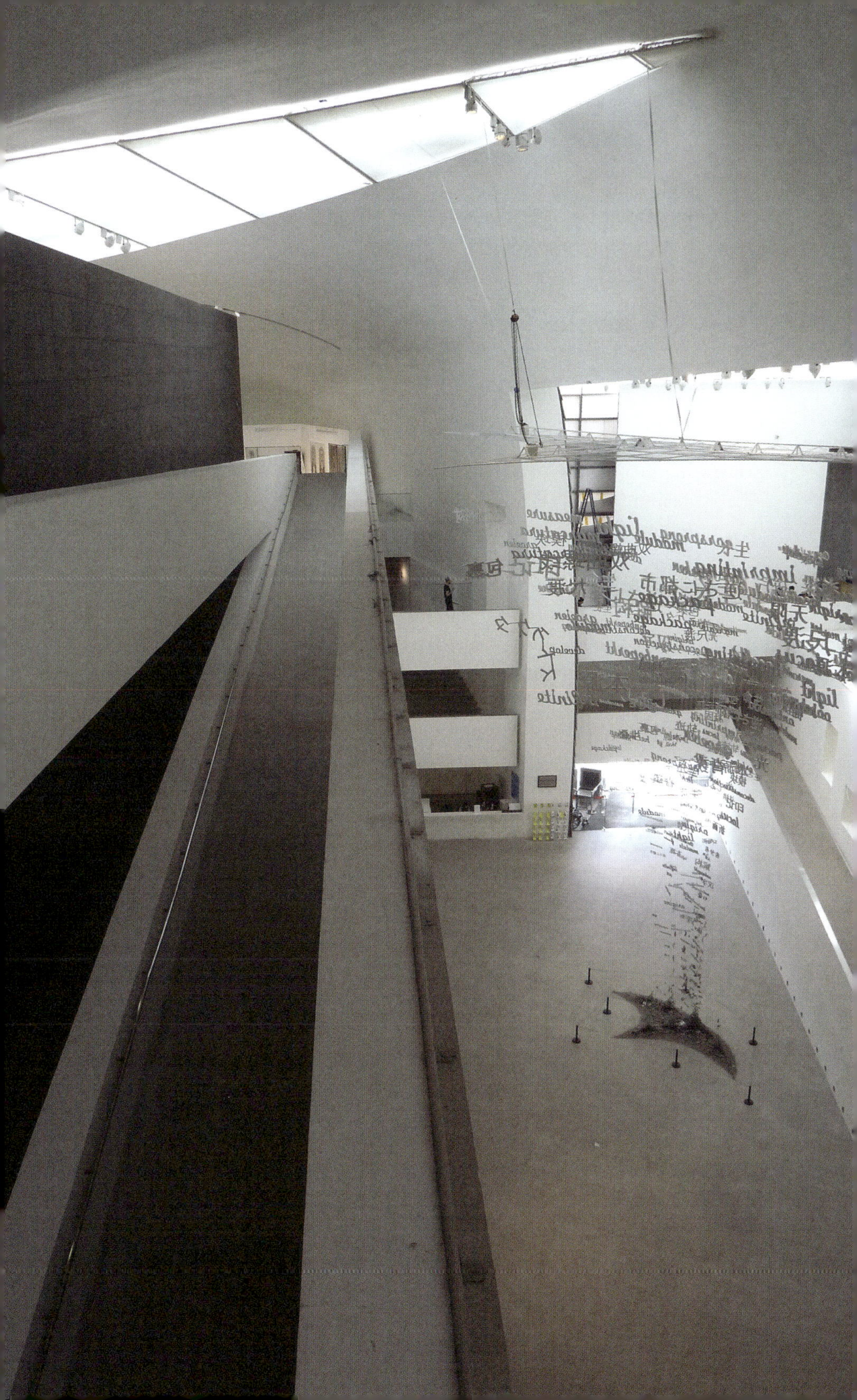

"My position would be as an educator first"

A talk with Arthur Solway
Gallerist, Shanghai

Arthur Solway, an experienced art dealer represents the James Cohan Gallery in China. The renowned gallery for contemporary art with its head office in New York, which represents, among others, established artists such as Bill Viola, Robert Smithson, Richard Long and Fred Tomaselli, is one of the pioneers on the Chinese mainland. It opened a branch there in July 2008 as the first gallery from the USA. The rooms of the gallery in Shanghai are on the ground floor of an old Art Deco villa with a picturesque garden in the middle of the French Concession district, an oasis with a post-colonial European flair. In the meantime it is reckoned among the top galleries in China and has held exhibitions of important international artists including Louise Bourgeois, Bill Viola, Richard Long, Alex Katz or Francesco Clemente, but has primarily shown the works of young Chinese artists.

The gallery owes this pioneering role above all to Arthur Solway, who has long shown a deep personal interest in the country and its culture. He comes from a family of gallerists and consequently regards art as "a part of my genetic code", as he himself puts it. Before going to China he worked for 30 years in New York, among others for the legendary gallerists Leo Castelli and Peter Blum. The changes in the "Middle Kingdom", whose language he speaks fluently, exerted a magical attraction over him. "I wanted to be in the front row while the transformation of China was taking place."

Shanghai seemed to be the most suitable place for the expansion of the gallery. The city has a long tradition and regularly attracts foreign visitors who do business there. But Arthur Solway was also thoroughly aware of the risks involved. The gallery did indeed have customers in Japan, South Korea and Taiwan, but China was uncharted territory. To open a gallery in China it was necessary until a few years ago not only to have a Chinese partner, but also to make deals with the authorities. So-called "wholly foreign-owned enterprises" could only be established after 2006. This was, therefore, the right point in time to set up in China.

At the beginning Solway saw himself in the role of an "educator". Unlike other gallerists who sell Chinese art to Western collectors he wanted to help well-known artists from the USA and Europe, who had a certain affinity with and sensibility for Asia, to make their début on Chinese territory and to bring them closer to the Chinese public for the first time. But this did not mean pushing business interests into the background. To ignore the market in a world involving the exchange of goods, information and ideas would have been naive. Arthur Solway was fully aware of this. Although at the beginning the gallery was dependent upon its foreign business connections, it could nonetheless build on the potential of the wealthy Chinese upper class.

"The gallery is and must always be a platform for ideas, and for artists who are transforming the way we see and experience the world" is Solway's philosophy. For him art is a language which is understood everywhere in the world, regardless of whether it is shown in the USA, Europe or China. At the beginning the interest was subdued, but in the meantime much has changed. The public is more receptive and the Chinese collectors are as passionate as their colleagues in the West.

The decision to open the gallery in the French Quarter and not in a popular art district such as M50 Moganshan Road was deliberately taken, as Arthur Solway emphasizes. The circle of people who come to the old villa is in his eyes primarily interested in art and in what the gallery presents and embodies. The presentation itself, in the original living quarters, and not in a cool, over-sized White Cube, is a symbol for the way one can live with and live art. It is inspiring not only for the artists but also for the collectors who can see here how one can live together with art.

We are especially interested in your relations with New York and Shanghai. Perhaps you can briefly tell us when you first went to Shanghai and what the reasons were.

The gallery in New York started in 1999. Both James Cohan and I had been working in the art world our entire lives. It goes back to my family. My father has had a gallery for 50 years. He shows artists like Nam June Paik and John Cage. It's been part of my genetic code for my whole life. Jim and I are related, we are relatives and he's my first cousin. When my father used to travel around the Midwest, he would sometimes go to Jim's house and would set up things to show clients in the region. It was kind of like working as a private art dealer on the road. I moved to New York in 1979. I had been in school and didn't know what to do. I grew up in a gallery. Of course the first thing I thought I would do is to get a job in a gallery, doing something, even sweeping that place up. I stayed in New York from 1979 forward up until about 2006 when I decided that I wanted to move to China. I studied Chinese. I was married to a woman from Taiwan for nearly 10 years. It was already part of my thinking. I had been in New York for 35 years and I worked for some great people. I worked for Leo Castelli and for Peter Blum, and I worked for

lots of other people. Jim Cohan had worked for Anthony d'Offay, Paula Copper, John Weber. Then he came back to New York in 1998 with his family. He opened his own gallery on 57th Street in 1999. Jim called me up and said, 'What are you doing?' I had finished working for Blum and was publishing some print editions and selling on the road, not unlike what my father did many years ago. Jim asked, 'Can you come and work with me?' I of course said, 'Yes.' That was early on. The first show of the gallery was early photographs of Gilbert & Georges. The gallery's program was beginning to be formulated with some cornerstone artists such as Bill Viola and the estate of Robert Smithson. But my serious interest in China would come later. By 2005 I was feeling ready to leave New York. We had clients in Japan, Korea and Australia. I thought, you know, something is going happen. I wanted to be in the front row while the transformation of China was taking place. Jim and I were in Tokyo in 2006 for the Mori Art Museum exhibition of Bill Viola. Jim said to me, 'Your Chinese is pretty good. Why don't you go to mainland China and see if we can take the Viola show to Beijing or Shanghai?' I immediately said, 'Okay' and jumped on a plane and came. I didn't care for Beijing very much. I didn't like the energy there. It felt sprawling and somewhat like Los Angeles. But when I got to Shanghai, I fell in love with the city. I was fascinated by the colonial, post-colonial history, the former French Concession area. The city was a lot like New York. And I said, 'You know what? This is where I want to be.' That is the short story in a nutshell.

Was there a problem for Westerners to get to Shanghai to run a space and to build up a brand?

No, I came... By 2006 you could open a foreign enterprise without a Chinese partner. Prior to that, in the 90s, you still had to have a Chinese partner.

Did you bring in Western artists?

The idea originally was first to bring a program of the gallery there showing Western contemporary art and Western European art. It is a platform for other artists that the gallery doesn't necessarily represent and where we can collaborate with other galleries, like Mark di Suvero, an American artist who happened to be born in China in 1933 and was part of the Jewish Diaspora. During the darker years in Europe, when Mussolini was coming to power, families like di Suvero's left and thus came to China. You could come to China then without a passport if you were a Jew running from the Nazis or the fascists. But to tell you more about it, these artists I invited to come to show in China were never shown there before. I like artists who are Western that have some sensibility towards Asia. That made sense to me at the beginning. I showed Richard Long, for instance. He came here and made work, using indigenous materials – local materials like stone and Yangtze River mud – and his work is simple to understand; it is universal. Stone, clay, circles. It is a universal language. Different, right? There were artists that I represented, like Yunfei Ji, who happened to be Chinese already. I didn't come there thinking that I would do something like what Lorenz Helbling did with setting up a gallery exclusively showing Chinese artists and selling a lot to Western collectors. That didn't interest me.

How was the reaction to the Western artists? Did you have a culturally educated audience?

It was slow at first. This is now our seventh year in business. In that short amount of time a lot has changed. The level of sophistication has grown more. The Taiwanese had been buying Western art already. The Koreans had been buying Western art already; the Japanese throughout the 1980s. The Chinese travel all over the world now. They go to Basel. They go to London. They go to New York. They go to L.A. They travel everywhere. They send their kids to college in Europe and America. They buy apartments in other countries. It is a different world.

What was your first experience when you brought Western artists to China? What changed in seven years?

It doesn't mean very much anymore, but we were the first gallery from New York to open in mainland China. Lots of people would come to the gallery and they would say, 'I've never seen Richard Long before, only in a book. The real thing is very exciting.' I knew that my position here would be as an educator first. I didn't know how business was going to go, not really. I thought it had potential. But I would of course need to sell things in other parts of the world from this side. Most of my business from the first year actually came from Japan, Taipei and Korea. In the first exhibition that I had in the gallery, a woman from Shanghai said, 'I like to be known as a Chinese who collects Western art.' And she bought something from our first exhibition. That was also important to her. That was in 2008. It just kind of grew from there. You have to realize it's only in the last 30 or 35 years that people have made real money. They

spend money on their life styles. They travel. They spend money to send their kids to school, buy apartments and real estate, go out for expensive dinners, spend a thousand dollars for a bottle of wine; but they don't always understand how collecting could also be an asset for them. They're starting now, but at the beginning it wasn't the case. But they are getting that now.

Do they see art mostly as an investment or as...

I don't really differentiate the Chinese much anymore from the Western collectors because collectors here are really passionate. I tell anybody who ever asks me, 'Should I invest in art?' I tell them, 'No.' Find your passion first, learn, make it part of your experience and life; engage with other people, open up your world to other people. The Chinese collectors who are at certain level now that are collecting contemporary art, they all know each other. They are all friends. It becomes a big social activity, which is great. Is that really any different? That is, like Western collectors? Not really.

How important is the marketplace Hong Kong for you or in general for the rich?

It's growing.

Perhaps compared to Singapore? Are there other important fairs? Perhaps more than in Shanghai?

It's a good question actually because it's something I am trying to figure out myself. I spend a good deal of time during the winter travelling to Southeast Asia, going to Jakarta, going to Singapore. I look at the fair in Singapore; I don't do the fair as an exhibitor with a booth. You have to make the strategic decision about where your clients are. But this fair, because it's Art Basel, people come from all over the place. I am not trying to sound overly zealous or flattering, but the truth is this is the most dominant fair in the region now, without question, and probably the one that matters most. But I still spend time on the road seeing collectors in Jakarta or Singapore because I want them to see me here and I make the effort to go visit them. It is a good thing. They come and visit me here. I do think there's growing interest because I meet people who live in Hong Kong that I didn't know before, and who are interested in collecting contemporary art. We meet people here. We make new friends. That's a big part of it. It's always about building and sustaining relationships. People buy art from people that they know.

I have one last question. If this is the frontier of the art market, the emerging market, what about the old art market in the U.S?

They are still very active.

What's the difference?

New York has much more business than I do, in terms of volume, yearly or annually. It has much bigger numbers. There's also a much bigger overhead in New York. Our gallery in New York has 13 employees. Here in Shanghai we have three. It's an exponentially wholly different thing. The galleries like White Cube that are opening in Hong Kong want to have a presence in the region. I came early, so I got a jump on it. I talk to my other Western colleagues who come here and perhaps they are not doing as much, if any, business and they are naturally disappointed, simply because they haven't spent enough time here. They haven't met people. They don't know many people. After seven or eight years on the ground... that's a different position. This is my home now. I've got a family. I have a life here. It's a different deal.

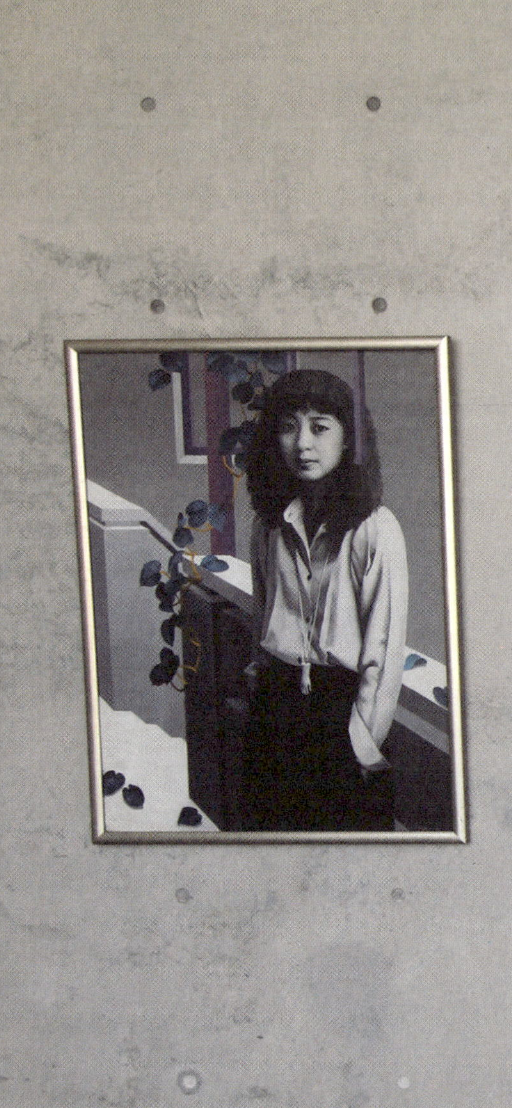

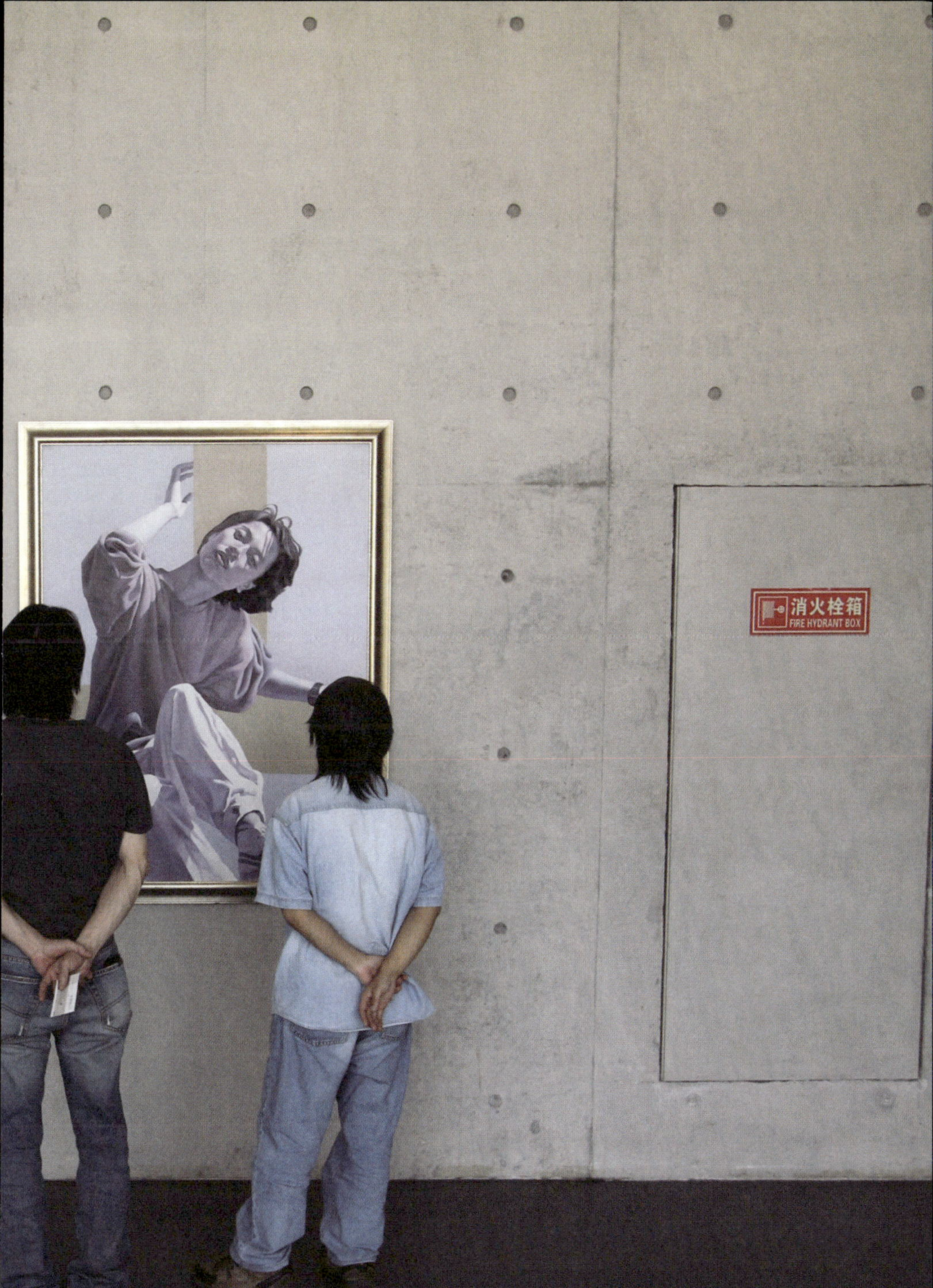
消火栓箱
FIRE HYDRANT BOX

"The best artists here are those who got their higher education abroad"

A talk with Robin Peckham
Curator/Gallerist, Hong Kong

In the course of just a few years Robin Peckham has become a key figure in the arts in both Beijing and Hong Kong. In addition to his experience as a curator and director in both profit and non-profit galleries, Peckham co-founded Saamlung, a gallery in Hong Kong that helped expand the purview of the arts in the city-state better known for its central role in the financial booms of the late 20th century. He moved to Beijing from the U.S. in 2004 and began his work there as a curatorial apprentice at Long March Projects (now Long March Space). In 2009 he relocated to Hong Kong to pursue research-intensive projects. Two years later Saamlung opened, establishing Peckham's central role in Hong Kong arts.

After years working in Hong Kong, Peckham is critical of the role of Hong Kong's education for artists and the disparities between the art market and the production of art where, he says, if you work hard, do your homework, you may be able to get together two dozen artists for studio visits. His insights are critical for the Hong Kong art field and have implications for cities hoping to develop their arts and culture. Peckham's approach, more common in Europe or the US, has always set him apart from his Asian colleagues. While many in Hong Kong clamor for attention from the few gallerists in the city, Peckham has worked to cultivate Hong Kong as a center of cultural and artistic exchange befitting a city with a strong middle class. His critical insights have aimed largely at expanding the scope of the art field in Hong Kong.

Peckham's reflections on Hong Kong offer insight into the ways that the commercial market for art was having a negative impact on the ability of Hong Kong to develop its own artists. Saamlung's closing after nearly two years, despite its highly positive critical reception, further underscored the difficulty for non-profit or artist run spaces to develop. Despite the clear necessity of a motor for new developments in art, Hong Kong seems unwilling or unable to support them. While Peckham is quick to note that there is rich ground for artists to produce cheaply and supplement their own income with fabrication work, his own role as curator and his desire to encourage a more complex international art field in Hong Kong still have not found the infrastructure or support they need not only to survive but to develop with a mature and sophisticated audience. Rental prices for artists and minimal space for experimental projects continue to hamper Hong Kong's arts.

Can Hong Kong, which has developed an image and infrastructure around commerce, create possibilities for artists? Peckham is skeptical. Artists, he insists, have to go abroad in order to be trained and exposed to other artists. Even as training for artists has expanded, he sees the number of artists viable for international markets as abysmally low. Considering how Hong Kong is seeing immense growth in its financial markets and growth of the middle class, this number is much too low. He warns that the pace of the commercialization of art in Hong Kong could be harmful for the emergence of an autonomous art field. For him the only hope is a new middle class, one that is both receptive and supportive of art, which is sensitive to art's relationship to their own cultural self-understanding.

What was the reason that you came to Hong Kong?

In 2009, having been to the fair Art HK and having spent time talking with artists like Lee Kit, Nadim Abbas, Adrian Wong and Magdalen Wong, I was quite interested in the way people were working in Hong Kong and decided to move there myself. It seemed to be much more of a research-focused environment, much more intellectual production. The fact that both Para/Site and Asia Art Archive were there convinced me that Hong Kong would be more amenable to a research mode of curatorial practice than Beijing, which at that time was about big production, commercial sponsorship, and things like that. I was quickly proven wrong. I found that Hong Kong was actually becoming even more ambitious and motivated than Beijing, even noisier than Beijing, with even less actual research going on. Again, I just went with the flow. I spent about a year preparing the idea of a commercial gallery, figuring out how it would look, what it would be like, who would be interested, if there were clients for it. Eventually I opened Saamlung in 2011, with the same group of artists that I have been working with since I decided to move to Hong Kong.

In the year before we opened the gallery we talked a lot about whether there was a need for a gallery like this in Hong Kong and why Hong Kong artists were unhappy with who was representing them. At that point it was really just Hanart and Osage and if you were lucky you could choose between the two if you were a young Hong Kong artist. The idea was to build something that would be based on a program, or ideas, or themes rather than defaulting to a simplified regional identity: Hong Kong artist, South Chinese artist, Southeast Asian artist. It was a community of like-minded artists who wanted to see their work being shown together. As we developed, and I think partially due to the work that we did with those artists at Saamlung, there was growing interest in those artists from other galleries and collectors in a way that made me feel the space was not as necessary anymore. A lot of artists began working with the growing number of galleries doing strong work and I started to feel that there was more of a commercial mandate to make their work visible. While our curatorial vision had always been to work with a group of artists that knew each other but weren't necessarily all in Hong Kong, the economic reality was that while shipping work from the US or Europe was costing us a lot and not selling whereas the Hong Kong art we would spend very little on and it would sell very well. I think all the money we made was from selling local Hong Kong art. At that point we had to decide: it was either continue to push the commercial gallery or try something else. We made the choice to back off from the commercial angle and focus solely on the curatorial project.

Can you illustrate how Hong Kong has developed in the art field in the last couple of years?

It's been very clear. There are very few people involved in the local art scene so you can trace exactly what happened, when it happened, and why it happened. I guess if you had to point to one instigating factor in Hong Kong, it would be Para/Site – which was first founded on a truly international model back in the 1990s – when they were really an artist-organized space. At that point, there was a different generation of artists who were representing

Hong Kong internationally, people like Leung Chi Wo. After a certain point, their careers were taking off and they didn't want to be involved in running a space so much, so they decided to hire an external curator. They eventually ended up with Tobias Berger. I think Tobias has done more than anyone else to really create a vision for not only what international art in Hong Kong can look like, but also what Hong Kong art can be. He invented or brought in a lot of the rhetoric that most young artists are working in now and really helped to create a new vision for people. Later on, of course, Art HK was the one institution that created change and it also opened the eyes of a lot of dealers and artists alike to the fact that Hong Kong could be an interesting place to exhibit.

From 2002 – when the Chinese art market really started to peak – there was this idea that Chinese artists are the future, that the Chinese market is the future for a Western dealer and that everyone had to get to Beijing. Later it was Shanghai and then back to Beijing, and now Shanghai again. There is no real connection with the rest of the world. At that point, collectors in Hong Kong were buying Hong Kong modernists and ink painters, basically, which was not an interesting market to try to break into if you are a dealer from elsewhere.

Beijing was very enthusiastic about bringing in foreign art, and it still is, even if they're not always as excited to buy.

What are the major delineations between Hong Kong and the Western art world?

Of course it really is completely different. I mean Hong Kong is still missing so many of the very, very basic links that would make it something you'd call an art scene. There are so few artists here. People often ask us to set up studio visits here and want to know how many interesting artists there are in Hong Kong. You can say there are about a dozen people you can go talk to. If you have some time and patience you can double that list. Maybe. It's nothing compared to what a city of this size and the level of education should be able to produce. People often talk about how difficult it is to be an artist here, but I don't really think that's true. The cost of living is high but production is not. But I think the reason comes from there being no strong artist-training program. I think that is one of the real reasons why there are so few practicing artists. An artist goes through a weak art program, comes out with a degree, and then there is no way to professionalize that kind of practice; there is nowhere to show new work or get feedback and exchange ideas. In addition, the focus is on technology and design in Hong Kong to the detriment of creative practices. I still think that the best artists here are those who got their higher education abroad; it allows them more exposure to working artists, kinds of galleries, and other possibilities of working. Artists trained here graduate and often don't have a vision for what the art scene could be; they ultimately end up with one of the galleries available to them and have the scene defined for them in that way.

What about the very strong commercial market side?

The commercial side is not so large either. There is a lot of untapped potential in collecting; there isn't a passion among collectors for young talent. The noise to action ratio isn't right for a city of this size; people don't do their due diligence. I think this is also because conceptually Hong Kong is very small. There is not much of an idea of free exchange with China or across borders like you would have as a young artist growing up somewhere like Vienna, where Berlin and Zurich are easy to get to because of geography, language, culture. Hong Kong people tend to want to stay in Hong Kong. Not just artists or col-

lectors but everyone. You don't hear about them going to Beijing, for instance, to develop their careers, so the sense of opportunity for artistic growth is affected, as is the potential to develop an exchange with other regions. Even as more artists come from abroad there is a very distressing idea about authenticity that limits their role here. Collectors will come from Berlin, for instance, where you have artists from 30 different countries showing and they come to Hong Kong and they only want to look at Hong Kong art. And next week they are going to Beijing and there they are only going to look at Chinese art. It is still this kind of peripheral identity that makes it difficult to break into this truly international way of being.

Hong Kong is a very PR-focused culture and it is hard to get attention for something that doesn't position itself in a particular way. What we may end up seeing are more artist initiatives that through collective effort will be able to get the same attention that one gallery in the right place and with good PR could get.

Well as we said, the art-intelligent population in Hong Kong is microscopic compared to the city as a whole. Art in Hong Kong for a long time was really the preserve of a very small group of people, a couple of big families, who had a full-time curator, who went and bought things for them around the world. Then it got a little bit bigger with the development of the upper middle class and the expansion of luxury branding and all of that, which in Hong Kong was really the late 1990s and early 2000s. In China it was pretty much after 2005. Now you definitely have a more populist interest in art. I think places like M+ are doing a very active program to encourage that, such as the 'Inflation!' exhibition, which was obviously intended to stir up some interest in contemporary art. The yellow rubber duck by Florentijn Hofman of course does an even better job. I think that explains why there is such an institutional focus now on emerging art. It is kind of this division of interests between the very elite and the fact that it seems okay now to make that desire public, because there is an audience.

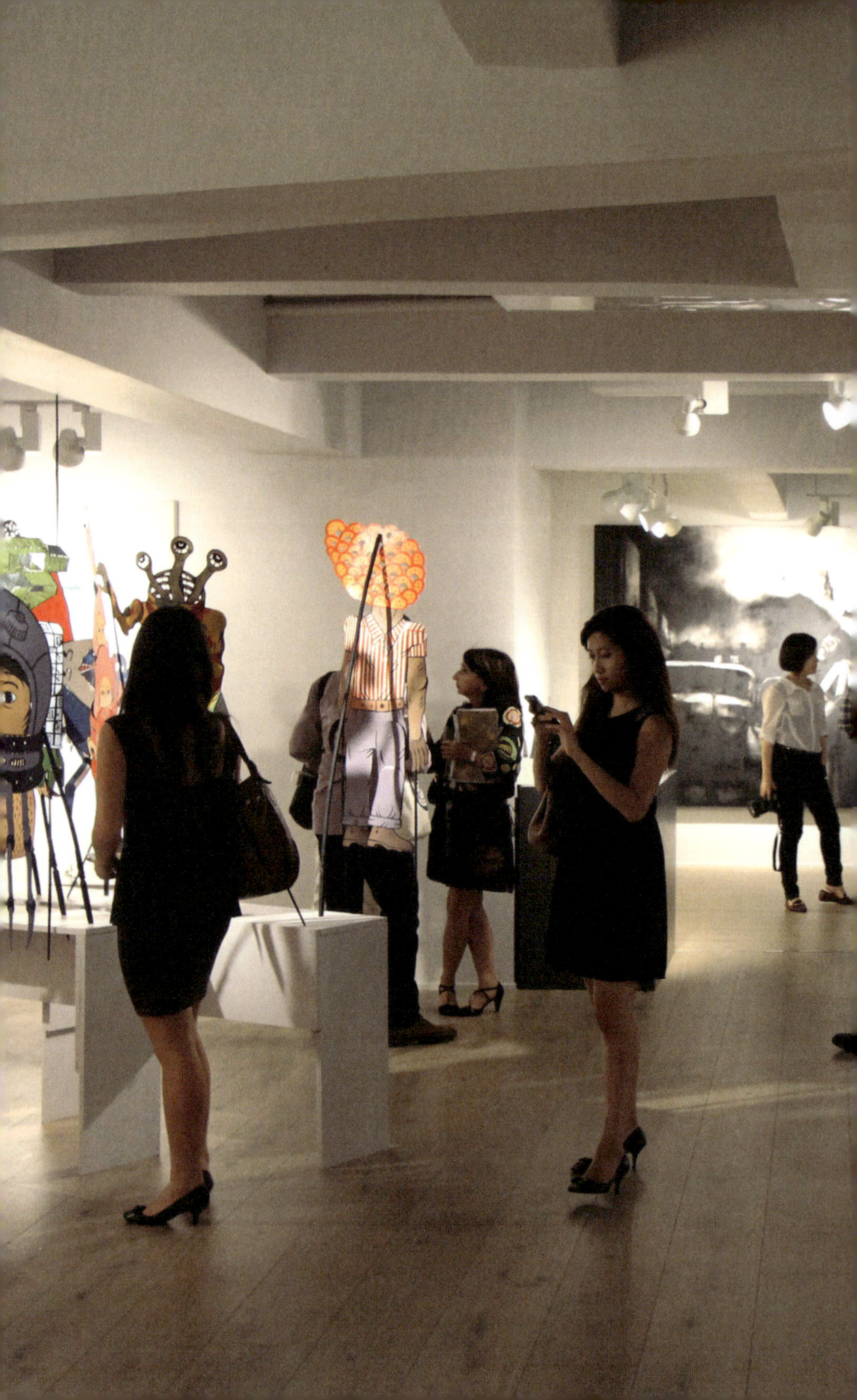

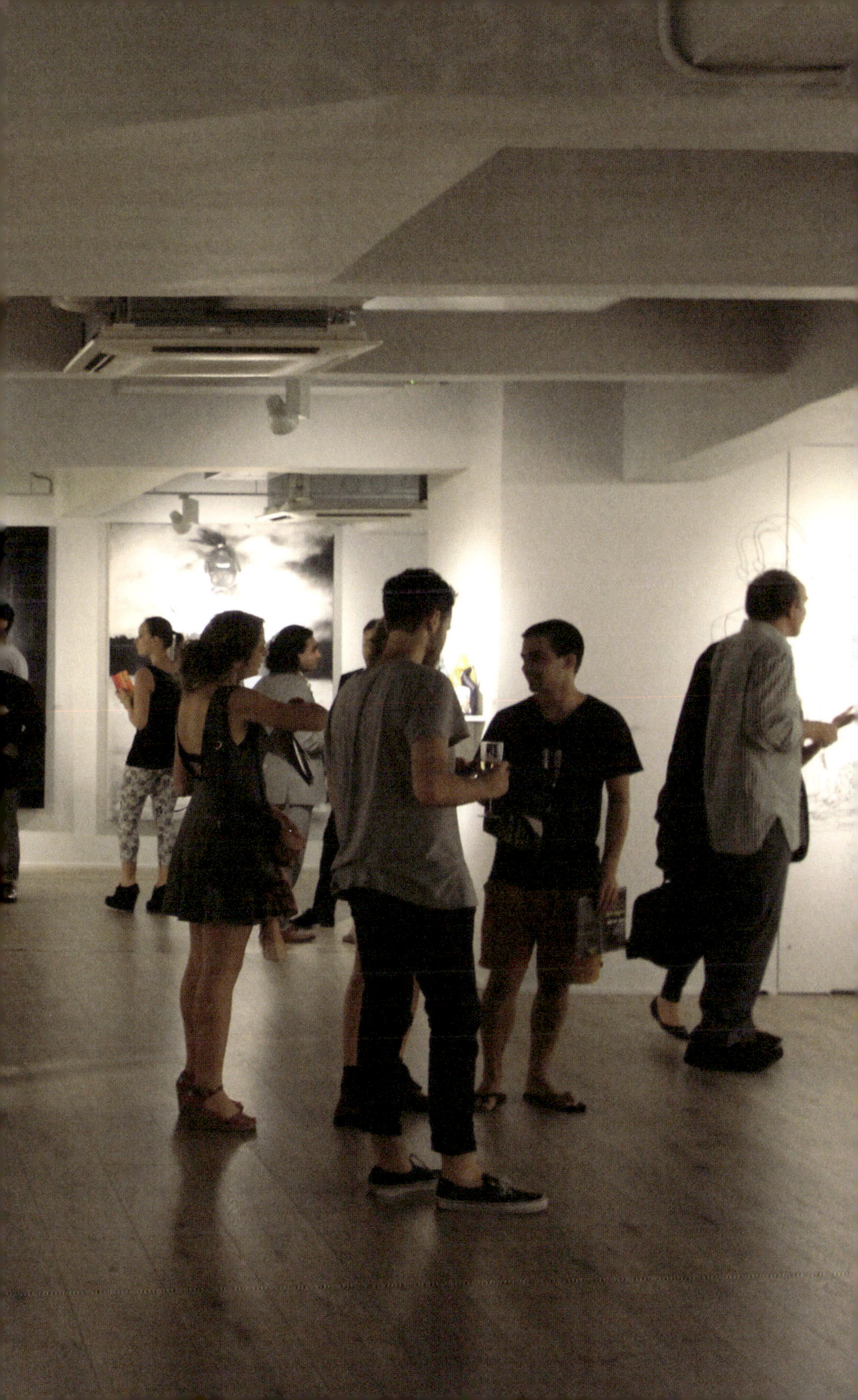

"I was asking myself: could I do the same thing in Hong Kong?"

A talk with Leung Chi Wo
Artist/Curator, Hong Kong

Born in Hong Kong in 1968, Leung Chi Wo is one of the first and most significant personalities to contribute to the formation of the arts in Hong Kong. Leung describes Hong Kong city as a multinational, diverse, fruitful, and dynamic place. He is internationally known for his own art work and as the co-founder of Para/Site – a gallery and exhibition space on Hong Kong Island that has been central to galvanizing the arts infrastructure in the city. Leung has also carried the Hong Kong art scene abroad internationally as a representative of the region in the 2001 Venice Biennale.

Leung's career as an artist and curator has proceeded in large part through decisions he hadn't anticipated having to make, a sort of causality, Leung identifies, that is as much a part of the city as the city's well deserved reputation as a rational and efficient model of urban life. When, for example, he finished his bachelor in fine arts, Hong Kong had no such thing as an "artist". A post-diploma scholarship in Culture of Photography in Italy gave Leung the chance to see what the arts are like in other cities. He followed his work in Italy with an internship at the Museum van Hedendaagse Kunst in Gent. In his time abroad Leung saw how the arts contributed to urban life but was unsure whether Hong Kong could be similarly affected.

Today Leung lives in a converted warehouse far from the business districts and high density housing in Hong Kong's picturesque New Territories. He moved to the Wah Luen Industrial Centre Building together with other artists in 2001, when the former occupants moved with much of Hong Kong's industrial business to China. Today, the area is known as the famous and vibrant Fo Tan Studios, the name taken from the little town they are part of. Leung stresses how lucky he is to have space and calm in a city known for anything but.

Part of what has made Leung such a central figure is his having been part of a first generation of contemporary artists in Hong Kong, who helped to establish some arts infrastructure in the face of a total dearth not only of exhibitions but also of interest in the arts. Hong Kong was going through its official handover to the Chinese and much of the middle class was emigrating elsewhere taking the money and support needed for the arts with them. Amidst these changes and difficulties, Leung connected with other artists, many of whom, like him, had lived abroad, to found Para/Site, Hong Kong's first art exhibition space. The space, though it has recently moved, remains a key institution for the arts in the city.

When asked about Hong Kong's growing art market and the growing image of Hong Kong as an art hub in Asia, Leung is critical and euphoric at the same time. Of course, he appreciates the diversity and Hong Kong's role and perception as an open harbor for new ideas, creativity and debate. However, despite these positive developments, he is quick to express concerns about the price of living and of art, which make it very difficult for a dynamic art scene to emerge. Leung stresses that the lack of a serious audience for art is also a major difficulty. He explains that most of the lessons about art are coming from the market, which in Hong Kong means largely the auctions. Strong educational institutions are still sorely lacking. This also explains the slight interest in conceptual art, since abstract and so called complicated works of art require better-developed educational programming. All these reasons force galleries to act very simply as commercial enterprises making space for progressive work difficult to come by.

Leung identifies the situation between galleries and auction houses as problematic for artists. He explains that he used to sell his work through galleries and always tried to avoid auction houses. However, this situation has since changed. Galleries cannot help him or others in Hong Kong in the ways they need, so he decided only to work with them for specific projects. Galleries are being further beset by difficulty as they compete with auction houses for limited attention. The situation, Leung explains, goes so far that auction houses are creating markets and then searching for work that fulfils the demand they've created.

Traditional orientations of the art market are changing dramatically in Hong Kong as audiences are thin and the market establishes itself as the driving force for the valuation of art. Leung sees new international institutions coming into Hong Kong as part of Hong Kong's hopeful future.

He alights on M+ as a potential force for change; M+ could for him have an impact internationally, it could be a real counter power to the strong market side and fill the missing educational role of the city.

When and what made you become an artist?

Well, I think I wanted to do something like being an artist but there was no such thing as an artist here when I finished my studies. After I finished my undergraduate university education in fine arts I was interested in continuing. Whilst studying I was looking into opportunities; there was a scholarship to Italy which I applied for and got, and that is how I started. I have to say that this was not the beginning of being an artist, but the beginning of me really considering becoming an artist. I learned about the possibilities of being an artist, and you probably know in Europe an artist is not something new, and also the whole environment was more encouraging. Then I got the chance later to do an internship in Belgium and that was very eye-opening, because I met living contemporary artists. That was very inspiring for me and I was asking myself: could I do the same thing in Hong Kong? For me, this time out of Hong Kong was very fruitful in a way. I would say, a very rich experience, being away from home for a while. But then it was the time to go back and to try myself. But even though I was interested, I think I couldn't be an artist until I saw examples and that's why I mean, I didn't see examples in Hong Kong. I mean here in Hong Kong as a student, of course, you met artists, but at the same time we all knew that art was more of a hobby. And always they said, 'You have to have another job.' I didn't really see examples that you could really do it as a career. Making it as a career means that a lot of people would review the work and write about your work and then I can see and could read book about art. And this was really missing.

Can you talk a bit about Para/Site?

A few years after I came back from Europe, I started my graduate study in studio art. In my first year of study I met a couple of artist friends and we had an idea just to do an exhibition together but then it was very difficult. The whole situation in Hong Kong was difficult then, and all the exhibition venues were not really user friendly or artist friendly. We liked to produce really site-specific work that meant we needed to have the flexibility to alter the space and so on. But it was very rare that we would be allowed to do so. At the time, the Hong Kong Arts Centre functioned more like a rental gallery, but it was just so expensive, and so we started to think about alternative options. For a while we just thought we should look for an apartment because there were three of us, so if we could find a three-room apartment, it would be perfect for an exhibition, and during the time, we saw different possibilities and then Para/Site – the old Para/Site in Kennedy Town. It was the space below our artist friend's studio and it was suggested that we take a look at it and it was perfect. It was huge and then also you would have to understand because you could not really rent it for such a short lease for one month. So we gathered more friends and we could do three exhibitions that made the lease for four months. This is how it started and then it was also a great time and timing. I remember that the Hong Kong Arts Development Council had just been founded. So we could also apply for a grant for our rent. That is how Para/Site started.

How do you sell your art? Do you work together with a gallery?

At first, I have to say, I don't sell that much. I usually sell always through galleries. That said, recently someone approached me directly and I did sell directly in this case because I find the situation a bit different now. My last solo show with Hanart was six to seven years ago and recently they do more paintings and so on. So in this case I sold the work directly, which was not commissioned. But I remember in the beginning, when someone approached me directly I would always refer to the gallery. Now I think we maintain more a loose relationship and my work with them would be more for specific projects, but not exclusive.

Because you think galleries are here not that successful for certain kinds of art?

Well, yes, at least for my art, because I haven't really seen that they have been helping me so much.

How did the growing Asian market affect your career?

Obviously everyone can see that there are more galleries. And there are more people buying art. Because my work is not entirely easy to be installed or to put at home, only some types of my work would be more appealing to those people, which is mainly photography. One thing you can see is that we are getting more diversity. I hope we could have even more. But at least, compared to the past, we have more galleries at different levels and also galleries showing different types of art. I am rather positive but also a bit uncertain, not about the art itself, but it is the environment. Because I really find that it is getting so expensive here, which is not so favorable for the growth of art when you consider young galleries having such difficulties paying their rent. Like Saamlung for example. That would really affect the future. Either they show something that would be more easily installable or they close it down and act as a consultant. This would be really sad, because it is a whole ecology, you need galleries, I mean, of course, we have this influx of money from the government. But you know it will not be long lasting, you always have this up and down of government expenditure on art and culture. Even though they promised that we would have a lot of money for the next few years, you would still want to see a healthier situation. This is part of the diversity, because you want artists who really want to work with different resources. I think this would be much healthier. You would have artists who would work with commissions from non-profits institutions. Or someone would work on commissions entirely from the commercial sector. Or some would really work with galleries only.

Do you see also a problem in the great impact of auction houses?

I know, this is something, to be honest; I keep my distance from the auction house. One time they asked me but I said I don't want that and that they could talk with the galleries. I think it is not a very good idea for artists to deal with the sales directly, even if the situation with the galleries is not helping so much, but it is the same thing with the auction houses. The auction houses should not be competing with the galleries either but it happens and that is what really makes it complicated. The auction houses create markets and then search for art, it shouldn't be that way. The market should be developed by this invisible hand. There are more galleries in China than in Hong Kong and I don't know their sales situation. There are a lot of auction houses in China. The international auction houses had difficulties to enter the Chinese market but recently they have done it. They have just started and are launching auction fairs. The China situation is difficult not really because of the auctions or the galleries, I would say it is more the government. I am not talking about the freedom of speech or censorship; I am talking about the funding situation, because basically you don't get funding from the government in China. So it is really a one-sided story in China that all sorts of institutions, even museums, claim to be not-for-profit, but somehow they still maintain profit activities. And this is what I find more problematic than the issue between the auction house and galleries.

Why are there few buyers or collectors that go to galleries?

I don't know. I think some do go, but probably to a few selected galleries only. You could imagine if you just want to sell the work and you know the buyers who would be happy to buy this work that has already exhibited somewhere then you have a job done. And that is the function of art fairs. But galleries do much more than just selling; that allows the full impact of the art. So it should be an original show in its best presentation and relevant context. However, if someone only thinks about buying and owning, this might be unnecessary to them.

What kind of an art place is Hong Kong?

Well, the obvious situation is that we don't have such a huge population of a very serious art audience. This is still relatively small. I mean, this is the background. So in this case, education would be a very strong component of the art market development. And I can imagine that not only the non-profit institutions, but even the galleries would consider it. The more progressive galleries would like to engage the audience to do something further, not just to sell things. Maybe the audience is happy with the way things are now, but galleries really can show them something that they haven't seen.

And this is what M+ can do?

M+ will do it, but I mean progressive galleries should also do this. That's the point I would like to make, if you have very international artists shown here, I mean they would also like to show something original here. Or they like to do something special for this place and for this cultural environment and that could be a very good role for the galleries.

In the West there is more a two-pillared system, of critics, museums etc. on the one hand and then the market on the other hand.

I think the situation would be like this: the focus is so much on selling and buying, because of the market, which is overwhelming. So, to be honest, this is also how the very general public is learning about art, because the art market has attracted a lot of media coverage. So this would be the chance to educate them, I suppose. I mean you must also admit the fact that now the gallery could have this ample opportunity to connect with society and but it is also true that usually we don't see this responsibility of the galleries to teach the general public, but as I said, the art scene here would not be healthy, if you only had the commercial sector. So for the galleries, if they would like to move on, they should also like to see the art scene evolving. So in this sense they are in a very important position if they would like to stay for longer.

Do you think Hong Kong will become the leading art market hub in Asia?

I don't know. It really depends on how much you expect from an art hub. I would say in Hong Kong we do have some advantages like free-

dom of speech. But it cannot be taken for granted that they will last. And I mean this is a pretty popular and hot topic these days, if you really don't protect this freedom of speech you could lose it. So this is important. I think Hong Kong could be a very interesting place for art, because historically it is more like an open port. And culturally speaking, people tend to welcome things from different places. Even things they don't understand. So this is a very good condition, but as I said this is just the beginning, you cannot just further develop with all the existing things, you need to improve. We are talking about the audience, the society. And yesterday, it was so silly what this legislative council member said. It was at a meeting about the West Kowloon Cultural District and then he was criticizing the acquisition of the M+. He said that artworks with explicit sexual content or graphic appearances involving political issues are not art. He is wrong. He is a politician and he said this.

Do you think this will have an influence on what they can exhibit?

So far we believe in the professionalism of the curators of the M+. I would say that there hasn't been any influence yet. But you can imagine this political party is very conservative. It is a very pro government party and they do have members or like-minded affiliates sitting on the board of the West Kowloon Cultural District Authority and the Hong Kong Arts Development Council. So in this case this could be threatening. They might say something, which could somehow exercise some pressure on the employees of this institution. So I think this is so silly and should not be said.

What thoughts went through your mind when Art Basel announced it would buy the Art HK fair?

I would say that, yes you see, this is globalization, yes branding. I couldn't find the right words, because you know, Magnus Renfrew is a good friend. And then he basically founded the Hong Kong Art Fair and ran it very well over the years. He is really recognized for doing all these things. But then you know the reality is that it has been sold. So I don't know what would be the better word, but somehow, I am sure that Art Basel is still a very important art fair for Hong Kong. So it is more a sort of naming and sort of belonging. So it is born here because of the place and now it is another city. I think it will also be interesting to see how much Art Basel will observe the special situation of this place here, instead of mak-

ing an Art Basel like an Art Basel everywhere.

What opportunities and difficulties do you see in this?

I could go back to what I mentioned before: if those institutions, private institutions, galleries and so on would like to stay here for longer, that means they don't consider Hong Kong as a shelter just for the economy as in Europe or America. That means they need to take roots here and they have to really consider what makes sense in this place. I don't know exactly, I am not familiar with Art Basel, but let's say like what would be the relationship between the art scene of Miami and Art Basel? I don't think that the government would notice the art development without the huge exposure made by Hong Kong Art Fair. For example if we talk about trade fairs, the government has done a lot for them. And on the other hand we have this Arts Development Council, which is unfortunately much smaller and has got less power than the Trade Development Council. If the latter had this interest or the possibilities to deal with the art market that could be something very good. For example the Trade Development Council could help people to get to know the business here and to do trade fairs overseas.

I think there is one thing we should take in account, which is: why we would like to have the impact in society not only economically is because we consider there is such a strong cultural character here that needs a dialogue with these market activities. Why am I saying this? I just read the first introduction here in this art magazine 'The Leap' and it talked about the so-called subjectivity. Because when we talk about culture, the subjectivity of culture has not really been considered in the past here. Mainly because Hong Kong was more regarded as a trade port and also people have always been considering this land together with mainland China until let's say like the last two decades. But homegrown people, artists, culture workers here, they would really think the culture of Hong Kong ought to be an entity in its own right, instead of just a sideline of the bigger culture in China. And in this case, cultural character has been developed for the art community here. We would like to see if there would be any artist in Hong Kong who has something special. Hong Kong galleries here would offer something special. Museums here would be really different from museums in other places. This is important because if we consider these things, people and institutions could be really rooted here for this special character and

then the art fair would somehow develop into something unique. This is why I mean, if we don't have this kind of subjective interest in the local situation then it will be more difficult.

Do you think it is a problem that there is such a high presence of mainland Chinese artists?

I think if we look into the concept of subjectivity here, let's say mainland China, it would be more like a national cultural character. If we were the same, we would always just be part of China. But, on the other hand, if we talk about a character, like that of a city-state with its multi-nationality, with its diversity and something fruitful and a dynamic, which is changing all the time, this is what Hong Kong is. Then why would we not allow Chinese art here? It could be very interesting if the Hong Kong identity included Chinese culture, instead of being part of the mainland Chinese culture. And at the same time we could see that artists of different origins, who are based in Hong Kong, would also create Hong Kong's culture.

The words you used to describe Hong Kong's character could also perhaps be used to describe globalization.

Well, globalization, I mean the negative meaning of globalization is that you just parachute in somewhere without respect for the local culture. What I mean is that Hong Kong could be very inclusive, but at the same time it could also have this cultural diversity exported to other places. After all we care about who the people are. I think it is very important not to adopt the homogenous national approach to the art discourse here.

How does the taste differ between here and the Western countries?

I guess there a very big difference. Conceptual art is not very popular here. It is the visual that is appreciated more, things that are easier to understand.

Would you say that enjoying abstract and complicated art such as conceptual art is related to the education of a society?

Definitely. We can see this here in China and Asia. The more the people get education, the more they start to appreciate art, and also more complicated art; art that makes you think and is not only representing something.

I mean we have observed this already in the last few decades. Contemporary art is a recent development here and is now being increasingly enjoyed. So we could also assume that in some years conceptual art could also be appreciated.

Yes, I would say so. We see more and more people that enjoy art and this is also because we teach it earlier. But still there are the masses, which are not included. There is a gap between them and the elite that goes to these events – the same people you always meet. It is not that it is not available for everyone. Actually it may be, but the masses do not know what to do with it. There we see a lack of education. This is why they prefer something more visual and not so much conceptual art. There is a gap, I would say, between people who are open minded enough to learn something new and people who are conservative about anything new.

But then you need something that entertains a little if there is no other way to include them...

Yes, as I said, I don't mind if they contain any entertaining factor, but this not the goal, this is only the tool. And after all they should not compromise the substance of this inspiring educational factor of a museum.

How would you do it?

Yes, education, we always had difficulties with education. I mean I work in a school and I could really tell how problematic it is to see all these kids who are applying to our school and they have no idea of anything about creativity and art. They should start earlier. It is a true never-ending story. The spectrum of contemporary art is very huge, but we are not just talking about contemporary art. This is the thing that has to be done in different sectors and different levels. For example I work with the government and they do a lot of educational activities, so they prepare programs. I suggest to them that they actually should do programs only for the civil servant, at least some special programs. Just imagine, if you have civil servants who are working in the water supply department who love art, then you would see art everywhere. Art shouldn't be confined to the museum in this sense. This is why we should deal with different departments for art projects. If this staff had some art appreciation, they would also maybe try more creative solutions for things. And that's why I find art education should, after all, be really like general education and be in different sectors and should not be confined within a formal school system.

This is a problem everywhere. But we don't talk about that as we have more threatening issues, because now the art market is growing very fast, so how could other things be picked up at the same time. This is the main issue. We talked about the art market relying so much on the role of the buyer, which in general is the growth of the art audience. I mean you always need this pyramid. You need this critical mass, and you have a huge base of an art audience and then have very good art collectors at the top, and now the art collectors are mainly from somewhere else. I think for public policy you need to consult the people, but you also need to consult the experts. You always have this situation, you would see further than other people and then you would propose to them why we need to do this. So if you put up this cultural policy, you would really need to elaborate and explain; and we know we are talking about sustainable society and this is education. And if you consider that a museum is part of education and then the collector system, the market system should be somehow as well. And for this reason it is really important because you don't want to have anything happening in Hong Kong that is nonsense. Everything that you do here needs to make sense. You want to understand why a very wealthy collector spends money on an artist. You want to know why even this is from somewhere else. So, I think, the reasoning is really important and we are already kind of like fed up with this monotonous idea of making money. You buy art. Yes it could be for investment and to make more money. But we all know that. To be a human being there are so many other things involved and I guess that makes art somehow more interesting than any other sector of the society or other businesses. Because I am sure that most people would say you buy art because you like that piece of art and that is the most important thing, because if you like that art you would never lose anything.

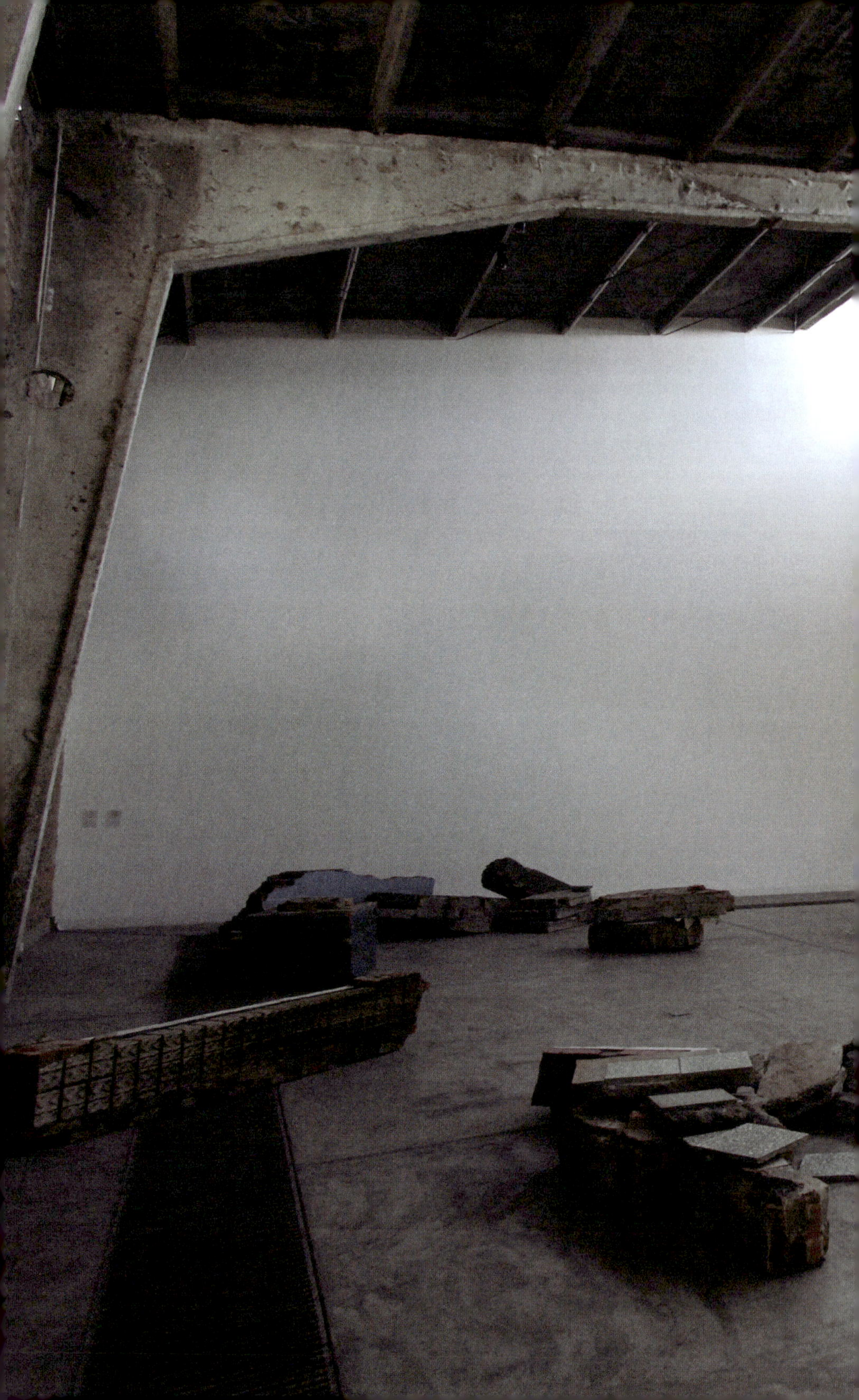

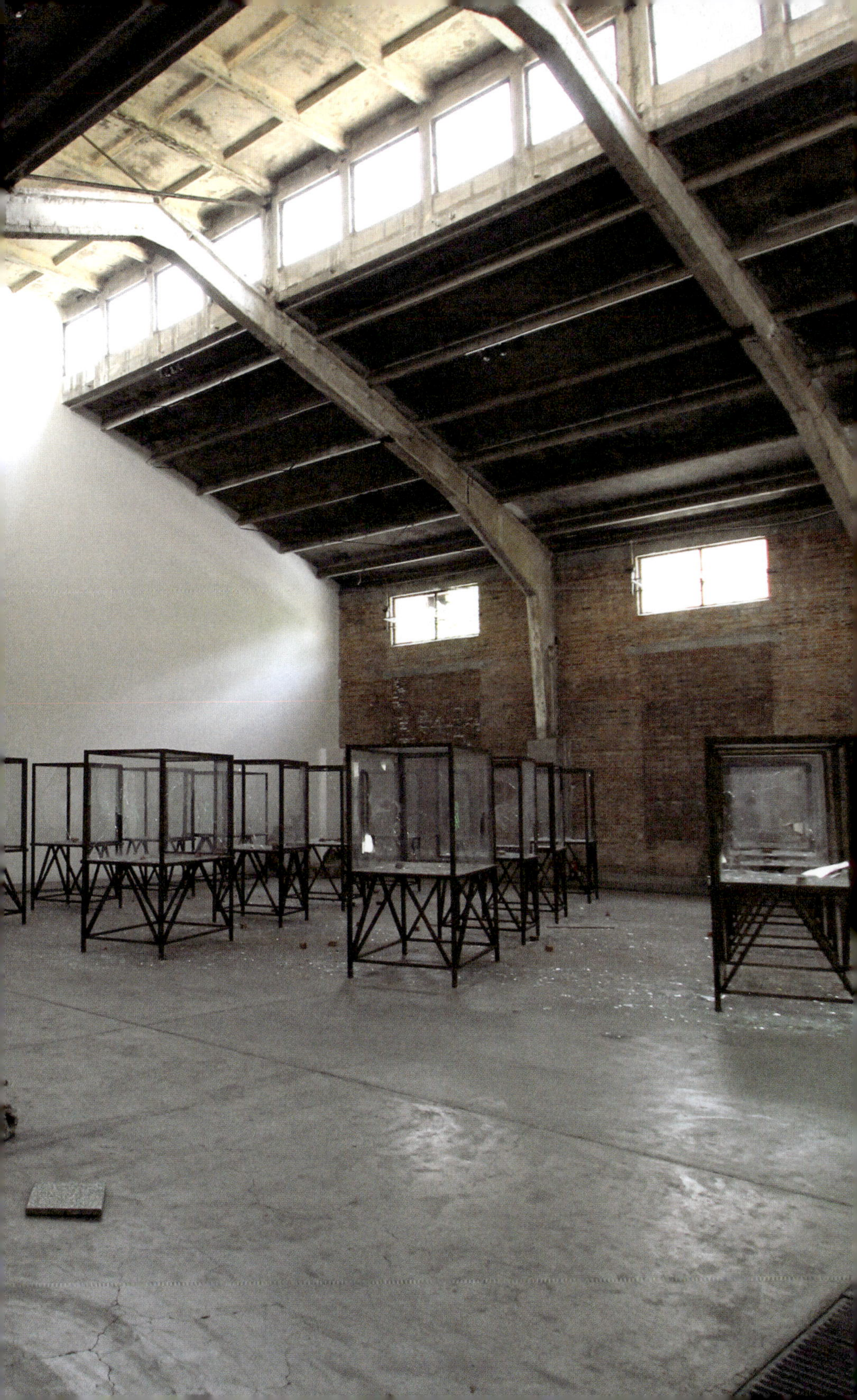

"Works of value are put into auctions"

A talk with Cedric Pinto
Collector, Singapore

Cedric Pinto is the managing director of Historical Land, a real estate advisory service in Singapore. His role there is overshadowed by his inclusion in a new generation of Singaporeans, who, after witnessing the way economic, cultural and social changes transformed Singapore into a hub for the arts, got themselves into the mix as collectors. In 2010 while travelling, he visited galleries in Ubud, Bali, and discovered his fascination for art. In the beginning it was Pinto's love of art that motivated his purchases. He decorated his living and office spaces with works of art and he liked to look at them for inspiration. Only in the last two years has he started to participate actively in art auctions, buying and selling art. He concentrates mainly on art from South East Asia but, Pinto says, he can't help but buy Chinese art spontaneously.

Collectors are known for their relationships with artists, for going to studio visits, for endearing themselves to galleries, and for being experts if not in art history then at least in the market value of art. Pinto, however, goes to auctions. It is a new form of collecting, the result of regional socio-economic developments that are allowing a new generation to find social expression and economic value in art. For Pinto, describing what it is to be a collector is to describe the social life, language, and specific and international cultural signs and symbols that he has learned to trade in as much as the actual works that he is buying. It is a trend, a lifestyle, and a class distinction. As described in other interviews, auction houses are for the newcomers easier to understand through their transparency and the open bidding processes.

To enter into Pinto's shophouse, an architectural type common all over South East Asia, is to be transported to a place more readily associated with the sublimity of art than the common building type; the two-stories are full of wonderful and colorful art pieces and each one has its own very great story.

Pinto is a newcomer without a family history in the arts. His interest in art comes from his own experience and art's growing visibility. The new cultural capital he has garnered through collecting is something new he shares with friends. But how Pinto and his friends access art significantly differs from how his Western counterparts might. The auction house plays a bigger role for Pinto than it would for similar Western neophytes to the art market. It is not, for instance, seen as a blight on the field as it is commonly held to be elsewhere. Auctions are highly valued by new collectors; here they learn that the value of art is determined in the market and not, as may have once been the case, by their own taste.

Pinto and his cohort of collectors enjoy the status that art confers on them. However, the way they consume art articulates a new and growing practice – much more commercialized – where the selling makes up new and important parts of the field. In all of this, the auction houses are the center for gatherings for this group and therefore play a very different role, worthwhile to collect.

When did you start to collect art?

Four years ago. Only about two years ago I started to collect more expensive ones and I started buying from auctions. Because I was… Maybe after collecting you get to know other people who are also collectors and we talk about better art pieces. I'm also influenced by friends who are collectors and dealers and managers for some artists.

Was that a certain trend in Singapore that people started to collect and that you started to talk about it?

Yes. About two years ago, I started going to auctions. At the auctions you meet like-minded people who collect the better works. I would say that only good works are being put into auctions, works of value are put into auctions. Auction houses in Singapore or Southeast Asia would not take in works that are of no resale value. When we go to auctions we get familiarized with the popular artists, talk to people who keep certain works from certain artists. Also, friends and all that, like friends in businesses from Indonesia, we talk about these certain artists. From there, I identified certain artists that I think it will be worthwhile to collect. During my one course of travel, I visit galleries, go to auction houses or even buy some art pieces directly from the artists and sometimes just visit the artists. The artists are introduced by friends or sometimes we meet the artists themselves in places like exhibitions. So I buy artwork pieces directly from those artists, the living artists. But, on average five times a year, I participate in an auction to buy and sell.

Is there a trend that there are more collectors? Is it fashionable to be a collector in this region?

Yes, now it's become a lifestyle thing here. Like when you have a home or a new home, you would have a couple of nice art pieces in your home. It's more of a lifestyle thing. It's a topic of discussion even among the professionals, among the rich. Art is something that, if you talk about art, it's not ordinary anymore. It's upper market. You are seen as more afflu-ent especially if you collect good art pieces.

What is your strategy of collecting?

For me, collecting is for the fun of it. But then, from time to time, be-cause I want to change the pieces and after a couple of years – a year or two – I may wish to dispose of one. I've already enjoyed enough of the piece and I want to put a new piece up. So the only way to turn around is to sell the pieces because there's not much space to store them.

I buy more through auction houses and in Indonesia, various parts of Indonesia, because I travel. Yogyakarta, Jakarta, Bali, Surabaya, Bandung. I go to these places and I do meet up with artists like Jeihan Sukmantoro, who is in Bandung so I buy directly from him. In Yogy-akarta, there are some other artists like Nasirun and Erica Hestu Wah-yuni who lives there. So while over there, there are a couple of artists I visit like Budi Ubrux – he's also in Yogyakarta. So there are a couple of artists here and there in Indonesia, living artists who I visit and I buy pieces from them directly.

Are there also other people coming to you and asking for advice?

Yes, I do have friends and relatives who are starting to keep them. They actually bought some pieces from me. Small pieces to start off. They do come for advice. I advise them to actually buy art pieces that can appreciate in value. The first thing to me about the artwork is, what are you intending to do? Are you intending to keep this work for a long time because you like the work? Or do you intend, after a few years, to sell it? If you intend to sell it, then you have to keep a work of which the artist is known, a known artist, a popular artist. So it's easier to sell at the point of time you want to sell. If you buy something just for yourself to enjoy and keep for a long time, without caring about the value, something to keep for an unspecific period of time, then it's okay to buy decorative pieces, something that you like, something that attracts you.

So you make a pre-selection by the popularity? And then the next criterion is what you like, or is it more that people tell you that this is a good person – you should buy from him.

In order to assess what is good first of all you need somebody to advise you on what is good. Then you find out more from auction sites and all that.

So you read a lot.

Yes. I go to auction websites like MutualArt, ArtTracker, Artprice, etc. which keep track on works by artists, for example. If somebody says you should buy works from this artist, what I'll do is search through auction sites and see how many works of this artist have already been auctioned, and what are the prices, to get an idea of the trend of this artist.

Do you sometimes compare with your friends?

I do. We do chitchat and find out what are the directions – they say this is good, why they are good, and sometimes to see how long it will take before this artist becomes very popular. That's the prediction. But I think, for me, what I always do is to look at the auction material, either in catalogs or auction sites. If I want to buy a certain art piece, I would do my research by going through the database of past auctions. From there you will know the trend. I want to gauge how well this artist fares in the auction. To me, it's very important to buy works that have potential.

So it's a bit like an asset.

Correct. For me, I see myself as a collector not as somebody who buys just for decorating. I'm a collector and I collect potential pieces, pieces which are of value either now or in the future.

In terms of the global changes in the art market, or in the art world in general, where do you see Singapore placed in the future? Or Jakarta or the region here? Do you think they will become more important on the global map?

Yes, I think, for Southeast Asia, Singapore will be number two next to Hong Kong for the next five year period. I think Singapore will still remain number two. But I don't know. It's hard to predict after five years. Whether Singapore will overtake or not is very hard to predict. Hong Kong has been very strong and will be very strong, because the main auction houses are there. If the Chinese art is very established, very strong and very popular and very valuable, Hong Kong for the next five years will still be the main art destination for sure. I do not know whether Singapore can, after that period of time, overtake that. I don't know. I think it all depends on whether the auction houses want to do the auctions in Singapore. If they do that – I mean the main auction houses, the top three auction houses – if they do that here, then I think we stand a chance to overtake Hong Kong. Then there will be more main activities here. China also has its own auction houses like Poly Auctions and all that. Chinese-formed auction houses Poly, Guardian, they are popular in China. They do their auctions in China in Beijing, in Shanghai, sometimes in Hong Kong So they control the Chinese art. If Sotheby's, Christie's, Bonhams do auctions in Singapore, then there is this competition between Hong Kong and Singapore. If they do set up here, we may stand a chance to grow further because Chinese art is dominated by the three big players as well as the auction houses which are already established in China.

Do you think that would also attract more people to start to collect art? Like more of the rich people that think, oh I should start with collecting?

Definitely. It is the rich people – so long as, when they buy the art pieces, they know that in the time to come, the value will appreciate, they will look at it as something viable.

Or a status symbol.

Yes. It is of course a status symbol that goes with the lifestyle. Status symbol – yes I mean you have a nice art piece – a very popular art piece to put in your home that itself already brings out the level of status. And the fact that they know that this piece, if I collect it now, a couple of years down the road it's going to increase in value. Definitely more and more rich people will start keeping art. Art will be like investment in property, for example. Maybe they won't put all their money in property after that. They will put some in art.

*But sometimes it's also the lifestyle of
your art – it's also a topic that people
like to talk about.*

It's a lifestyle thing. Sometimes a
topic of discussion. You talk about
this artist, you talk about his work.
You talk about other artists. You
talk about what are the pieces that
are worth keeping.

*If you are in a certain circle, you
should also know what is happening
in art, right? Do you think that's
become more and more important?*

Yes, you need to be well-informed.
If you are a collector, you need to be
well-informed of how certain artists fare. How much interest there
is in certain artists. So you can also
collect the works of these artists.
You won't be left out. What I meant
by left out is that there are certain
times that you buy works from certain artists, because the price is still
reasonable. But if you wait a few
years down the road, the prices of
these pieces escalate and it's hard
to catch up. The value keeps going
up. There are some certain art pieces from certain artists – the prices
keep going higher and higher.

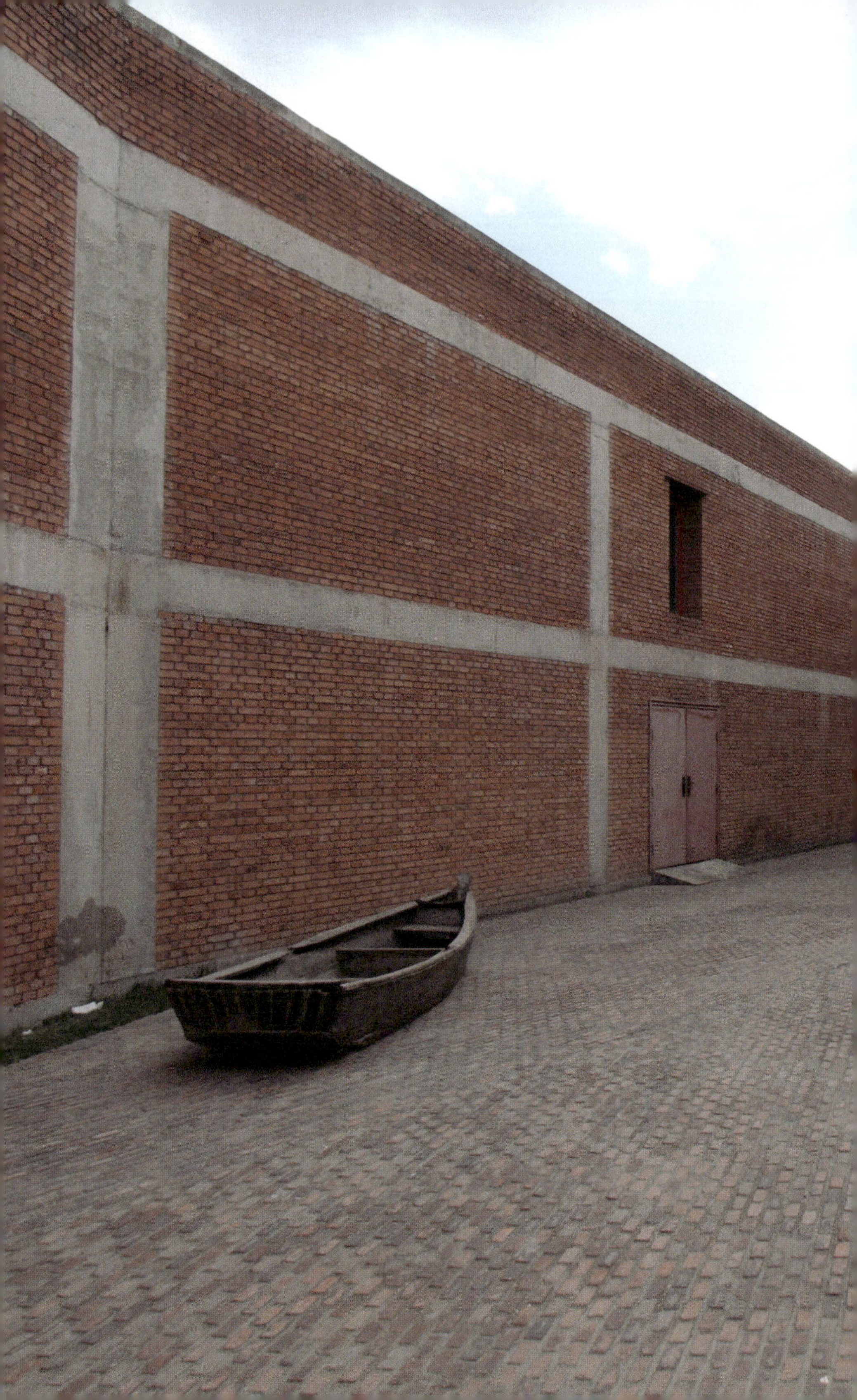

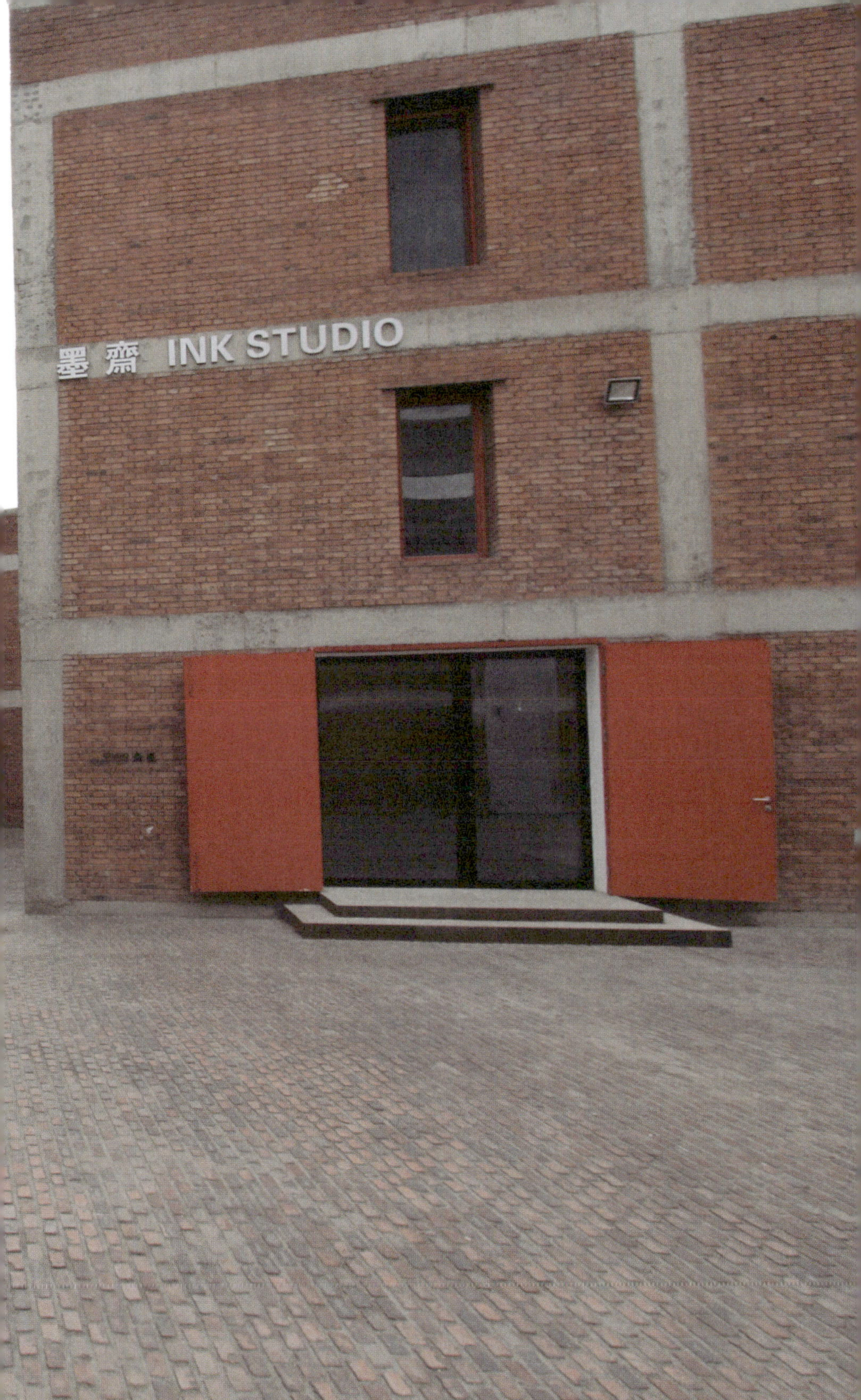

墨齋 INK STUDIO

"There is a market, but there isn't perhaps necessarily the cultural life"

A talk with Nick Simunovic
Gallerist, Hong Kong

Nick Simunovic has been interested in art history since he was a teenager growing up in Canada. While studying at Harvard University in the US, he enrolled in a number of art history classes, and upon graduating he moved to New York to work for McKinsey & Company. While working at McKinsey, he took on a pro bono assignment for the Guggenheim Museum – his introduction to the museum and art world in a professional context. Later on, he joined the Guggenheim Museum full-time, where he stayed for five years over two separate stages. During his stint at the Guggenheim, he traveled extensively to Asia, particularly Beijing and Shanghai, where he got the impression that an increasing number of people were interested in Western modern and contemporary art, and that this was a trend that would continue to grow. At the same time there were no Western galleries to work with collectors in the region. So he approached Larry Gagosian and suggested that he should think about doing something in Asia, and Gagosian agreed. Shortly after, in the summer of 2007, Simunovic joined the gallery and moved to Asia, to set up the gallery's operations in the region.

As director of the Hong Kong branch of the most famous art gallery with the highest turnover world-wide, our dialogue partner is in an ideal position to sound out the market there for contemporary art. Established in the best and most expensive city location – Pedder Street – and operating in the immediate neighborhood of other big and noble galleries, and select wine and tobacco dealers, Gagosian is a lighthouse on the booming Asian art market.

Simunovic gives us a differentiated picture of the situation, characterized by asynchronies and contrasts. Unlike the typical clientele of

Gagosian in New York or Geneva, his customers here are newcomers and novices in matters of contemporary art, who, however, have often already collected classical Chinese art. Their first contacts with Western art were usually made in auction houses, which, paradoxically, are apparently at one and the same time powerful competitors on the market and pioneers who have opened up the market for the gallery system.

According to Simunovic's assessment the galleries are, however, gaining more and more influence as the sophisticated Asian collectors place increasing value on the price advantages of the primary market in comparison with the strongly competitive secondary market. In his opinion, which he illustrates with an entire list of locational advantages, Hong Kong is an absolutely ideal hub for the entire Asian continent, whereby he distinguishes clearly between the art market and the field of art production, seeing Hong Kong as a less interesting terrain than mainland China for contemporary art production. He explains this, among other things, with the strongly mercantile tradition and mentality of the Hong Kong population, which leaves little room for art and culture, and by reference to the overwhelming fascination mainland China and its political, economic and cultural development in recent decades exerts over Western observers. This damns the Hong Kong art scene to a shadowy existence. As far as the importance of Hong Kong as a location for Gagosian and its business strategy is concerned, our dialogue partner sees no dissonances in his assessment of the overall situation. He is in Hong Kong, as he candidly confesses, in order to sell Western art and not with the purpose of discovering Asian artists for the Western market and importing them. Is this perhaps a reason why he has such a low opinion of the Hong Kong art scene?

Can you tell us about the differences between the places, New York, Geneva and so on?

I have not worked for the Gallery in those places, so it is hard for me to say exactly what the mentality of the collectors is there versus here. Maybe I can give some suggestions anecdotally: 95 per cent of the clients I work with are located in Asia. In general, I would say that most people in Asia who are collecting work from Gagosian have had some experience with Asian classical or contemporary art, and are now expanding the scope of their collections towards Western art. This of course is a very different situation compared to somebody working in the gallery in New York or London, where collectors probably have always been collecting Western art and are simply adding to their collection. In many respects, we are meeting people who are thinking about buying Western art for the first time and then slowly growing from there.

What was the main reason that you chose Hong Kong and not another place?

There are three reasons why Hong Kong made the most sense. The first is, the city has a very welcoming and liberal tax infrastructure. Secondly, Hong Kong is very well situated geographically, in terms of being oriented towards northern Asia and being on China's doorstep, as well as being close to Korea, Taiwan and Japan, which are all major centers for art collecting. Hong Kong is also not far from Southeast Asia, which is, I think, more of an emerging region for Western art. In short, Hong Kong is extremely well located in the heart of Asia. The third reason is that there was already a momentum building here; the auction houses were already here, for example. Again, I think this points to the open and transparent framework that Hong Kong allows. So the fact that there was already the beginnings of a market through the auction houses suggested that Hong Kong was a place where collectors from across the region liked to come to look at and to buy and perhaps even sell art. So Hong Kong has a hub status that I think other cities in Asia do not have, even if those other cities have a deeper tradition of artist production. For example, Beijing has many more artists and a better art school than Hong Kong does. But from the market perspective, Beijing is very difficult for a Western gallery.

In Europe, when talking about the market here, we always hear that it is quite difficult for galleries to exist because people seem to prefer auction houses. There is no long tradition of galleries in this place, although it is emerging now. Do you have the feeling that it is developing?

Very much so, the response was actually quite profound and quite immediate. Collectors in Asia are very sophisticated. Perhaps the original default way of collecting art, if they are buying contemporary art or classical art, might have been through the auction houses. But again, very sophisticated collectors know that they can work with Asian galleries to get works by Asian artists. So it is rare that you would have someone who would be buying solely at an auction, or is unaware of the fact that a gallery can create value for them. I think that there is also a growing appreciation for the fact that primary market pricing, in this day and age, is perhaps more attractive in many cases than the secondary market pricing that one is faced with at an auction house, where there are many people competing for an artwork, which will drive the price up, and there is a nice and very healthy premium that the auction house charges on top of that purchase. The fundamental structure and dynamics of the gallery pricing model is very different from that of an auction house. I think collectors are starting to understand that.

We've been talking about the practices in Europe that enterprises install art works in all their rooms and it is part of their business culture, a part of their corporate identity. Does it work in the same way here?

I think that we are seeing the beginnings of that sort of thing. In Hong Kong for example, property companies are trying to draw closer to visual art or to contemporary art as a way to differentiate among their competitors. Swire, which is one of the big property companies here, had Frank Gehry do some projects for them. So there is a sense that working with a brand can confer a certain kind of advantage. There is another property company called New World Development, which has developed K11, which has been branded as an art mall. And they are actively expanding this project in mainland China. I think they want to have another half dozen or more of these K11 branded art malls in mainland China. They are sponsoring major exhibitions around the world, such as the current ink art exhibition at the Metropolitan Museum in New York. I think we are seeing the nascent beginnings of this idea. But it is not yet like Deutsche Bank with its 15,000-artwork collection.

And what kind of private collectors do you know? What are they doing? Are they constructing collections mixing Asian and Western art? Or do they specialize in one of them?

There is a selection bias in how I answer this question because I know the people who are only interested in Western art. I am sure that there are many more collectors in Asia who are not interested in Western art that I just don't meet because they are buying bronzes or Tang Dynasty furniture or scroll paintings. The number for this type of collector in Asia is always going to dwarf the number of people who are buying Western art. But of those collectors who buy Western art, some of them can be expatriates living in Hong Kong, and maybe all of their collection is Western. And maybe they just happen to live here because they are making their career here. But in general, almost everyone we work with has Asian art, or has been collecting Asian art. And they are complementing or supplementing that collection with Western art.

You said you were here to transport Western art to another region. Conversely, does Gagosian take back from Hong Kong to Geneva, New York and so on some of what you find here?

Yes, I think we do a little bit of that but I think the gallery will be always primarily known as the gallery of Western art and that is what we do best. Our goal in terms of establishing our presence here in Asia is not to rush off and find 15 Chinese or Korean or Taiwanese artists, and become something that we are not. But we are very selectively adding new artists to the program.

And what about Hong Kong artists?

I think it is a complex situation that is difficult to disentangle. On the one hand Hong Kong artist were more or less overshadowed by the artists of mainland China. I don't think the galleries of Chinese artists or the galleries in mainland China were any better than the other galleries in Hong Kong. But I think that somehow there was this kind of interest in works coming out of mainland China in the 90s. So I think, partly because of that, Chinese artists like Zhang Xiaogang, Zeng Fanzhi and Yue Minjun received a lot more attention than artists in Hong Kong who were also active during that same period of time. The other issue is that I think art and culture in general in Hong Kong is not as appreciated or supported as it is in mainland China, which has a 5,000-year history of supporting arts, letters, poetry, theater, opera and so forth. I think to go to art school and be an artist in China is a lot more acceptable and a lot more encouraged than it is in a place like Hong Kong, which is 100 years old, and much more built on the idea of trading and mercantilism. What I am trying to say is that I am not sure if it is a reflection on how good or bad the galleries or the gallery system are in Hong Kong; rather it is the fact that aspects of what is important to create a thriving art world do not exist in Hong Kong. There are very few art schools, there are very few artists, there are very few writers, and there are very few journals. There is a market but there isn't perhaps necessarily the cultural life that you have in a place like Berlin or New York or London.

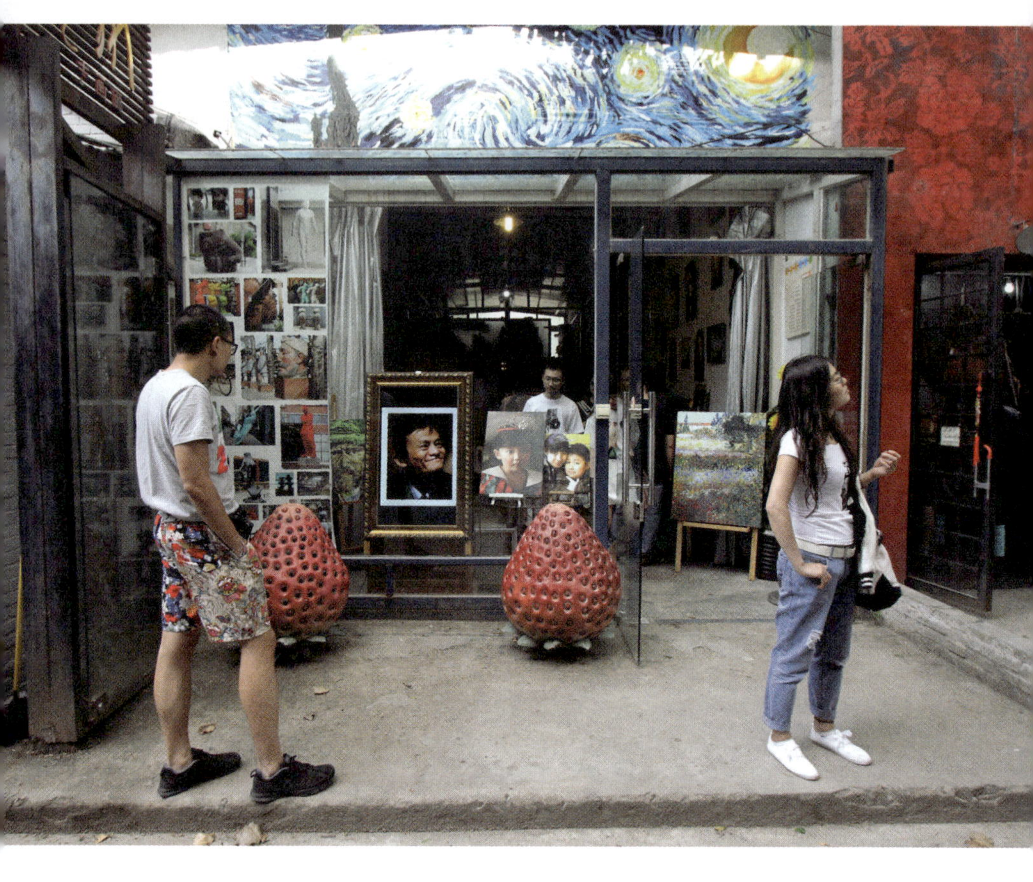

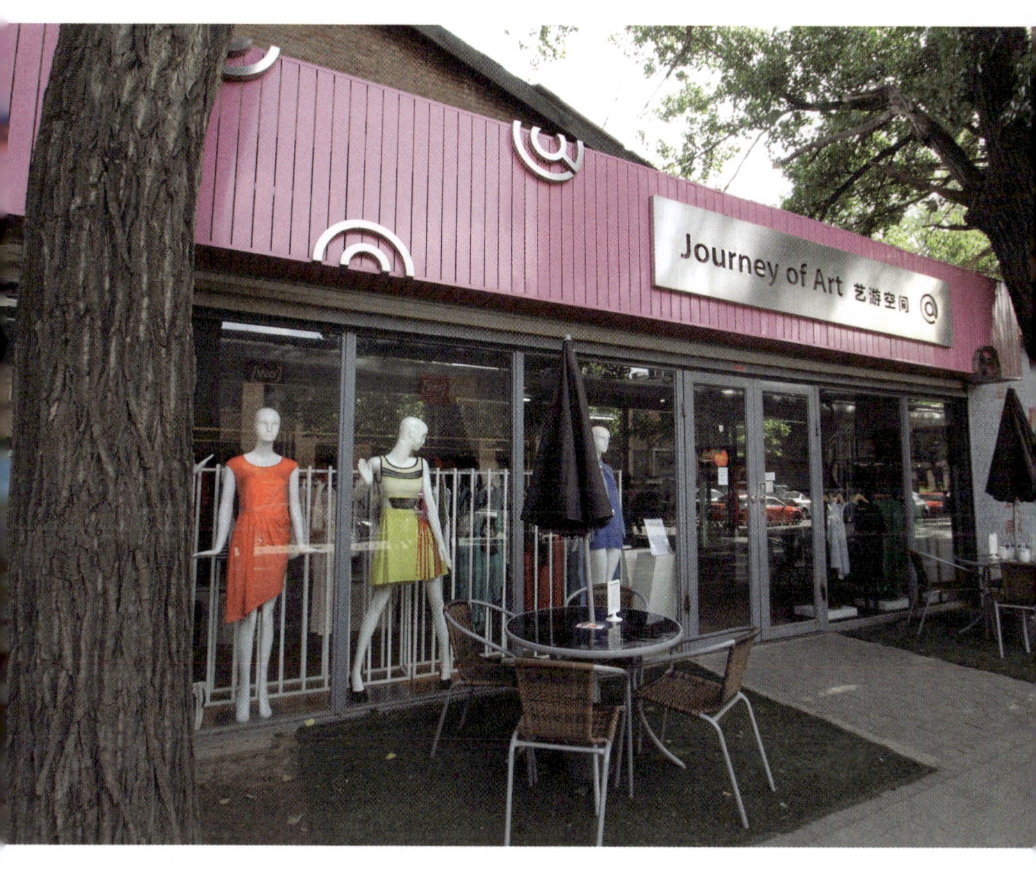
Journey of Art 艺游空间

"The auction has been much more at the front of the development of the art market in Asia"

A talk with Jonathan Stone
Auctioneer, Hong Kong

Jonathan Stone is the Chairman and International Head of Asian Art at Christie's in Hong Kong where he has worked since 2011. Stone was born in 1960 in New Zealand as a citizen of the UK. He studied business and history at Cambridge University before going on to work in marketing in Japan where he stayed for several years. He found his way into the arts through a postgraduate degree in art history in London before finally joining Christie's. He worked for the auction house for nearly 10 years as a specialist in London in the 1990s. He moved back to Japan where, for five years, he was the managing director before moving to the Hong Kong branch as the managing director for Asia.

His career with Christie's and his many years in Asia make him an expert in the Asian art world. In his interview he gives detailed insight about the role of auction houses in Asia, the regional diversity and the collectors who frequent the auctions.

Unlike in the West where galleries and artists make up the majority of the art scene, in Asia, Stone explains, the auctions are in the vanguard of the market. With the arrival of Sotheby's in 1973 and Christie's in 1986 in Hong Kong, auction houses became very strong forces in the Asian art market, a clear indication of which is seen in the ways that they helped Hong Kong to achieve its status as the second biggest Chinese auction art market and the world's fourth largest by total turnover. Galleries, on the other hand, arrived only in the last few years and are still struggling for acceptance. Stone explains this asymmetry historically, citing the lack of infrastructure for a more robust market. Indeed the modernization process in Asia, which has also enabled it to catch up with the modern and contemporary art of the West, has skipped 150 years and to a certain extent several stages of art epochs which have developed the structures of the art field in the West. Today it has almost arrived at the peak of the latest development from the West, with tendencies towards commercialization and structures that are beyond the traditional and classic gallery system.

Auction houses are a much more widely used vehicle for collectors new to buying, says Stone. Both transparency in the auction process as well as competitive bidding are incentives for new Asian buyers since they are both mechanisms that are easier to understand than the sort of deals made in secret which characterize markets dominated by gallery sales.

The centrality of galleries is a tremendous shift in the market – auction houses are not, as they are in the West, relegated to the secondary market but serve as the primary market and even take on the development of artists through funding new work. This is, for emerging artists in Hong Kong and elsewhere in Asia, generally thought of as being detrimental to the development of the arts, as emphasis is put on the financial viability of artists in the market rather than artistic expression and development. These changes can also be seen in the West, where open sales with cutting-edge artists or new emerging artists are becoming more common. We are witnessing, especially in the East, a change in the art market such that old divisions are breaking down and the role of various actors are changing.

However, in the last few years Hong Kong has attracted many galleries, which are gaining importance. Stone reports this casually, making clear that it is not so much of a threat to the auction houses but is, instead, having a positive impact on the overall art market. This sort of positive feedback and collaboration was most pointedly seen when Art Basel pressed for the fair to be held both at the same time and in the same convention hall as Christie's auction. Art Basel in Hong Kong and Christie's auction were held in 2013, were profitable, and had considerable spillover effects. We are seeing restructurings and shifts that were long thought impossible.

Which role do the auction houses have in China? How is it different to Hong Kong? And how is it different to the West?

I think the role the auction house has in China, and I don't think it is so different in Hong Kong, is defined by the fact that there has not historically been the same level of infrastructure in the art market in terms of the number of galleries or dealers, nor the historical presence of dealers and galleries, as there has been in Europe or North America. The auction has been much more at the front of the development of the art market in Asia. I think that, given there isn't such a long continuous history of dealership or galleries in Asia, the transparency of the auction process is something which has appealed to people who are fairly new to the art market. At auction you have clearly a published estimate, and the price achieved is in the public record. When you are bidding, there is a justification for the price because there is competitive bidding – you have other people bidding as well. If you are not so familiar with pricing, or do not know why this piece should be a thousand dollars or a million dollars, the fact that you have somebody else bidding is a validation of the price, plus the transparency of the auction process is appealing. I think in the field of contemporary art, for example, in the last five years there have been far more galleries, particularly in Hong Kong, coming in. There have always been galleries but recently the number has increased considerably. I think that the auction houses played a role in developing the market, in a way that the auction houses have not played a role in developing that market to the same extent in the West. I think the auction houses have always been the secondary market, but I think they are a little closer in Asia to being part of the primary market, where you might offer new artists to a greater extent than has historically been true in the West. Having said that, I think this is changing in the West as well. For example, Christie's has the 'First Open' sales where you have cutting-edge artists or new and emerging artists. I think worldwide the more traditional division of the art market between the auction houses, galleries, and museums is much more fluid now than it used to be. But I think it has become more fluid first in Asia. The degree of movement between all the different aspects of the auction world is actually much more advanced in Asia than it is in the West.

Will the growing number of galleries become competitors to the auction houses in Hong Kong? And do you have strategies similar to gallery strategies, which would exactly reflect what you said about breaking down the boundaries a little?

I think the answer to the first question is yes. Because I think the number of galleries has grown. And one of the greatest things that has happened to the art market is the presence of the art fairs in Asia. You have had the Hong Kong Art Fair, next March you have Art Basel Hong Kong, which is great, and although it is competition for us it is also a development for the market. It is about the overall market growing and not about competing for a market which just remains the same size. So there are lots of opportunities for growth. And when the Hong Kong Art Fair began in 2009, they positioned their fair alongside our auctions, which I was very happy with, because I think it actually brings more people to Hong Kong and it is a win-win situation.

You talked beforehand with Art Basel about having your sales and their fair at the same time? Is future cooperation planned?

No, when the Hong Kong Art Fair set up, they came to us and said that they would like to have their fair at the same time as our sales. And clearly there were certain pros and cons about doing this but in the end we felt that the pros outweighed the cons. And in terms of the second question, yes, we are developing private sales. Private sales have always been part of the sales we offer, in the sense that if you know that somebody is selling a piece and another person is looking for that piece then it is quite simple to make a connection. But we are developing this much more rigorously now. And we have a series of selling exhibitions. Here in Hong Kong there is a gallery space downstairs, which we opened in the beginning of this year. And that is the opportunity to have selling exhibitions, where you feel like we are in fact a gallery.

How would you describe your Chinese collectors? Do they belong to a certain group or come from a certain milieu? Is the number of collectors growing?

First the number is growing, particularly in China. We had recently our third sale in Shanghai at the end of last week. There were a significant number of new buyers. And in Hong Kong sales every season, and indeed in the sales of Asian art and other categories as well, in London or Paris or New York, you see new buyers coming in from China consistently. So there is a growing number of Chinese buyers. I think it is much more difficult to categorize them in terms of the type. I mean clearly by definition anybody in the art market needs to have a certain financial viability. So you are dealing by definition with a particular segment of the greater world. I think one of the things you have seen is the development of museums and private museums in China, such as the Long Museum in Shanghai, which opened this year, for example and there are other examples. So you have people who are buying in a sense of creating a museum, clearly you have people buying as private collectors, you have more corporate institutional buyers and I think in China there is this awareness of the investment potential as well. People talk a lot about art as investment. One shouldn't overemphasize that but I think it has to be acknowledged that people are aware, especially in China, of the potential for a return on art.

Which are the biggest differences between the typical collector in the West and here?

I find that quite difficult because I think, in a way, the similarities have been greater between the collectors than the dissimilarities, in that collectors have to have that kind of passion for collecting. So that is what the biggest similarity is, which really answers the questions.

Are there spontaneous buyers? I would like to go into the topic of the special social psychology of those few buyers who come and in the end don't buy. We read a lot in the newspapers that after the sale is over, they say they actually can't buy. So we have the whole topic of 'losing face' in open competition. Aren't there sometimes difficulties in dealing with that?

I think there are two things. One is that nowhere in the world can you be sure that there won't be somebody who will not have buyer's remorse. It is certainly not a unique Chinese characteristic. And I think the second is that given the volume of business that the auction houses handle, although I know there has been quite a lot of coverage of the payment issues, it has really been quite small. I can't really speak for the auction houses in China but for the international houses. And I think that the other thing too is that it is part of an educative process. Newer buyers, whether they are in China or in the other parts of the world, increasingly understand that the fall of the hammer is the agreement, that is a binding contract, so that is a behavioral and educative process. People, as they understand the auction process, understand that this is how it works. And I think the other thing too, again here I can only speak for Christie's, is that over the years we have developed a way of ensuring that the buyers are absolutely bona fide, which is part of our duty and obligation to our vendors, so we take that really seriously. And I think we are all quite thorough in doing that.

From an auction house perspective, how will the art market in Hong Kong and China develop? You said already there would be probably more collectors and more people buying.

I think we are still in a fairly early stage. As the wealth grows in Greater China and as we do our job in finding new people, getting people to understand how the art market works, then I think it has the great potential to continue to grow.

In terms of branding, name branding, now that you have opened a branch in Shanghai, do you already see that people buy from Christie's because of the brand, that the object becomes more valuable for Chinese, for example?

I think there is element of that. Because we would like to think that people can buy with assurance. When you buy at Christie's we offer a warranty for a piece we sell so people can feel comfortable when buying. I think again, as I said, the auction process is a very transparent process. I think all of that helps, and I do think that there is a security about buying at Christie's because of the international presence and of the two and a half centuries of history, all that contributes to and supports our brand.

And do most of the Chinese already know Christie's or do you try to do a lot of advertising?

One still needs to continue to market the brand. In a way the best marketing is the results of the auction itself and the integrity of the auction process, which is, I think, hugely important. It is not that everybody is aware of Christie's and I think that in Asia, because you don't have 250 years of history, we are a comparatively new brand. Both Christie's and Sotheby's have been in Hong Kong for 30 to 40 years, and we have been in Japan for 40 years. It is quite a long time but it is not 250 years and still we are another service provider and maybe not as yet so much part of the cultural mindset of people as we are in Europe.

*How would you describe the art field?
Who is a stronger player, who is weaker,
how do they interact and how does this
differ to the West or what we have in
our heads?*

I think with some noticeable exceptions it is about the comparative newness of the art market in its broader sense. As we were saying earlier on, a lot of the infrastructure of the art market is comparatively new in the sense of the development of dealers, galleries, and of auction houses and institutions. I think in Asia it varies a lot. It is a little different in Japan, where the art market has a longer history perhaps. China has a very long and really extraordinary cultural history but you also have a sort of a hiccup in the early 21th century. You get the redevelopment now of a lot of institutions. But it is happening very fast. There are 3,500 museums in China or something like that.

And if you look into Hong Kong?

I think Hong Kong is a little different in that the focus of Hong Kong has been perhaps more overtly commercial. You know the role Hong Kong has often played as an entrepot of the region. It is a very easy place to do business. It is very open, there is a very equitable tax structure, import-export is very easy, and you don't need an export license, whereas you do in most European countries or in China. It is a very easy and flexible place to do business, where there is a clear jurisprudence system, so again people can feel absolutely comfortable doing business here.

*And if you look more to the South,
to Singapore and the region there.
Do you think that will develop as well,
as fast as here?*

I think it will develop. I think that Hong Kong has established itself very quickly as the hub of the art market in Asia. Part of it is the ease of doing business, the reasons that we said. Singapore has things such as a Goods and Services Tax and so on. I think another reason for Hong Kong is the geographic position in the region; it is three hours from Singapore and three hours from Beijing, four hours from Tokyo, four hours from Jakarta.

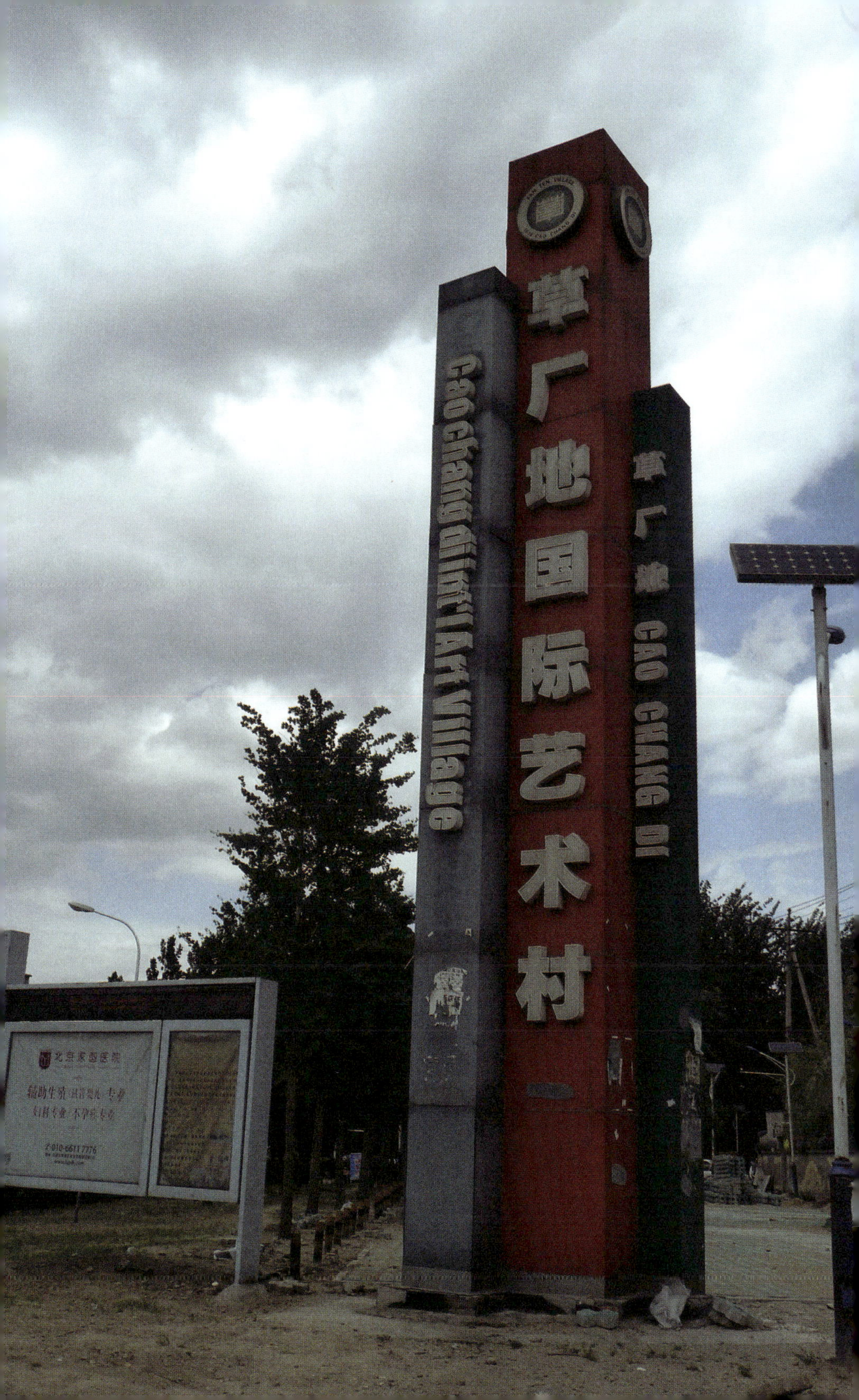

草厂地国际艺术村
Cao Chang di Art Village
草厂地
CAO CHANG DI
北京家圆医院
电话 010-6611 7776

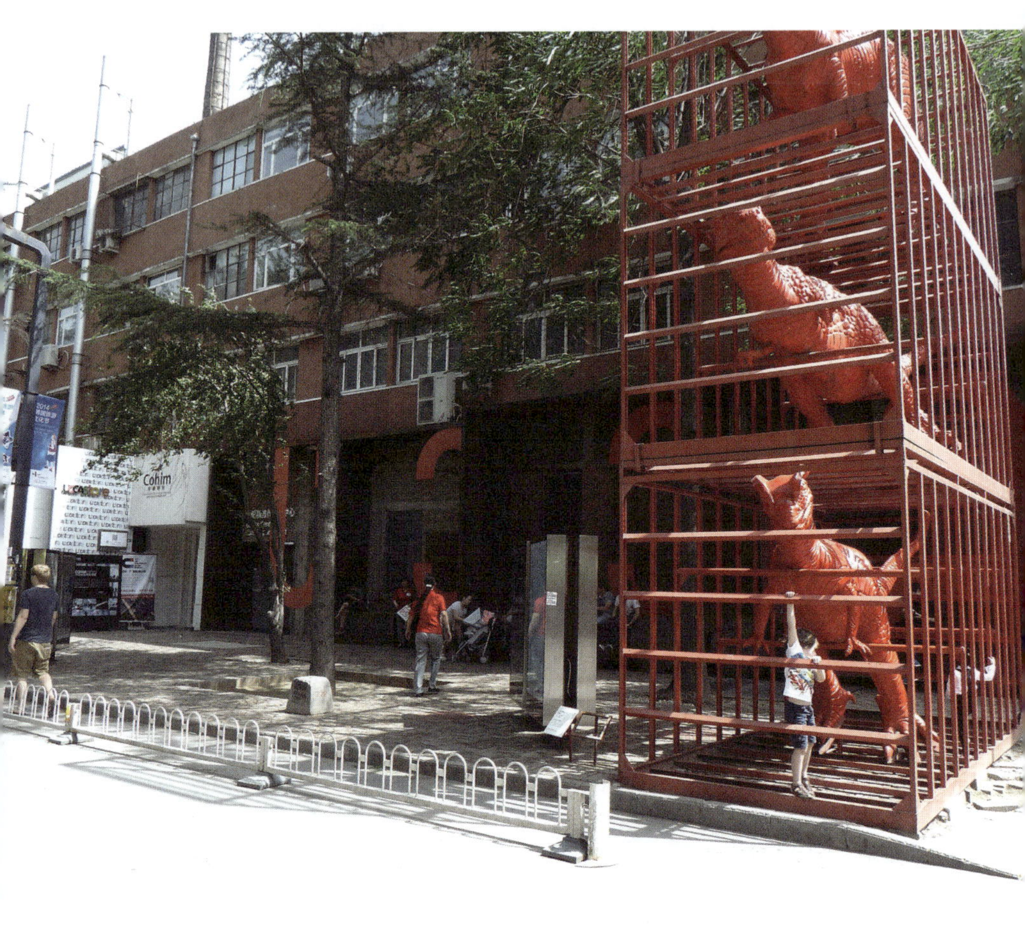

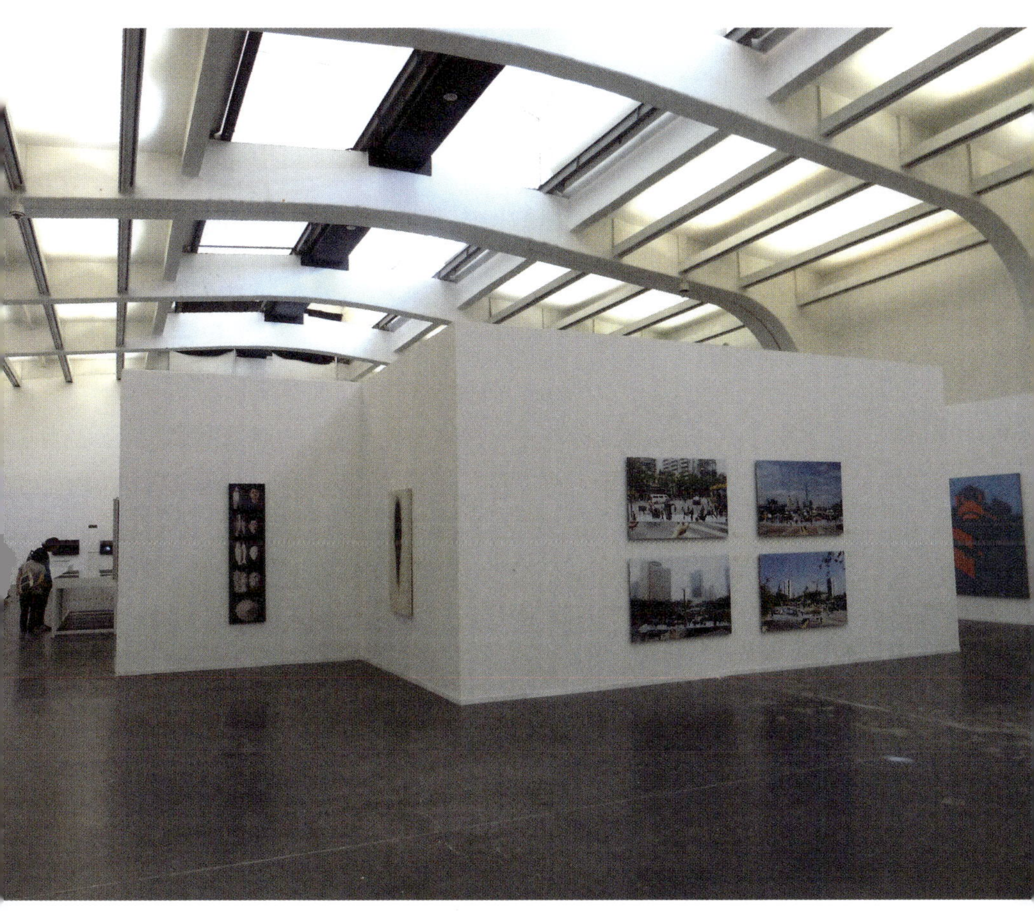

"It is an emerging market, it is an emerging situation"

A talk with Colin Chinnery
Artist/Curator

Colin Chinnery represents the ideal type of a cultural bridge-builder between different worlds, between China and Great Britain. The curator, cultural manager and artist grew up as the son of a Chinese mother and a Scottish father first in Edinburgh and later in Beijing, where he has lived on and off since since 1979. After studying Classical Chinese in London he worked, among other things, as an arts manager for the British Council in Beijing and as the chief curator and deputy director of the Ullens Center for Contemporary Art (UCCA), where he played a decisive part in its development as one of the most important institutions for contemporary art in China. From 2009 to 2010 he was the director of the SH Contemporary Art Fair in Shanghai and since 2013 he has been working as the artistic director of the Wuhan Art Terminus (WH.A.T.). As a conceptually oriented artist he was a founding member of the artists' collective Complete Art Experience Project, which includes high profile Chinese artists such as Qiu Zhijie and Liu Wei. Chinnery's works have been shown at several important exhibitions in China, the USA and Europe.

During his time as curator at Ullens and as director of the Shanghai Art Fair Chinnery already found the global perspective particularly important. Hearing different voices and confronting different perspectives from the Asian-Pacific region, the USA, Europe and other parts of the world is, in his opinion, an unconditional prerequisite for the cultural exchange of positions and regional "DNAs". The question as to what constitutes global art is being discussed with increasing urgency in the art world around the globe and is also relevant for both the new public and the collectors in China.

In China there is scarcely any state support or structures for art foundations and non-profit making organizations. This is, Colin Chinnery says, particularly bitter. There are a couple of institutions, but they neither form nor determine a structure. It is not least for this reason that the art field in China continues to be strongly dependent on factors outside China. Everything rests upon the commercial sector. Domestic collectors are the driving force and the backbone. Some of the around 600,000 people with a fortune of a million US dollars wish to know more about art and are becoming more sophisticated. They are searching for a way to art but often do not know how to go about it. Or they buy expensive works at auctions, which is, however, becoming increasingly unattractive for them. Like Chinnery has said on another occasion: "What these people lack is not money – it's trust. It's a way into the market without being taken advantage of."

Colin Chinnery gives a detailed insight into the development of an emerging art field which is rapidly changing on account of the powerful dynamics behind it, and is characterized particularly by an expanding art market, a low but growing density of art institutions and an unbelievably large number of young, aspiring artists. A part of this story is closely linked to the booming economy of China, which has also enabled an exponential growth of the art market in recent decades. The nature and the speed of the political, economic, social and cultural transformations which China has experienced and run through since the end of the Mao era determine the conditions for the current and further development of the art world in the country and put their own distinctive stamp upon it. The relationship between artists, their cultural inheritance, their understanding of the present and their vision of the future are also profoundly influenced by these transformations. It is enough to cast a glance at neighboring countries like Japan in order to ascertain that the differing conditions in each case have led to specific peculiarities and characteristic features in the respective art fields. And as it is difficult to read a past which is subject to continuous reinterpretations the future remains incalculable – this seems at least to apply particularly to China. Colin Chinnery adopts the following viewpoint: "After all, the questions don't change; they only change with their context."

Can you say a few words about your background?

I am half-British, half-Chinese, I am based in Beijing. I am an artist and curator and a critic. I have lived here on and off since 1979.

You studied art?

No, I didn't study art, I came into art quite late in my thirties.

Are you an independent curator or are you associated with a special institution?

I have done institutions but I guess I see my curatorial practice as more of an institutional practice rather than being an independent curator curating thematic shows per se. I work as an artist so I associate myself mostly with artists more than anybody else but just one example is that UCCA, the Ullens Centre for Contemporary Art just across the road. I was one of the founding directors. I was the deputy direction chief curator who set up the organization. I was in charge of the artistic program when it first opened in 2007; then I ran the SH Contemporary Art Fair for a couple of years in 2009 and 2010; at the moment I am setting up a new institution, a Kunsthalle-type of institution, in the city of Wuhan. In terms of art curatorial practices, it seems that I have more of an administrative, no not administrative, I would rather say a conceptual approach to saying what an institution is and how it should be thinking and acting and operating in a social space. That's the way I think, I curate shows as well, but I don't operate as an independent curator of thematic shows. I like working with artists on solo shows, especially artists I know very well because I know their practice and it feels more comfortable for me.

How is the institutional setting in China? Are there enough institutions here for artists? Are they developing?

China is a developing country, which means that contemporary art as our global cultural phenomenon is also a beginning thing. It started in the 1980s with the Stars Group and the '85 New Wave movement and continued in the 1990s. '89 was the beginning of a more pragmatic commercial path as well as the starting point of a much more international conceptual or post-conceptual artistic practice of artists that were in China. Then I think the art market started in 2004 to 2005 when the 798 Art District opened and all these galleries started actually being able to offer art properly as commercial galleries, supporting artists and their careers. The market started first because that is where the money is. There is no financial support for institutions otherwise. It has only been since private collectors have become more active in society, institutions or non-profit organizations have become more prominent in this ecosystem, or whatever you want to call the art world. So there are not enough institutions, there are too many galleries and not enough non-profits. It is not that I have a fetish for non-profit or that I am anti-commercial in any way. I used to run an art fair. I just think there needs to be a balance between the two things and we haven't reached the stage that we are at a balance yet. We are still at the stage where the non-profit is just beginning; it is developing very quickly but still just beginning and the commercial sector still has a lot more power than maybe it should have.

Can you tell us something about the gallery scene? Are there a lot of gallerists coming from the Western countries?

Galleries started out in about the 1990s with a couple of galleries dealing in contemporary art. There was ShanghART in Shanghai and Courtyard Gallery in Beijing. I am talking about contemporary art rather than modern art or different forms of it. Contemporary art is an international domain. Western galleries started becoming interested here quite early on, for example, a Japanese gallery BTAP, Beijing Tokyo Art Project, which is still in Beijing but not really operational any more. That was the first commercial gallery in 798; they started right at the beginning. And the experimentation in business models by Western galleries in China is continuing a lot today in that they try to inject more capital and try to experiment and see what model they can use as non-Chinese galleries to build an operational business in China. Given that if they want to sell non-Chinese art, if they want to import and export artists' commodities into and out of China, all these things, then there are lots and lots of obstacles involved. The galleries are in town, there is Pace Beijing, that is one model. There is the Faurschou, which is next to Pace too, turned from a commercial place into a foundation, so this is no longer running as a commercial space. Then there is Continua, which doesn't really attempt to sell here; it is a showcase for their international artists in China and they don't really sell their work here; they give their artists in the West a kind of a wonderful place to do projects. And then they have new work for their clients back in the West. So each gallery has a different model of how to operate in China.

The gallery owners came from the West, from the Western world. Did they have an influence on the taste?

Western galleries?

Yes.

No. They are not really operational here yet, so they can't, they don't; if they are not operational in China they can't really have a say in the market or how the market is directed.

You have talked about galleries as mostly commercial. Is there an understanding that the galleries are very important for the development and the career of an artist?

Yes, of course. As the galleries are becoming more sophisticated, there are galleries who are able to do that. At the beginning I think a few years ago, the market was very strong and it was the time of the bubble and I think, everyone just wanted to make as much money as possible at that time. And that supported artists' careers in a different way. It gave them the means to make more different kinds of work, gave them the means to be more confident about their work.

Some artists thrived in that kind of market environment, some artists sank, some artists overproduced. Some artists were much smarter about it and then used that as a path to make more interesting work and further their creative energy. Now there are a number of Chinese galleries that participate in Frieze Art Fair, Art Basel in Basel and in Miami and these galleries represent the most interesting contemporary artists in China. They know how to operate a gallery. It is not just about selling works; it is also about supporting their careers; it is about promotion of the work among institutions, curators, interesting collectors, and it is not just about selling as much work as possible. Of course, there are some very good galleries in China now. Of course, they are outweighed by lots and lots of beginning galleries or less-sophisticated galleries but that is normal in any kind of emerging situation.

And it is a learning process for them...

It is a learning process for everyone. It is an emerging market, it is an emerging situation. China is in a situation where things are developing very quickly and in Europe things are in a kind of stagnation, a little bit, and so it is two different directions.

Are there a lot of people interested in conceptual Chinese contemporary art?

Chinese art has been introduced in the international context for many years now, ever since the 1993 Venice Biennale that included a large contingent of Chinese artists, mostly painters, but still that was the first big introduction and since then it has been pretty constant. Chinese artists have participated in Kassel every time and Venice every time and lots of shows around the world. Some are just Chinese shows, but some artists such as Yang Fudong or Cau Fei, Xu Zhen or Liu Wei prosper as artists in their own right, not as Chinese artists. Now they are represented by Marian Goodman or White Cube. Major blue chip Western galleries are now representing these artists who are on the creative edge of working of avant-garde contemporary practice, or whatever you want to call it, in China. I think it has become, I wouldn't say completely normal, because there isn't such a thing, but there is enough interest in China for a steady stream of coming and going between China and the rest of the world. Of course there are types of art that are not so easy for Western curators or collectors or gallerists to really comprehend. That more difficult work will take a lot longer to become recog-

nized outside of China but that is because China is not yet really on the international circuit. It is a big country that is still off the beaten path in terms of art and the international art circuit because China hasn't become international yet in that way.

And if you look at the collectors, are they mostly Western collectors?

There are some artists whose work is still beyond the comprehension of non-Chinese collectors or curators or gallerists. There are some artists whose work is very good here and well respected but still a little bit too different for people to understand outside of China. On the other hand, there are artists who are recognized by critics, collectors, curators and gallerists outside of China; there are both sides. It depends, some work is much easier for them to understand quickly and some work takes a lot longer.

We were in Hong Kong at the Art Basel art fair last week. One member of the Art Basel direction told us that there are a lot of young collectors here in China.

I think right now we are seeing the second generation of....

Collectors?

No, let's say the first generation got rich, they have kids now who have grown up, so the first generation that made the money, very few of them are going to collect art. Then the second generation inherited the wealth and power of their parents and their enterprises and very often they have been educated abroad, they have a much different world view, very international and savvy, cosmopolitan. It makes sense for that generation of young rich people to get involved in contemporary culture like they do in the West. The way that money operates is very globalized and also the way that people operate; they travel, often being educated in the West. So these collectors are going to be having a big effect on the art market and, as you previously said, even as taste makers.

If you look at the art institutions, there are not a lot of museum here. What is the role of private collections in contrast to these art institutions?

Because private collections have a different prerogative than public institutions, in China there are no public institutions for contemporary art yet. There is one big one in Shanghai and there are a few around maybe, but they don't really operate in the way we understand them in the West. As they take public money they have a responsibility to the public to collect, to research, to analyze and educate the public about a certain body of work. There isn't such a thing yet. What you have instead are private institutions mostly run by either private collectors or real estate organizations. They have the prerogative that they don't have the responsibility to the public, they only have responsibility to themselves. There is nothing wrong with that; it is just a different model. Private collections and museums are wonderful and support lots of artists and do good shows. It is a different kind of thing all together. We don't have, let's say, what we perhaps lack, maybe the intellectual side of keeping archives, the research, the caretaking of the body of work, the recent history and education. That role, the role of dissemination and education is still very much what the media is doing. Of course, the media are still much more interested in the commercial side than in the intellectual side of art; that's just normal at this stage and I think it is understandable. So that is what I think is still lacking. And very few private organizations can really fulfill that task, it is just simply not their role.

From your point of view, can you tell us something about the role of the auction houses here in the Chinese art market?

Well, I am not an expert on the secondary art market. I have never been involved and never worked in that sector so I really can't speak from any kind of position or real knowledge or experience. However, from observation I have never really been a big fan of the secondary art market. In Asia and East Asia in general, the secondary art market is still rather the place to go to than the primary market. Because it is seen as being transparent, it is seen as more user-friendly and also because they deal with brands. The secondary market it is much more brand-friendly. In an emerging situation like in China brands are much more powerful but we have seen that happen also in the West when we see the return of the power of the auction in the West. In the past two years, since the last financial meltdown, we have seen that the secondary market has become very powerful. First because lots of people go bankrupt and they need to sell their collections; on the other hand those who don't go bankrupt know how to work within the system or create their own systems for creating even more wealth. The second remark of mine is very

much a part of that game of cumulating, investment and so on, which does have overall a negative effect on the careers of the artists, let's say the balance of the art system as a whole. But having said that, it has a role to play and we can't ignore it; we have to be aware of it, we have to even sometimes work with it. Even though I am reluctant to do so, I think that it is almost impossible not to.

What is the impact of institutions such as Ullens Centre for the art scene or the art world in China?

It is the only game in town. I mean basically, and I mean the only game in town when talking about non-profit. We are talking about a role of creating exhibitions that are not for profit or not for sale. It has an educational function that creates exhibitions from artists all around the world, not gallery size or institutional size; these are all really important functions. One must have that kind of institution in any kind of an art system in an art scene. This is the only one so far. I would say it is not the only one in China but incorporating a certain scale and a certain quality you can't argue otherwise.

And if you look back over the last 10 years what was the main transformation in the art scene?

Well, that is pretty easy to answer. I think it is the role of the market. And it was exactly 10 years ago when the market really started to be a factor. Galleries started opening up, blossoming I would say in 2004. I think 798 Art District went from having a handful of galleries to a 100 galleries in just over a year in 2004, 2005, 2006, let's say in two years. That is really when things started picking up and that obviously had a very positive effect. On the one hand it enabled lots of artists to actually build long term careers so that is really positive. On the other hand it has had a questionable effect on the young artists who have just graduated and they see art now as a career rather than just something that you possibly do. Before there was a market artists didn't choose to become artists because there is no money in it. Or they just loved it and wanted to do it. They might have failed and done something else in the end but those who didn't persevered and did very interesting work. And now these artists are very well known. In the West, where there is a much more mature system, it is still very hard to be an artist. It is still very tough and the other thing is that you have got quite an array of options in terms of different forms of support, different kinds of practice. You can be an artist who works on commission, or does projects; you can be a painter who works with a gallery; there are all kinds of different options; you could do a whole range. At the beginning of the market there is lots of investment and so on. At this stage I think lots of young people have seen being an artist as a way to earn money. Also, the other thing is that the career side of it has become a very prominent factor, more prominent than what we wish. I would say, on the one side, it supports many more artists than before. It helps the whole art scene to blossom now; because of this commercial situation, there are the collectors who then can buy artists' work and support the practice. There are the galleries who can do a lot more for artists because they can accumulate a certain amount of wealth, which they can put back into creating a project. There are magazines and journals, which are disseminating the work beyond the commercial media. And there are institutions, private collectors who open museums and so on. That is all because of the market, so that is all very positive. But the only thing one would worry about though is the imbalance of the market in relation to the number of artists.

Kids who are just going into school or are just graduating are feeling the pull of the market so strongly that it is almost difficult to extricate themselves from that. Don't be too cynical about it; the only reason why I am worried is that in the last 10 years we haven't really seen a new generation of great artists like we saw in the previous 10 years of artists that are now very established and very influential in China. Where are the equivalent of those artists now? I mean there are good artists but we are not seeing the seminal ones. I don't know why that is. We are speaking among ourselves and debating this issue. It seems likely that art as career has a certain detachment effect on the quality of work.

How would you describe the differences between the Western art scene and the Chinese art scene? Are there differences? Only looking at contemporary art or the contemporary art scene.

Well, the differences are huge so I don't know where to begin. It comes down to having a mature institutional ecosystem on one hand in Europe. It is stable and secure but it is also starting to stagnate. There are a lot of problems associated with it now. In China I would say it is a new, much more energetic and commercially orientated system that is developing its ecosystem. Or it is in the form of becoming, it is not set, so I feel that at the moment there is lots of potential in China; I feel like there is more potential in China than in Europe at the moment.

How is the relationship between the official sector such as the public institutions and the private sector like galleries? For example the CAFA, is it important?

In the educational system there are two art schools that are very important, the CAFA and the China Academy in Hangzhou. Of course, they are incredibly important. CAFA not only produces students, graduate artists, but they also have an important museum where they put up shows like the CAFA Bang, which was just a couple of months ago. And the Hangzhou Academy has some of the best Chinese artists working there as teachers and producing with their students, building an interesting collection. They have an entire Bauhaus collection for their design school. That on one hand is very interesting. I think CAFA and Hangzhou Academy play a very active role in the contemporary art scene. On the other side of the institutions, there are museums like the Museum of

Contemporary Art Shanghai or the Power Station of Art. That hosts the Shanghai Biennale and that is also important. I don't know so much about other shows but that is something else. There are a few of these government-run museums which do host these contemporary art shows but I would say that the government-run museums are far less involved and far less influential as active participators in the art scene here. And the government as an entity doesn't generally get involved; it is not so supportive or it doesn't really actively participate. Since I am in 798 I thought we could see a couple of shows together. On that level I think there is far less participation of the government per se but there are the schools; I think they are the most active participants.

If you can give an outlook from your point of view, in what direction do you think the art scene is going to develop? Is it an ambivalent development or is it going in one direction?

I feel very positive as a whole because I think that the fact that the money is being injected through the commercial sector means that we have the ammunition that we need to develop interesting projects. And these private institutions are opening and I think some of them will become very interesting, just like UCCA, and more artists will be able communicate with the audiences in different ways. And not only in Beijing or Shanghai but in other cities all around China. We are seeing that happen now; it is already in the process of happening so I think that is really the kind of energy we want to tap into at the moment, because it has a lot of potential.

Can you say that it is a very fast development?

I think it is fast. China has sometimes developed an unfair reputation as being secretive or full of unknown secret police kicking down artists' doors and stopping shows. I think we can work pretty much as we want to work. We understand that there are barriers and obstacles and we negotiate like one negotiates obstacles in everyday life. When you encounter a problem with your girlfriend or boyfriend you don't just quit because of having encountered the problem. One starts through things and that is what life is like and the most important thing is that we get things done and we are active and we think about things. I think that is the energy that is in China at the moment. It is this kind of idea of getting on with things, being positive and tapping into some energy. Even though China is not a democracy like India, its contemporary art scene is far more active than in India. And it is not just because of the commercial side, it is also a question of how much international art has been introduced to China. The first major show of Western contemporary art in China was the Robert Rauschenberg show of 1985; I think the first major Western contemporary art show in India was in 2008, 23 years later. So it is very interesting that there is very little relationship, if any between the fact that China is not a democracy and that contemporary art is thriving. It has a lot to do with the commercial model that China is operating under, the economic model that China is developing because then contemporary art can tap into that energy. I think China has a very strong dynamic so that is why it is developing very quickly.

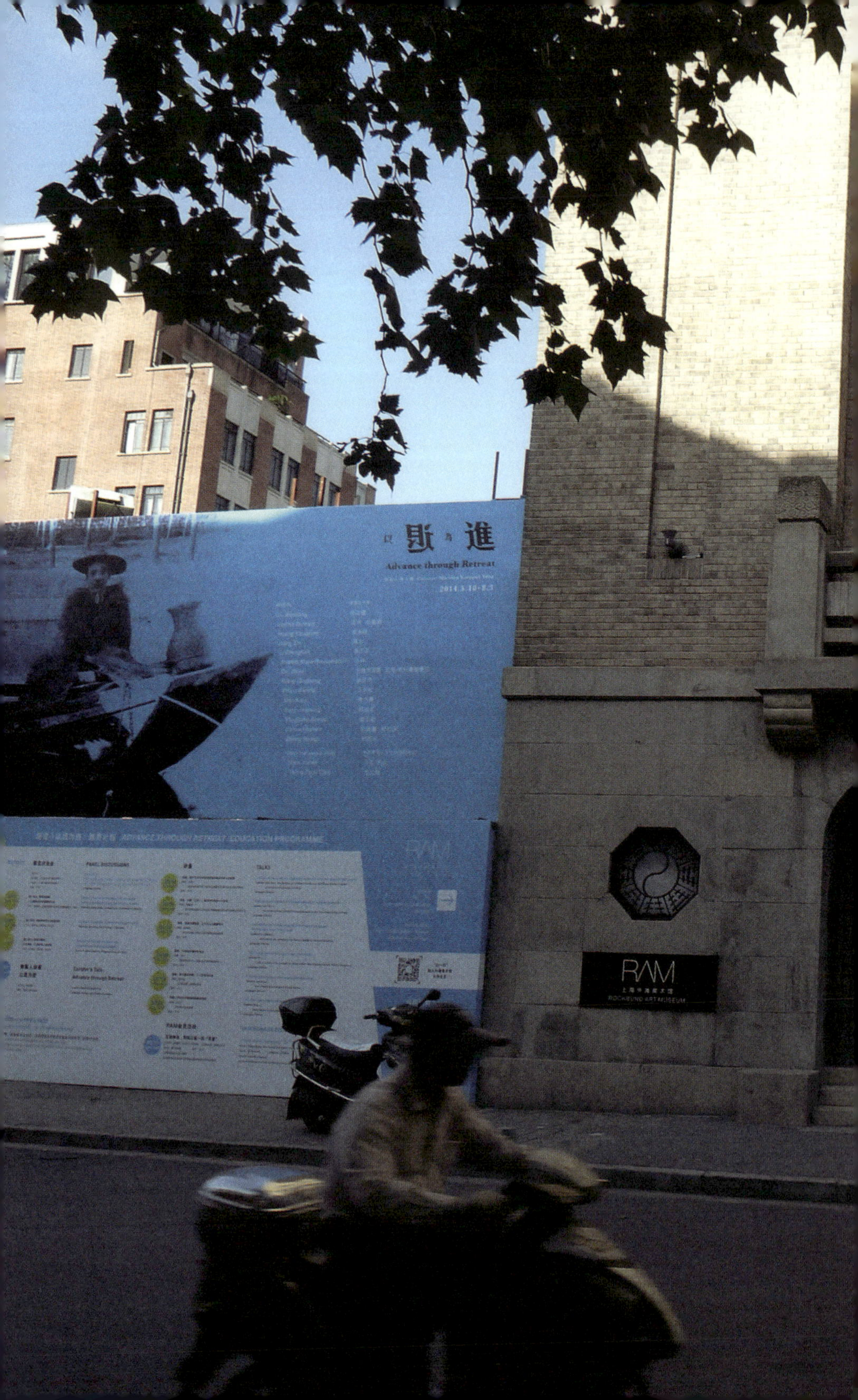
以
斯
為
進
Advance through Retreat
2014.5.10-8.3
RAM
上海外滩美术馆
ROCKBUND ART MUSEUM

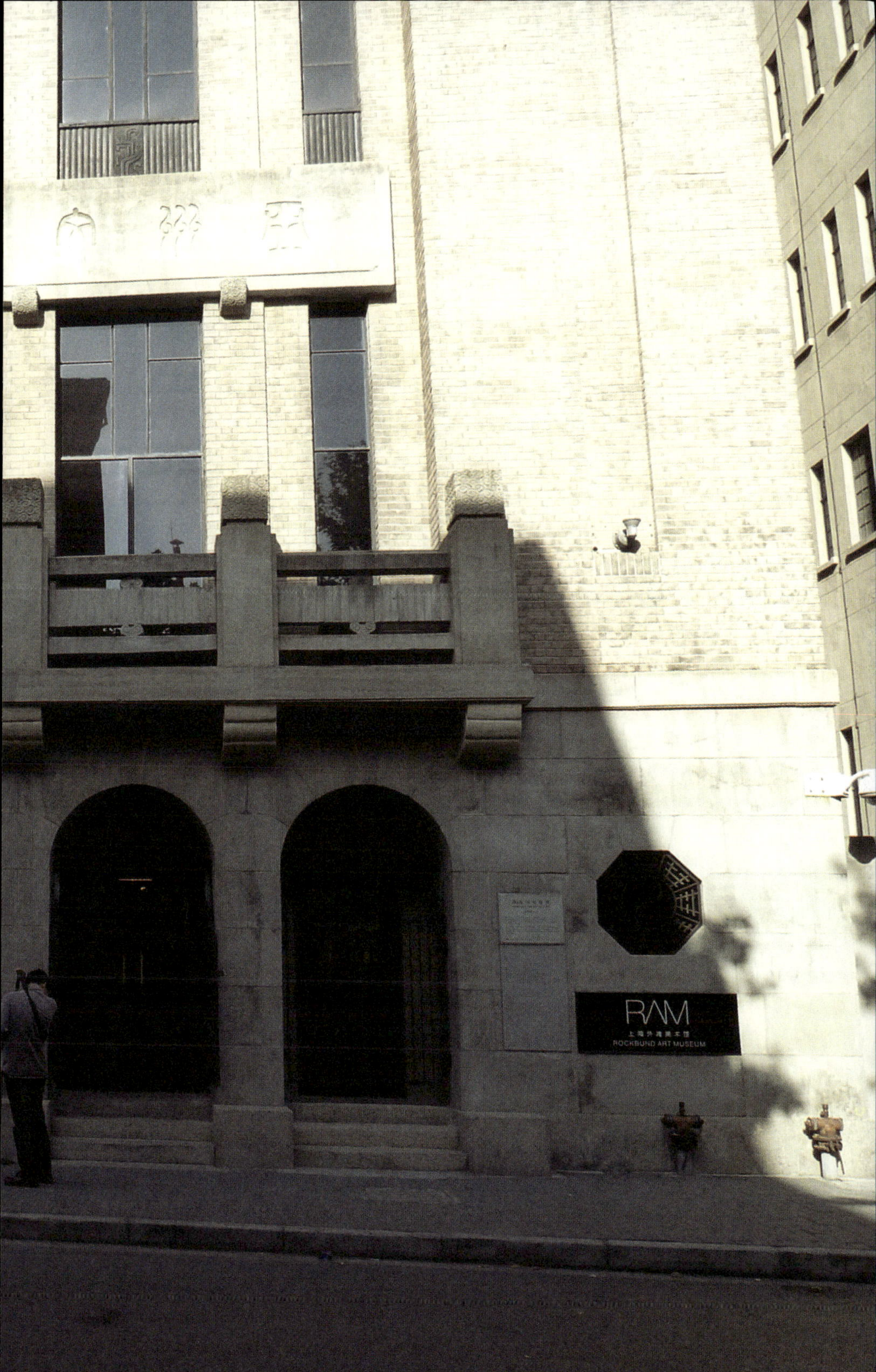
222
RAM
上海外滩美术馆
ROCKBUND ART MUSEUM

"We really support artists' positions, which is rare in China"

A talk with Gu Ling
Museum management/Journalist, Shanghai

At the time of the interview Gu Ling has been a member of the staff of the Rockbund Art Museum (RAM) in Shanghai for three years. She is the manager responsible for the development and communications work of the museum. She studied cultural management at a university and is also active as a journalist. She writes freelance articles on the Asian art world and is the Shanghai editor of Randian Online, an online platform which "seeks to promote independent cultural debate in China and to foster intellectual exchange between China and the rest of the world."

The Rockbund Art Museum occupies a special place in the Chinese art world. It is not based – like many of the private museums which are being set up – on the permanent art collection of a rich patron. Instead it shows the works of Chinese and foreign artists in changing exhibitions, in the style of a Kunsthalle, for example those of well-known figures such as Zeng Fanzhi, Zhang Huan or the US-American Mark Bradford. The production of new works of contemporary art is the core content of the museum. In particular the art should have a relationship to the Art Deco building which was renovated by David Copperfield in 2007 and has housed the RAM since 2010. The foundation of the museum can be traced back to a city development concept "which aims to renovate heritage buildings and revitalize the cultural milieu for the north end of the Bund through arts, fashion, business and leisure programs", and is to this extent similar to other cases of city branding in other metropolises.

Gu Ling represents the claim of China to participate in the global art scene on an equal footing. She speaks very openly about the weaknesses of the Chinese art world, for example the lack of quality, as she sees it, of the works exhibited in the museums or the frequently far too casual approach of the management in the art institutions. But in the interviews she nonetheless very decisively rejects the impression that there is a need to catch up in development. She speaks out instead in favor of an autochtonous development which only needs time. "We need time to test the whole thing", she dryly observes. The knowledge and the tools needed to produce and mediate contemporary art are, in her opinion, available, as she herself nonchalantly demonstrates with her own expertise.

Gu Ling presents a view of the contemporary art world in which she and the RAM have an important role to play. For her the actors in the art world are embedded in a pluralistic post-global context, which is indeed informed and influenced by a Western culture, but in which Chinese contemporary art definitely seems, nonetheless, to be keeping pace with the times. In this context the RAM functions as a so called bridge of communication between international and local artists who are on an equal footing. For her the boundaries between Western and Eastern art are fluid. "There are no boundaries, there is no absolute boundary", in her opinion.

Could you describe shortly how you got into art? And what does your institution do, what is the philosophy of your institution compared to other institutions in Shanghai or China?

I studied cultural management at a university in China, in Shanghai, and I started working for the Rockbund Art Museum two years ago. The Rockbund Art Museum is a contemporary art museum committed to fully supporting new production of contemporary art. We are quite different from the private museums which are now opening up very quickly in China and are usually based on private collections, on corporate collections. We are a non-collection museum. The core content for the museum is the production of contemporary art. We curate three exhibitions per year and for each exhibition, especially for the solo exhibitions, more than 50 per cent of new production is required. The new production usually connects very closely with the space of the building, as you can see; it carries a very strong history and it is a very unique architecture. It was originally the Royal Asiatic Society so this was one relationship for the artists to consider when deciding whether they want to do a project here. And the second relationship is in regard to the local context. In Shanghai and in China, for example, we just finished the solo exhibition of Bharti Kher, an Indian artist. She really looked into the formalization of the history of Shanghai and also the connection with maps. The maps coming from the East Indian company which dealt with the opium during the post-opium war were the point she looked into. But we also have different artists, for example Ugo Rondinone, the Swiss artist based in New York, who has really looked into the architecture. He is inventing a full horizontal wall painting to draw a contrast with the vertical structure of the building. This is the core we are looking at, the context in which the artists makes new projects, which is not only in favor of the museum development but also for the career of the artists themselves. For example, for Udo it is actually the very first project for him to consider one exhibition as one art project. And also for Bharti it is actually the very first solo exhibition for her on such a scale in Asia. We are creating some innovative projects to combine very closely the artist's practice and then the museum strategy.

The questions is, how important is this institution for the art world in China, for the development in the art scene?

The museum started in 2010, so we started with established Chinese artists, Cai Guoqiang, Zeng Fanzhi, Zhang Huan, etc. And then in 2012 we had the new director Larys Frogier join the team and then he initiated the new mission statement and the new four platforms for the museum's development, that is to say the exhibitions, which is the core, education, research and development. He also started communication and trying to find more consistency and a system to support the museum's running. This year, in the exhibition I introduced, we really support artists' positions, which is rare in China. We can't really find such a way and just full involvement to support artists' practice. The other side is education: we are actually thinking about really rephrasing it. It is not learning because the programs we are curating now alongside the exhibition programs have a bit more variety and are very frequently happening. There are very active programs of public activities. We have lectures, performances, seminars, workshops happening every week. Usually weekly there are two to five different activities, so this is really a very strong platform for us, for audience development but also for activating the local cultural scene. To create a space where the public can go to and discover new things to find new perspectives of seeing the world or thinking about the same. The education or the learning department platform is also very important. I believe this carries a very strong meaning of being in the museum. The educational function has to be easier. Actually, the museum organizes an annual forum: in 2012 the annual program is focused on the topic of educational function in the Chinese contemporary museums, so we invited more than 10 museums from China to discuss how to improve and facilitate the educational function of the museum.

But you normally support conceptual art works and conceptual production, more than drawings and...

No, depending on the definition of conceptual art. If you see conceptual art and contemporary art as equal I would answer this question as it is.

How do you describe the level of awareness of art in China, the level of knowing about contemporary art? Is it something really new to the public? Is it just for a small elite?

I think, actually, I agree with you, that on a certain level contemporary art is in this paradoxical situation, when at the same time it is trying to build its own system and its own community and its own circle, while on the other hand the core spirit of contemporary art is about questioning, throwing up questions, refills, protests and trying to find alternatives. I think this is the spirit very much connected with the problem as well, for us especially for the museum. Even though we are funded by a corporation we are a public museum. We are opening our gates to the public, we are very much trying to connect with our audiences. We are trying to communicate the content rather than close it to the so-called elite community. This is the way we choose to act so to ask whether contemporary art in China is well known in the public, I think the answer is no. Maybe there are 0.1 per cent of the public that knows about what contemporary art is. For the majority of the public, they still believe art is painting, sculpture, something purely aesthetic and visual rather than connected to concepts.

Do you think this is changing rapidly or is it a slow process?

I think it is changing quite quickly. I can give you a rough number on our audience development. In 2013 compared to 2012 we had a 65 per cent increase. And then, the visitor number of Bharti Kher's exhibition, just one exhibition audience, is similar to the number of the annual visitors in 2012. By the rise of the numbers we can see how very rapidly people just join and try to understand.

I think the cityscape is somehow similar: you have private museums which are the latest thing. Are the art academies considered more contemporary or more modern or traditional institutions?

It depends, there are some art academies; in Shanghai there are no pure art academies. There are academies within a college or a university or they have more of aesthetics or culture, literature and alongside is a college for art instead of independent Royal Art Academies institutions. In China there are in total eight main art academies, for example CAFA, the China Central Academy of Fine Arts in Beijing, which is very active; they do a lot of research, they have a contemporary art museum, which is the CAFA Museum. They also launched a biennale for young artists who are very much in the contemporary art practice. There is also the art academy we call the Chinese Art Academy, which is based in Hangzhou, so they are also very much active. There is one college contributing to what they call total art; it is very

much connected with the Bauhaus tradition of considering 'Kunst', in that everything is art, total art, architecture, painting, literature, film. They have also another college contributing to the new media such as video, video installation, time based art. Talking about Shanghai we also have Shanghai University, which has been collaborating with John Moore's Foundation from England for more than three years and they founded an award for painting, but painting in the contemporary art sense. I think the academies are also moving. Maybe the majority of the art academies or universities are still considering art as modern or have a more classical definition just like the public.

How would you describe the quality of the new artists? Are they developing or could they be compared to Western artists? Are they very good in different media? How would you describe it? It is a very general question, I know.

We are living in a globalized society, even our director focuses on the post-globalization meaning that we are already involved in. The development of China in the past 30 years is within the globalized context, very much so, also the young artists. If we are talking about the new artists, maybe born after the

1970s, they are very much influenced by the Western culture, the commodities they use...

So they went to Europe?

Maybe they traveled, maybe they received the information from the Internet. They are very much in communication with the Western artists.

How important is it for you to work with galleries, to communicate and cooperate with galleries? Are art schools more important than galleries?

For the Rockbund we are always very conscious about selecting partnerships. If a gallery tries to have an impact on our selection of artists by offering sponsorships we would be very conscious about such a cooperation. If we already selected the artists and the artists have cooperated or are represented by a gallery, if they are open and willing to contribute to the production of a catalogue or be a specific part of the project, we are open. But we refuse to accept any level of sponsorship with the intention of influencing the autonomous production of the museum in conceiving and implementing the project. So this is the stand that we take. This is the same strategy as with any other kind of partnership.

How developed is the gallery system in China?

There are a lot of galleries. It started from the 1980s. I think the first gallery opened in Beijing in 1982, so it has been 32 years. So it is quite a long time, according to the Chinese speed in developing a system. There are some galleries, for example, in Shanghai there is the ShanghART Gallery, which has been running for more than 16 years I think. They are an agent for most of the established artists coming from Shanghai and there are also branches of international galleries based in China like Pace or other international brands. But also I guess the market started maybe with the auction rather than the gallery in terms of international acknowledgement so I guess the galleries also sometimes carry a sense of education as well in their works because they need to educate their collectors, they need to educate the clients, the clients who were already there. The clients are there looking for luxury brands but not for the art, so they need to educate the local market, so they need to be putting more efforts into communication. I think galleries are more important. Galleries started before the museums. At certain periods of time, I think they took up the task of educating the public about what is art and what is the value of art at a certain level.

But now there are public institutions like this.

For the Rockbund Art Museum we are trying to advocate the museums as a space for debating, for thinking, for provocation, for criticizing, for questions. Also when we curate or produce a program of the exhibitions we are trying to make this opening visible so the public won't miss it.

What was the reason that you show artists here from all over the world and not only Chinese based artists?

Do you put the same question to Guggenheim? Or other institutions from Europe or America? Why they show non-American or non-European artists? You do not ask them these questions, so for us it is the same thing. I mean why do we need to show only Chinese artists? We are showing art, the space is for contemporary art and I mentioned the function of education at a certain level. We need to present what is going on internationally, what is going on in the local scene; if possible we are trying to provide bridges of communication between the two groups of artists and a lot of times there are mixed groups; they are

not completely separate. Chinese artists are very much influenced by the Western artists as well. So it is a flow and they are very much connected, not separated. For us here what we see is not separated, there is no Western, there is no Chinese absolutely, there are no boundaries, there is no absolute boundary.

Do you think there is no difference between Western taste and Eastern taste?

Of course there are differences but there is no clearly distinguished one, telling us what is West and what is Chinese. There are always differences and I think at this time we are very much emphasizing pluralism. Pluralism is about diversity, about diaspora maybe at a certain level, about different specialties coming from different regions, with a different history. We allow the existence of differences rather than the philosophy of just being binaries like one another, black and white, West and China, no. I believe it is the right way to go. I think reflection is also one spirit coming from contemporary art but we don't necessarily reveal or reflect on the roots only by looking at so-called Chinese artists. And what is even Chinese now?

It is a good question.

And actually we have been questioning the local arts community as well. A lady who was very much a senior and experienced curator, she asked us, why do you do so few Chinese exhibitions, why don't you mingle much more with the local art community. Maybe we need to do more mingling, I guess, but we are very much focused on balancing our programs, so we really look at the international programs, the Chinese programs, solo exhibitions, group exhibitions and the possible communication between both Chinese and international artists. Also here for the current exhibition, we were questioned by the media, saying that the Chinese artists we invited actually emigrated to Europe many years ago and have been living abroad, and asking whether they count as Chinese artists. We don't consider that as a question.

So you think contemporary art is a universal language?

I think contemporary art would refuse to be seen as universal. I mentioned pluralism, diaspora, different variety and different localities and we want to encourage different localities rather than putting up one standard and one language. Martina Koeppel-Yang in her curatorial practice of the exhibition mentioned

the concept of lingua franca; maybe you have heard about it. It is a standard to try to apply to all languages. Is there something which could be really applied to all?

Of course there are some differences between the so-called East and West, but I think the differences are getting smaller.

Yes, and this is a danger we need to prevent maybe, the homogenization in the process of the globalization. This is a homogenizing process, in which everything everywhere will look the same. There are also artists who tell me, if they go to different exhibitions, even the exhibitions look the same. And we need to prevent that, we need to prevent that danger of becoming similar that will kill creativity. So one part of our programming is also to encourage contradictions. We don't consider consensus as the core of contemporary art. We consider the dissensus as the core of art.

Can you tell us something about the visitors here at this museum? Where do they come from, are they mostly highly educated people?

Eighty per cent of the visitors come from local areas, Shanghai and China, but we also have around 20 per cent tourists and then in the 80 per cent there are about 20 per cent expats living in Shanghai. Regarding education we have 90 per cent of the visitors graduated from universities and have more women than men. We have 60 per cent women visitors, we have 78 per cent of the visitors who come with friends and also the same percentage who come for the first time to the museum, which makes for rather new communications.

Do you think the number of the people who are interested in contemporary art has increased in the last year?

In Shanghai I guess the basis is growing for sure. Not only for us – we had the growth of visitors – but also for the Museum of Contemporary Art in the People's Square, because they did this huge Yayoi Kusama show. They had people queuing in front of the gate, they had thousand visitors per day. The basis is growing, especially with young families; young parents bring their children to the museums.

How is the quality of the museums in China?

Usually the architecture of the museums in China is fantastic but the content is very weak. There is no organization or strong ties to run or keep the institutions operating. I think there are a lot of issues that need to be discussed and tested in regard to the education mechanism: how we train at the human resource level, how we could build teams which could successfully run a museum in a contemporary sense, and then how we do audience development, how we develop communication, where does the money come from, from private collectors or corporations, how can the government support more. It also needs to be considered more as a culture career, as something you need to build on rather than a business and industry. In Chinese it is called 'shiye', not industry. The target of running a museum is not to earn someone money. It is for cultural growth. But of course, the public is looking for places where they could get knowledge, where they could search for knowledge. So I think ultimately it could get money, because the public is the market. The museums are young; this one is only four years old. We need time to test the whole thing. Now it is hard, everyone is building up, but in 10 years we will see how many are still running and how they are running. By then I think we can talk about something problematic. Rather than now when everyone is happy.

As you said you have to have good quality artworks.

For us it is more interesting, for example, to see how we could build effective liaisons between similar museums. To build the partnerships to help each other to define where or what are the problems or what are the obstacles that we need to counter and maybe we could help each other. If we all want to find the more developed consistency rather than, as the media is always trying to do, to create conflict by asking us to compete with each other, asking us which is the best museum in Shanghai. No, this is not the way.

How would you define quality in an artwork?

I can't answer this, sorry. It takes preparation to answer this question. But I think this question is about meaning, whether the piece is meaningful or not but then what is meaning anyway. This is a huge topic, I can't define it. But I think the quality is something really in details. Especially for institutions like us who are fully supporting production. We are looking into the details, how we build the captions on the wall, how we consider the lighting, the space, how we make the audience comfortable so the audience at the same time observes the artworks from different levels, just details. And I can't answer it now, it is a lot of details. To make sure that the presentation of the art is right. I think now, for contemporary art, very often, I don't know if it is a video installation, it also depends on the part of your presentation, how it is presented in the space.

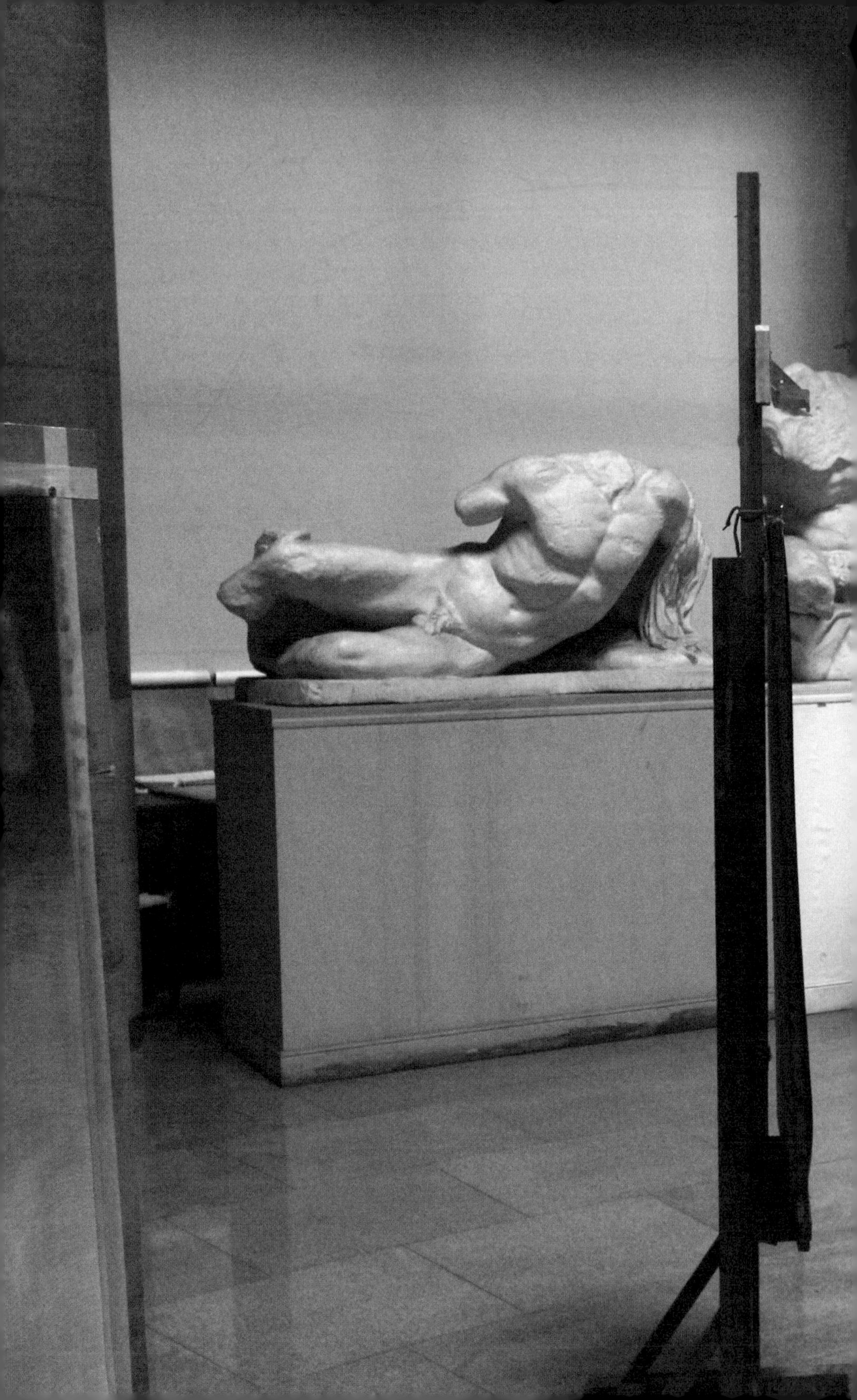

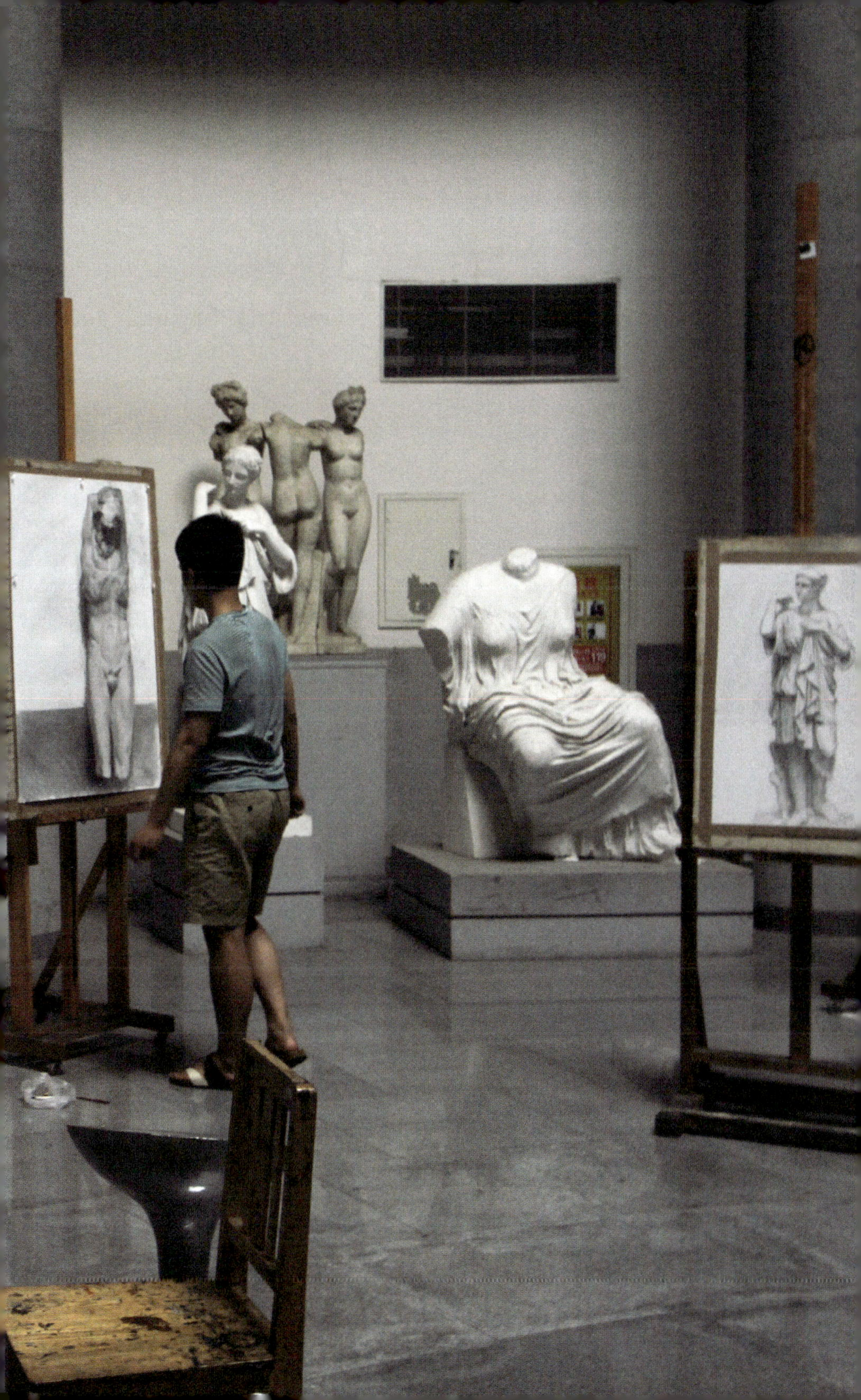

"Here it was really the art market that has changed the whole ecology of art"

A talk with Tobias Berger
Curator, Hong Kong

The image of Hong Kong as a metropolis rapidly entering into the game of the global art world, which our dialogue partner sketches, is based on profound experience. Because of his long-term personal involvement in this region Tobias Berger knows what he is talking about and thanks to his biographical projectory from West to East he can described the local developments as a player intimately involved in the game and as an observer with the critical and reflective distance and comparative view of an outsider. Berger has certainly played a key role in the Hong Kong art scene as a result of his first stay as head of the Para/Site in 2005 – an institution which, as the first body with a non-profit orientation, was a central force in the shaping of the Hong Kong art scene. After working for a time in Korea as the curator of the Nam June Paik Art Center he returned to Hong Kong and took on his hitherto most influential position as curator of the nascent M+ Museum, the position he held at the time of the interview. With this institution, which claims to be more than a simple museum of the customary kind and also aims to be different from the classical sites of consecration of contemporary art such as the Marmottan Monet or Beaubourg, Hong Kong is attempting to create an unmatched and matchless site for various art forms. According to Berger's interpretation the metropolis wishes to realize the idea of a creative city as a self-experiment and to use it for the purpose of city branding in the competition with the other claimants for the occupation of this geo-political key position in the South East Asian art market. This "more-than-an-art-museum" is meant to become, within a few years, the focal point of a new art district, which is to be built from scratch, and will house Uli Sigg's unique collection of Chinese contemporary art. But, as so often under the contradictory political conditions prevailing in Hong Kong, the Damocles sword of governmental unpredictability and uncertainty hangs over this ambitious mega-project.

According to Berger's depiction of the situation political-administrative decisions can quickly lose their validity, and as an experienced observer of the Hong Kong art world his assessment is: "We have no idea what is going on".

For a comparative cultural analysis of the dynamics of art worlds the insight he provides are highly informative, especially in regard to the thesis of a reversed development of the Asian art world in comparison to the well-known processes of historical development in the West. In Berger's opinion the art market in general and the global market for art products in particular were and are in fact the driving developmental factors in Hong Kong rather than the non-profit sector of the local primary market for art. This thesis critically questions the ethnocentric viewpoint of the Westerner on the situation there and his projection of a quasi inevitable epigenetic development of the art world in accordance with the European model. And it also relativizes the customary Western notion of the incompatibility of the worlds of art and commerce.

Berger sounds very optimistic as far as the self-dynamics of the Hong Kong art world is concerned and praises its open structures, which enable the actors to take on the most varied roles and functions one after the other or even parallel to one another, instead of their being assigned to strict categories as in the Western art scene. His conclusion: if Hong Kong was until recently cut off from the global discourse of the art world, this metropolis has within a few years blossomed into a leading player in this "discourse space". In other words, presence in this "discourse space" means visibility and audibility, which generate the attention capital so highly desired in a globalizing world, and for which the metropolises compete in their efforts to position themselves as so called creative cities in the international struggle to attract big companies and highly qualified workers.

Can you introduce yourself and tell me how you ended up in Hong Kong?

I ended up in Hong Kong twice. I came in first in 2005 after I was running Artspace in Auckland and one could say that paradise got boring and so we – my partner Yuk King Tan and I – left. Para/Site was looking for a curator and that was interesting because they were an artist-run space, one of the few interesting artist-run spaces in Asia. In 2005, I think after the 2004 biennial in Guangzhou, which was very important for a lot of artist-run spaces, they decided that they wanted to become more professional and they were looking for a full-time curator. I applied and I got the job and so we moved to Hong Kong in 2005. I ran Para/Site for three and a half years, putting it more on the international map, making it more curator-based and not so much artist-run-based. Putting it out there, making it more international, there was a lot of discussion; in the end people said I did an okay job there. Then I was approached by the Nam June Paik Art Centre in Korea to become their chief curator, so I went for two years to Korea from 2008 to 2010. After two years in Korea I came back and got the job I have now, as curator at M+.

Can you illustrate in regard to positions that you have or had here, how Hong Kong has developed in the art field?

In 2005 people were talking about Hong Kong as a cultural wasteland. Culturally it was never a wasteland, but for contemporary art, especially international contemporary art, there was very little there. There was very little exchange, very few places where people could go and see contemporary art from America, or from Europe, or from other Asian places. I remember the first auction preview I went to was from Sotheby's, which was in the ballroom of the Island Shangri-La; it was totally small and non-significant, and that has all changed. There were different things that changed. First it was the auction houses that exploded. People understood that there is money in art, in contemporary art, which is always the thing in Hong Kong. Then Asia Art Archive (AAA) became more important; I mean they were there before, but they basically upped their game, Para/Site upped their game, Osage opened, which was kind of big because it was the first big gallery that did a bit more international shows. We at Para/Site did a thing that was called October Contemporary, which put all the non-profit spaces together, which was good especially for communication. Then it was the Art HK that hit the ground and changed everything. It's quite different from Europe or from North America, especially from Europe, where we always think that the non-profit sector is the leading force in art and is really making the changes or something like that because we all grew up with museums and with a non-profit sector, but here it was clearly the art market that has changed the whole ecology of art. It's a private enterprise. Interestingly when the people who later founded the art fair first came sniffing around they wanted to found an Affordable Art Fair because that's what they had done in, I think in Melbourne and in England somewhere. They didn't come to found that extremely sophisticated contemporary art fair. Then people talked to them and said that it made much more sense, that what they needed was an art fair, that they should forget that affordable stuff. And that's what they did and they luckily got Magnus Renfrew. There were a few very lucky things in it and hiring Magnus for that job was one of the lucky things that happened and from there on it became something interesting.

And do you think that because of this the project of M+ got...

No, M+ started earlier. The original project of the West Kowloon Cultural District is like 10 to 15 years old. But the first concept for the cultural district was a developer lead project, but around 2005 people finally understood that the whole project would mean, that in the end property developers would finance it, or possibly influence what would happen in these cultural institutions. People got very nervous about it and the government needed a way to get out of it, so they basically put a very high price on, the clean way was to put a very high price on the whole structure, or area, so all the tycoons would say that they don't want it. And then the whole thing came to a stop. But in that time four museums were planned: one for art, one for architecture and design, one for moving image and one for popular culture. Then this museum advisory group was formed, and there were a lot of really good people on that. They then planned for this new museum around 2006, 2007 and the first art fair was in 2008 or something like that. So actually it was an independent decision.

But probably somehow, well not related to the fair, but maybe to the awareness of art, that it became a bit more important.

No, it was the awareness that Hong Kong has to change to become or better to keep being attractive as an international city. It came more out of the idea of Richard Florida's creative cities where all the cities change the way they work. It came out of a strong competition with Shanghai and with Singapore because these two places are the competing areas. It came also out of an inner understanding that Hong Kong needs more of these spaces. The art fair came out of a booming auction market and the tax-free environment. It's different and certainly these things somehow now work so nicely together, which is fantastic. But I think the origins are very different.

What kind of an art place is Hong Kong today for you, or how would you describe that place?

That's a good question. The thing is it changes so fast and one doesn't realize it. If you had asked every half a year, one would have given you another answer. Half a year ago, or eight months ago, we had two young, new Hong Kong galleries; they were doing great stuff. We had the Police Station going forward in a nice way. We got the Uli Sigg collection. Everything was fine. Now, only half a year later, one of the two galleries is closed, the

Police Station is re-evaluating its position, and we are getting a huge backlash for the Uli Sigg collection. There is no final answer and that's the great thing about Hong Kong. It is continuously changing. That was two weeks ago. Now, yesterday or on Sunday, we had 26,000 people at the exhibition, so again it changes so fast. I think that's an amazing thing that one doesn't know. We have no idea what is going on. We don't know who will open galleries, how the new Art Basel Hong Kong will be, how my exhibition will work. Nobody knows.

Yes, nobody knows. But who would you say are the main actors at the moment. Probably still the market is the...

I think there are different actors, but these different actors are not so easy to define as in Europe. I mean, just look at some people like Mimi Brown, doing Spring Workshop, she is difficult to define, establishing a non-profit art residency for a limited time of five years. Look at Johnson Tsang. He's a gallery owner but he is also one of Hong Kong's most important curators. Look at MAP Office, who now have a show in Beijing, but who are not really recognized as visual artists here in Hong Kong, even if they have done more biennials as Hong

Kong artists than any other artists. Everything, and that's the beauty of Hong Kong, is not like it seems. People play very different roles and you cannot just say Johnson as a gallery owner is maybe not that important, but Johnson as a curator is very important. What is Para/Site at the moment? It's not really important as an exhibition space, but it's a very important place as a place of discourse. What is the Police Station? All these things are very difficult to define. Do Gagosian or White Cube play any role in Hong Kong? Not really. They are a little like duty-free shops, generic places that are plugged in somewhere so you can have tax-free shopping. It's perfect, nothing against duty-free shops, they are beautiful.

Well but at the same time one could also maybe say that even if they are duty free shops and maybe not that significant for Hong Kong it still brings attention.

Yes, it brings attention and it brings collectors, I mean you just have to see how much the gallery scene, or what the galleries show, changes during the auctions. Would I say that Christie's is important for the Hong Kong art environment? No. But would I say that Christie's auctions do bring greater shows into the galleries? Yes, definitely. I think it's a mix, it's not many people, maybe 10 to 15 people that make the difference.

If we go back to the kind of the environment in Hong Kong, what kind of position should M+ have once it is really open?

I think Lars Nittve was tested when he had the first interview with the politicians here. They said they wanted him to build a museum Asia doesn't have. It's basically about building a world-class museum like Tate or Centre Pompidou in Hong Kong, so a world class museum from the Hong Kong or Asian perspective. I think what M+ should be is this independent platform of negotiation, a place where different ideas, different art and different research can come together independently and talk. Especially if you talk about Asia or Europe, East and West, and all that. We need a place to talk, to put different things together, to bring different art out and to compare. It's not about who is better or not, but to just have a decent discussion, a dialogue or whatever, but at the moment we don't have that place. And we don't have that place because the only two countries that could do it, that are free to do it, are Japan and Korea. And they are very introverted, I think that they will not do it. And most other countries are too much government ruled. Hong Kong always had an international perspective, but still is grounded in China. I think we should build that platform, that place where things can come together and things can happen.

And so you want to combine kind of being a global museum and having its roots in Hong Kong?

It's the idea, it is actually in this museum advisory paper that is actually really good. It says, 'From a Hong Kong point of view, it is a global perspective.' We are not going to completely reinvent the idea of a museum; we are going to challenge it but we are not going to reinvent it. We're going to change perspectives. We change it from, the MoMA is about New York, and the Centre Pompidou is about Paris. So M+ will be about Hong Kong. I think it's more about changing perspective.

And how do you want to make sure that, how do you want to engage people, or get an audience? Do you already have like a number of visitors that would come, like an estimate?

If you get 26,000 people to a place like the current West Kowloon Park for the 'Inflation!' exhibition, a place that is super difficult to ac-

cess, in a day, I don't worry. I mean the art fair is one of the best-visited art fairs per day in the world. It has like 55,000 people in 3 days. I don't worry about that.

And how did you react to comments like 'art is art and culture is culture'? How do you deal with such critique or comments?

Yes, that was said by a member of the Legislative Council of Hong Kong last week, trying to tell us not to present any political art. I guess you have this kind of people in every parliament. For us it strangely came exactly at the right time; we opened the 'Inflation!' exhibition, we were nervous about the Complex Pile artwork of Paul McCarthy, we were nervous about being a bit too controversial. Then this guy just says a day before the opening something that unwise and everyone certainly had to support us because it became a matter of freedom of speech. I mean one should never be happy about ridiculous politicians, but that was just perfect.

Because it gives you attention.

Yes, it gives you attention and it also makes people understand what's at stake: that a free society needs a free museum, without governmental interference. What I think a lot of people in that moment understood, and it was pretty clear in the reaction in the press and so on, was that it is good to have a museum like we plan it. Whatever we do, they don't agree with everything we do, but it is in the right direction and it is the right thing to do now.

I mean a lot of artists say that conceptual art is not yet much appreciated. Was it a strategic approach to bring something controversial, in regard to the 'Inflation!' exhibition?

Yes and no. I think the Yau Ma Tei exhibition was much more conceptual. And the Song Dong performance event, even though it was rather popular, was more conceptual. 'Inflation!' is not. It's a nice concept and there are a few works in it that are conceptual but it's not that hard-core, I wouldn't take that, I would like to take that credit but I don't think it is.

I mean it is somewhat conceptual but also very easy to understand.

I mean, when you look at the successful Hong Kong art, Hong Kong art is successful because it is highly conceptual and partly political. I mean, Lee Kit or Tozer Pak, or Doris Wong Wai Yin and Kwan She-

ung Chi and all the people we really like, or even Erkka Nissinen or Leung Chi Wo. All these people they are hard-core conceptual artists, they are not painting big canvases or things like that; they are doing really challenging art. I always said Hong Kong art will have a longer success time than Chinese art because they work in a much more different way than putting huge canvases out.

Would you say that with a museum and then the artists, it is really important to counteract the market here? Is it really also necessary to promote Hong Kong's own culture here?

But the market here, it really depends what kind of market we are talking about. I mean look at Johnson Tsang, who is an amazing curator and a good gallerist, and he plays both games. Look at Vitamin Creative Space, probably China's most successful gallery, and they are both playing every game. The things in Asia are not so divided; I mean it's not that there is a gallery and there is an art market. Our curator for Chinese art Pi Li, he was running and owned a gallery before, but we hired him anyway, which you would never do in Europe. I think it depends much more on people and if you trust people here; and it's not so much about in which box you fit and if you are once in there you will never get out. And here you can be a designer and an architect and an artist, or an art collector and an artist, or you can have different hats. You can run a gallery and work in a museum and go back, whatever. And that's really the great thing about Hong Kong or about Asia at the moment, that it completely questions this whole idea. We have to relook that and question it. I think that if the world and the art field should learn something from Asia, then it is the fluidity. Where things should not be seen so much in boxes, because it doesn't work anymore. A lot of artists are doing film, a lot of design is quite arty.

So the structures that we know from the West are not here.

No, they are questioned. You don't question the whole idea of art, you question the idea of how a museum works, how we see commercial and non-commercial. How commercial is a small young gallery and how non-commercial is something like the Kunsthalle in Bonn? Or at MoMA where everything is done because of money? I mean we can rethink that.

You would probably say that it's more like a globalized place for art but at the same time not because of all this interaction between the big players and the small ones.

Art is always global in the end and that's what matters. It matters to the few people that are there. It works in a global context and you are much more connected. I think in the end that is what happened. Hong Kong got much better connected in that global context in the last five years, if we come back to your first question. Because it wasn't part of the global discourse and there is something like a global discourse nowadays. And that's what completely changed, that it became a major player in that global discourse.

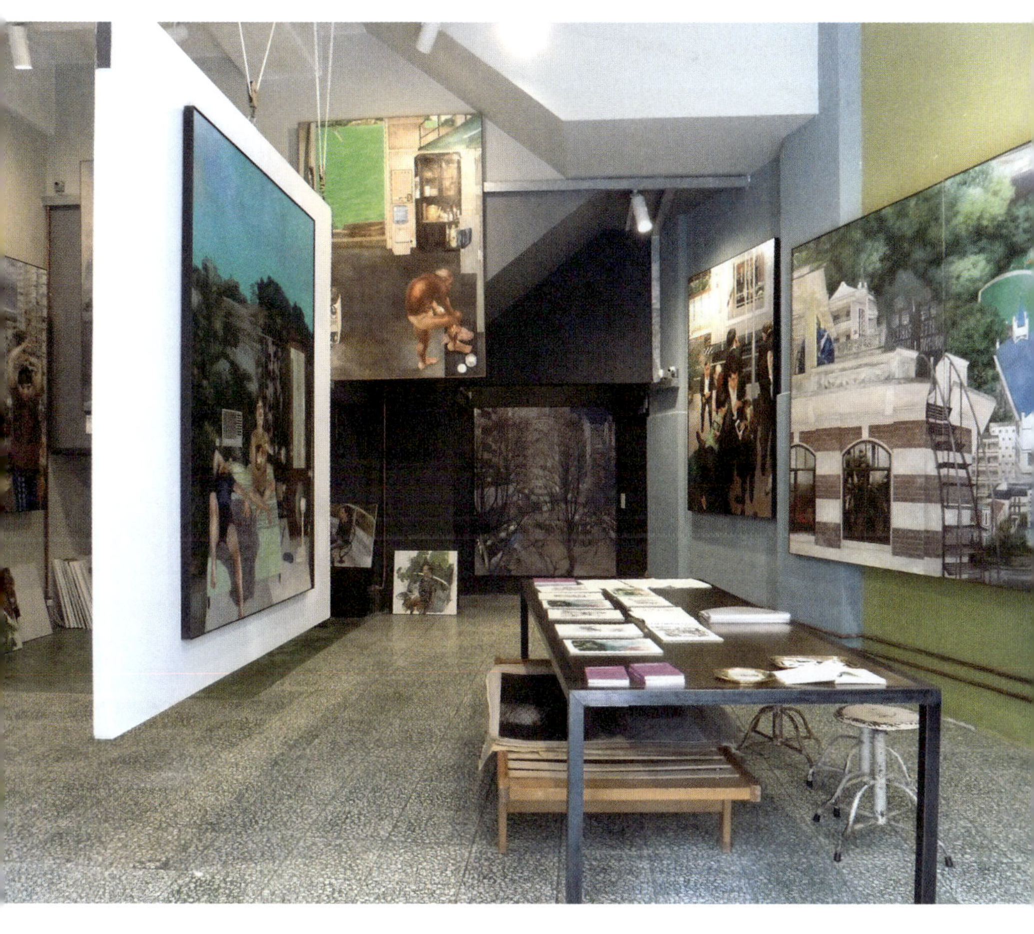

"We have much to offer.
We need more chances"

A talk with Ferdie Ju
Gallerist, Shanghai

Ferdie Ju entered the emerging field of galleries in Shanghai at a late stage. At first active in the global finance economy, for example in London and Hong Kong, he ended his successful career in order to devote himself to his "hobby", to art. He first set up a gallery in Bangkok, but failed on account of the financial crisis of 1997 and of his "otherness" in a country unfamiliar to him. Finally he used his savings to open up the Gallery 55 in 50 Moganshan Road, the well-known art district in Shanghai. His modestly furnished rooms are situated between shops that peddle mass merchandise to tourists and a number of galleries acknowledged in the world of art.

In Shanghai Ju encounters a public which seems to be very unfamiliar with contemporary art. He is consequently dependent on the foreign market, on customers who are interested in "concepts which are new, which are not concluded" and not merely in decorative works. There is no specifically interested public of this kind in China. And so it is important for him to exhibit his artists at art fairs abroad and in cooperation with galleries in Europe and the US.

Ju understands the mechanisms of the field and does not reject them, attempting instead to use them productively in the interest of his artists. Participation in the Art Basel in Hong Kong is, therefore, essential for him in order to be visible in the world of art, even though he obviously does not feel very happy about operating in this field. He accepts the need to earn money for projects, but always justifies this by referring to the support of his artists.

With an explicitly anti-economic gestus Ju attempts to support young, often "unwanted" Chinese artists in their development and to promote their visibility. These artists work predominantly in a conceptual way following up new ideas and developing their creativity without the driving force of commercial success. He pursues his program with a kind of missionary zeal, accepting the financial risks it involves.

For Ju the state of art is a symbol of the development of China. No matter how technically gifted the young generation of artists may be in copying works and ideas, there is nonetheless a lack of innovative power and new conceptual projects. The economization of Chinese society is blatantly revealed in the art world. Ju complains that a majority of the university graduates who take up a career in art see it primarily as an opportunity to earn money quickly and directly. They have no understanding of the intrinsic meaning of art. In his account his gallery appears as an ideal-typical alternative model running counter to this development. His model involves a process of catching up, in which he plays the part of an avant-gardist representative of "L'art pour l'art", who places the conceptual work of the artist in the foreground, strictly separated from all economic and profane incentives.

How did you get into art?

I didn't study art. My major at university was Mass Communications and Languages. Luckily, I got a decent job and had a little bit of cash to spare, so I started collecting art during my younger years. As time went by, I got a little bit more and more interested in collections. Maybe it's fun to do something about art, one day I told myself. So by chance, I entered this business, from a sheer hobby to a career with a mission.

Can you briefly describe your gallery and compare it to other galleries in Shanghai? What's the philosophy of your gallery and what's the program of your gallery?

We promote young artists with new, interesting concepts. Those concepts are not based on or inspired by the text books or reference books. Many young artists in China try to find some influential trends or masters to study well. Then they make something similar. They might be able to make excellent copies, but to me, they are very good students only, not artists or innovators. In terms of art, one needs to be creative. Concept is not just like ideas. I try to promote artists with concepts which are new, which are not concluded. The most important part of art experiments is to expand the boundaries of art. What is art really? Could this be art? Is it impossible this is also art? That's what 55 has been doing.

How do you find these young artists?

From all over China. Most of the artists I found were unwanted because their works lack commercial possibilities. To me, what they are doing is very valuable in terms of art, particularly in a country like China. I have to say China has been a manufacturing giant for the past few decades. By exporting all kinds of cheap commodities, some have made some very good money and become rich. But copy cats are copy cats after all. Art is all about innovation and break-through.

In art?

Not just in art, in almost everything. We are a manufacturing giant. As far as I know, among the top 500 businesses in the world, most of the entries from China are manufacturers except only one – Huawei, an IT-satellite innovator. We really need to make an effort to change from a manufacturing giant to an innovation leader. I always believe if we think we are clever enough, we should do something about it and prove it, not just always making copies. That's what I hope.

Can you compare your gallery to the other galleries in this area? It looks like most galleries here are for tourists, and they just sell decorative art.

That is a fact which nobody could deny. Judging by the fact that contemporary art is still new to this country that's allowed but no excuse to let it last forever. I am very proud of the progress we have made over the past nine years. In China, the art market has been reshuffled several times and we have survived. Sometimes, I thought it was kind of a miracle because we have very little patronage from China. We rely on overseas patronage. We never had any money given by foundations or institutions. I have always used my pocket money on the gallery, as I think art direction should not be restrained by anything, especially money. I think if I am good enough, the gallery business will survive and flourish eventually. If I can't make it, that's tough. That's why we always try hard to make progress. Making money out of doing decorative art or commercial art is not for me. Following the path one believes in and keeping on meeting new challenges keeps me going forward.

What do you think about most of the art which one can buy here?

Well, people are from different walks of life. I think having people coming in here is a victory because we need people to come to see our art. One time, we were showing a video work with the artist smashing things with hammers. Someone became very emotional, yelling: 'Tell him to stop. What a waste! It's very expensive.' Obviously, this audience is not coming for conceptual art. Most people are like him, coming here to take photos, or to feel art works with their hands.

It's a process.

After that, I always put a small statement next to art works, telling people what they are about. I don't like brainwashing people. I don't like to impose my understanding of art on people. I want people to read the statement and judge for themselves. Talking about process! I showed one video work entitled 'One Slap'. So many people asked why this lunatic artist wanted to get slapped in the face by a stranger. I said, 'Good question. Think about that yourself.' I hope future generations could learn something from our experiences. We have had bad experience before, but they could really cut the learning experience short, so as not to experience the worst. Even though I think on the other hand, they need to learn from lessons.

Are there a lot of galleries from the West in Shanghai, with directors or owners from the West?

Yes, very interesting. Shanghai, because of its history, has always been very friendly with foreigners. Chinese people absolutely adore foreigners. That makes it possible for foreign owners to do well with their businesses. As you know, the owner of the most important gallery in Shanghai, ShanghART, Lorenz Herbling, is from Switzerland. He came here with nothing much. Over the past two decades, he has become the gallery representing China.

Does China profit from these Western people?

Yes, absolutely. Somehow in Beijing, there isn't much room for foreign galleries. They have tremendous challenges from the locals. In Shanghai, foreign owners of galleries, restaurants, etc. are in a better position, simply because local people are more open-minded and friendly to foreigners. People here love to make contacts with foreigners. That's traditional. There is a large expats community. There are over 100,000 legal expats living and working here, in addition to thousands of temporary workers, who might have come here as tourists and then decided to work in

Shanghai for a short period of time. Shanghai is a place for business. The Chinese can afford expensive imports now due to the economic success. They think shops owned by foreigners are more superior and more reliable. I don't blame them because not so many Chinese shops or galleries are trustworthy.

But your gallery has another concept than ShanghART. The focus of ShanghART is to sell Chinese works to Western collectors.

Things have now changed completely. Ten or 15 years ago, when ShanghART was first established in Shanghai, and for many years on, I was told that their patrons were mainly foreign tourists or foreign expats living in Shanghai. But now because the economy in China has boomed, many rich Chinese have entered this field. Literally, they take art as an investment. The majority of them could not really be regarded as collectors. They don't have much understanding or passion for art. They just want to buy things simply for making a profit in the short term. They don't treat art as a part of their lives.

Can you give us an outlook generally on the whole art scene and in particular on the art market in Shanghai?

More and more people are now aware of art. At the moment, the majority are buying commercial or decorative art. Some people have already ventured into art with more depth. Of course, new quirky things could always attract some attention in a city like Shanghai, where people are more adventurous or curious. Conceptual art has to wait for a bit longer perhaps.

A collector in Hong Kong we interviewed said he began collecting as every collector does and it was a process of learning, so now he is interested in conceptual art.

That's great. That's very encouraging. Yes, it all takes some time, I suppose. Some Chinese collectors think very highly of themselves. They think if they could be so successful with their businesses, they could do well with art too. They ignore professional art consultation. The reason I think is that there are too many con-men around posing as so-called professional art consultants. They ruined the reputations of a profession. But in a new market all of this is normal. An American collector once told me that some decades ago there were plenty of these con-men around in the States too. People will learn their lessons. Now it is time for the Chinese collectors to pay a few fees to learn their lessons.

What do you do to push your young artists in their artwork and also in the art market? Do you make books, catalogs, exhibitions or do you work together with public museums?

China is a very interesting place. Shanghai, compared to Beijing, is in a very disadvantaged position because the focus of Chinese art is in Beijing. Unfortunately, I am from Shanghai, so I didn't open the gallery in Beijing. But I don't think it is a problem. We do regular shows at the gallery for our artists. For example, last year, we started two new projects: yellow.ants.art.lab and front.room.loop. Artists were invited to present one focused project in a small project space of 30 square meters. The purpose is to give these emerging artists a chance to show what they have. Over a period of nine months, we realized eight projects, very serious projects in different categories, such as video, installation, photography, interactive and 3D photos. For the video project, we showed works by young artists, including someone who was nominated for the Hugo Boss Asian Awards. I am very happy that in the end it became a very nice attraction for the audiences. Whenever people passed by our doors, they would immediately stop and step into our gallery to see what the video was about. That's very encouraging for me. Besides gallery programs, we regularly get in touch with museums, curators and art media professionals by sending them newsletters and profiles of new artists. Some of our artists have received invitations from museums to show already.

What role do auction houses play? Are they for collectors who just want to invest?

Very much so. We haven't entered this field yet. In China, just like in the West, many galleries have very close relationships with auction houses. For us, it's way too early. We'd rather focus our attention on art work instead of art price.

You said the government is not promoting art at all?

I just heard the government will spend millions of money setting up foundations. I really think it's a very good initiative. But how much money will really come to us? The money probably, just like in many other fields, would be diluted over the state, the government, the provinces, the districts, and all these people involved. Nevertheless, I still think setting up foundations is a good initiative. I hope on the board of directors there will be some really responsible people.

How do you see the role of private museums and private collectors? Are they important?

They should be. The Chinese government encourages rich people to set up private museums. Some museum spaces were built by the government for appointed collectors to house their collections. It is a government move to show off the economic success.

Is there a border between Western and Eastern taste?

Generally speaking, Chinese prefer the meaning behind or within art while Westerners opt for the visual effect. It has things to do with cultural background.

Do you think there is something like global art?

Yes. Art should have no boundaries. People buy art because they see something in it which makes them happy or inspired.

What was the reason for you to go to the Art Basel fair in Hong Kong?

Art Basel has a very high reputation. In Asia, Art Basel Hong Kong is now the best art fair. For a gallery based in Shanghai, Art Basel Hong Kong naturally becomes the best

choice. We don't have many expectations about selling our conceptual projects in Hong Kong because the majority going there will be Chinese or Asians, who will only buy paintings. But if we did well, I hope it will become a stepping stone for us to reach Art Basel in Switzerland eventually where more collectors are Europeans and Americans. Anyway, Hong Kong is a good start. Our artists have been working very hard and they deserve such a chance. I will try my very best to find the money to sponsor those projects.

So it is important for your reputation and for the reputation of your artists?

It's very important. Both the gallery and artists need to be seen and heard. Otherwise, people will think Chinese galleries sell only those big smiley faces. Chinese art is changing slowly but firmly.

Do you think Art Basel is promoting conceptual art very much in Hong Kong?

Very little. More people prefer colorful things in this beautiful world anyway. People who spend money on buying art naturally want to make sure the art works look nice and decorative at home.

The Art Basel is not only a market place, but also a place to make connections, and to meet up with other people.

Yes. Hong Kong is the very place for people to make connections for a long time. We hope to meet good people too. We have much to offer. We need more chances. Art needs to go forward. Art doesn't only have the function of decorating homes. Art makes statements. Statements show us the way to go forward.

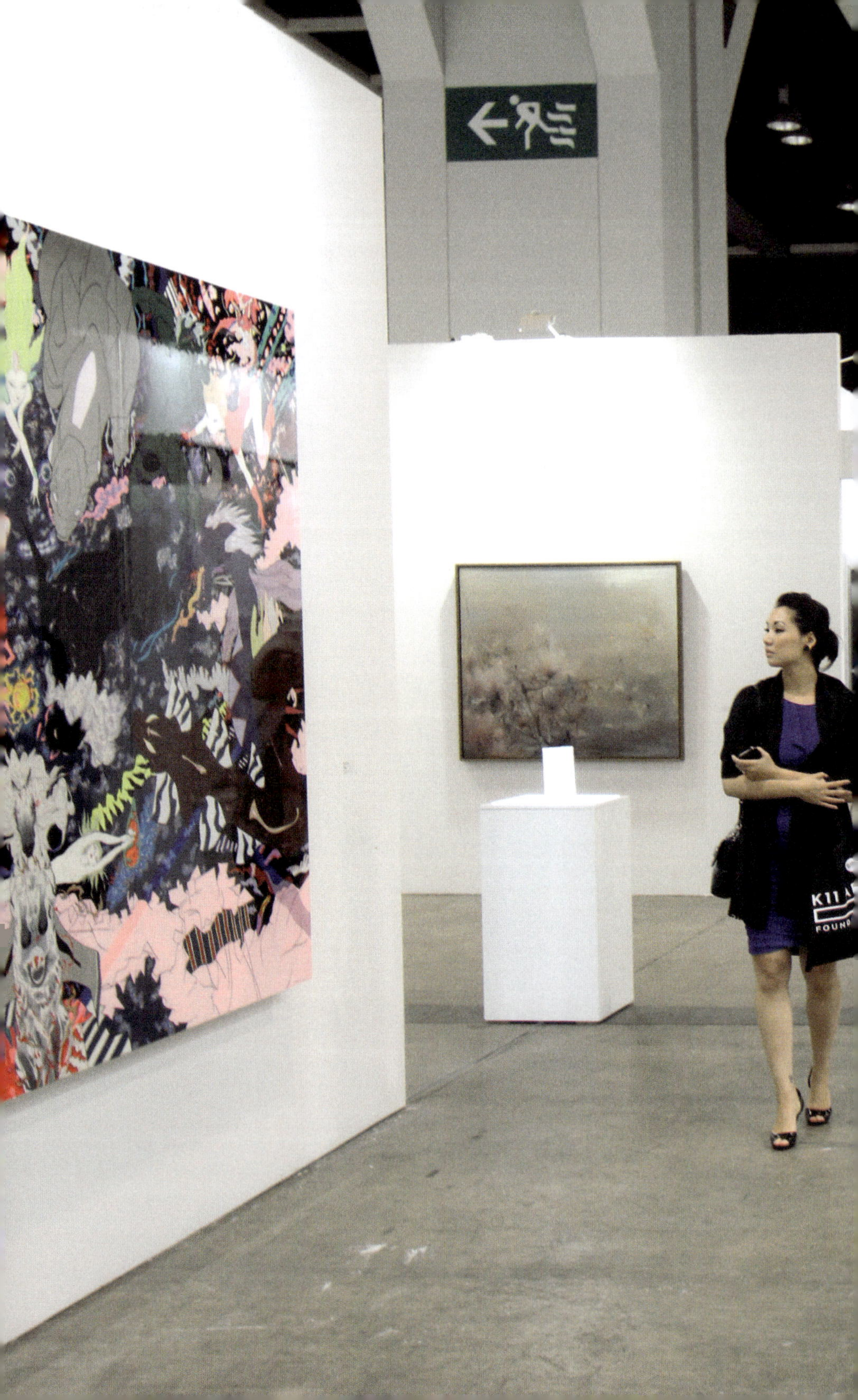
K11 A
FOUND

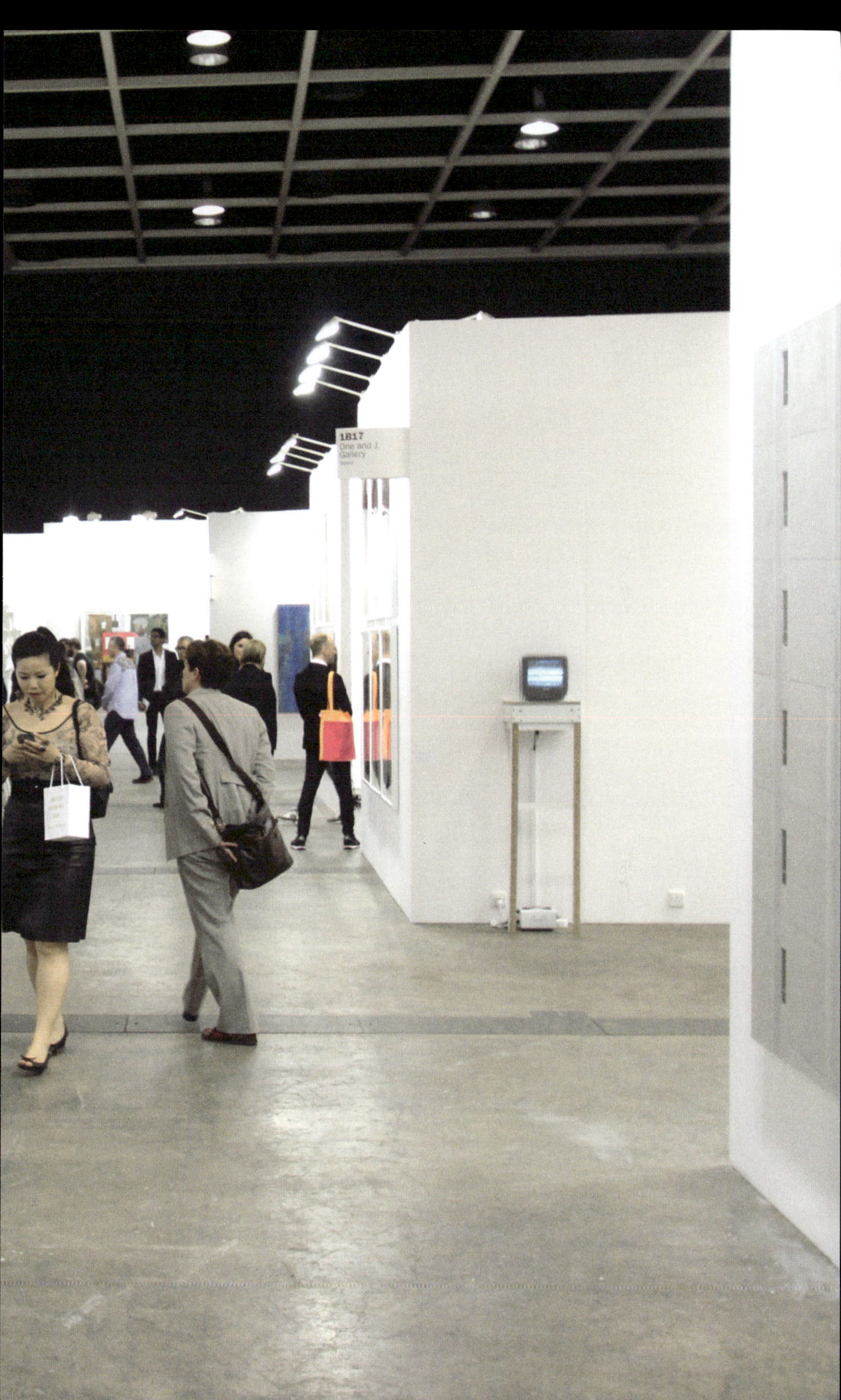
1B17
One and J.
Gallery

The Olympics of art in distant realms

The view of the gallerists on the Art Basel in Hong Kong

In the framework of our field research on the Art Basel in Hong Kong in 2014 it was possible, as in Basel and Miami Beach, to carry out a questionnaire with the galleries participating in the fair. The same comprehensive survey was used, which enabled us to make some comparisons in regard to intercultural convergences and divergences in the statements of this central group of actors. For the sake of simplicity these findings are mostly presented with the relevant per cent values in each case. Their validity and import should not be overrated, but in the framework of this pluri-methodological study they provide an interesting supplement to the predominantly qualitative research methods we adopted. The 80 galleries that participated in the survey, were almost exclusively newcomers to the "Art Basel Universe". Only five had participated in the fair in Basel in 2011 and only two in Miami Beach. One gallery took part in the fair in Basel in 2012. They cannot, however, be characterized as newcomers to the art field. Approximately half of them had already gathered experience in previous years at the art fair in Hong Kong. Nine galleries had attended all five fixtures of the Hong Kong International Art Fair, and 13 had been there four times. Only 35 of the 80 gallerists had never taken part. Fifty-two of the galleries questioned came from Asia, the greater part (20) coming from China.

As with the gallerists attending the fairs in Basel and Miami Beach, economic reasons played the decisive role in the decision to participate. For 86 per cent of the 80 galleries in Hong Kong "getting into contact with new customers" was "very important", as was "selling artworks for your gallery" for the same number. For the gallerists in Hong Kong the "presence of your main clients in the same place at the same time" was less relevant than it was for the galleries in Basel (36 per cent in Hong Kong, 69 per cent in Basel). This indicates that their primary interest lay in increasing the circle of their clients. In comparison to the economic factor the discovery of new artists and trends is not particularly important for the gallerists; and this is even more seldom the case in Basel. At 24 per cent the agreement of the galleries with the item "discovery of new artists/trends" was 10 per cent higher than in Basel. This suggests that in comparison with the establishment dominating the original fair in Basel with a well-known repertoire of artists, a larger number of less well-known galleries representing more or less unknown artists participated in Hong Kong, which left more scope for surprises.

Whereas for the gallerists in Basel the special significance of the fair lay in its "intrinsic" aspects, and specifically in the "quality" of the gallerists represented (96 per cent), the works presented (82 per cent) and the "cultural level and connoisseurship of its clients" (75 per cent), these factors play a clearly reduced role in Hong Kong. Only 65 per cent saw the quality of the galleries represented as a special feature of the fair. In regard to the quality of the works presented agreement with the item was only 53 per cent. At 46 per cent the rating of the "cultural level and connoisseurship" of the clients was also clearly lower in Hong Kong than in Basel. These statements also point to a certain hierarchical differentiation between the two fairs. Whereas Basel self-confidently defines its "corporate identity" in terms of the "outstanding quality" of the fair, the newcomer in Hong Kong shows greater reserve both with this kind of self-labeling and with the qualification of its customers as "connoisseurs".

Even the business side of the fair does not seem to play such a prominent role as in Basel according to the statements of the gallerists in Hong Kong. In regard to the relevance of "clients' buying power" the fair has a rating of only 57 per cent compared with 75 per cent in Basel. Significantly the location Hong Kong itself seems to be more important. For 66 per cent the "location Hong Kong/Asian market" is important. In addition, at 32 per cent, the "fiscal terms (e.g. taxes)" are clearly more important than for the galleries in Basel (7 per cent), even though Basel enjoys highly privileged conditions in this regard in comparison to other locations in the Western hemisphere. It seems as if the Art Basel in Hong Kong is judged in a quite pragmatic and utilitarian way according to the criterion of optimal business conditions, i.e. purely in terms of the market economy – a standpoint which is in accordance with the expectations and assessments expressed by the gallerists we interviewed at the Art Basel in Basel in 2012.

According to the interviewees in Hong Kong the works for the exhibition were specially chosen in order to take the specific local conditions into account. Sixty three per cent of the gallerists stated that their choice of the works of art was determined by the location. On the one hand they refer to the Asian clientele: "presence of Asian collectors", "tailored to Asian audience" and "Asian taste and culture". The preference was for "big objects", "more colorful", "not so conceptional" pieces, "high quality works, with an emphasis on calligraphy" and "artworks that won't offend Chinese people". On the other hand the works of Asian artists were consciously offered for sale: "We represent Korean artists around the world", "to feature the work of an important Hong Kong artists" or "most significant/potential artists from China" are some of the answers given. Reference is also made to the "bridging function" of Hong Kong. Statements such as "presenting the East/West aspects of program" und "global/universal language in the artwork" are very popular.

The presence of the interviewed galleries at fairs is concentrated on the Asian area. This is not surprising in view of the sample, in which the Asian galleries form the majority. For the gallerists we interviewed the Art Stage Singapore (31 per cent) is the most important Asian Fair apart from Hong Kong. It is followed by the Art Taipeh (22 per cent), the Tokyo Art Fair and the Shanghai Contemporary Art Fair (both 17 per cent). In the West the galleries are most frequently represented at the Armory Show in New York (20 per cent).

The thesis that the art fairs are of pre-eminent importance for the galleries is less strongly confirmed in Hong Kong than in Basel. They are "very important" for 41 per cent of the gallerists questioned in Hong Kong as against 61 per cent in Basel; they were "important" for 55 per cent (in Basel 38 per cent) and "not really important" for four per cent (in Basel one per cent). A possible explanation for these differences could lie in the fact that we are dealing here with less cosmopolitan galleries with less experience of the global art market than is the case with the "big players" who set the tone in Basel.

The factors influencing the development of the art world are located above all in the area of demand: new types of collectors influence the development "very much" (69 per cent), followed by the private collections (66 per cent), new groups of buyers (62 per cent) and the relatively declining purchasing power of public museums (39 per cent). Twenty nine per cent of the galleries interviewed agree "very much" with the view that the market price increasingly influences the evaluation of art.

According to the interviewees the Asian region will gain importance among the leading market places in the future – a conviction they express even more strongly than the Western gallerists interviewed in Basel. First place is accorded to Hong Kong (91 per cent as against 85 per cent in Basel); Shanghai follows with only 41 per cent in comparison to 58 per cent in Basel and then Seoul at 25 per cent and Tokyo at 23 per cent. And according to the galleries South America will also grow in importance, above all Sao Paulo (48 per cent) and Mexico City (32 per cent).

The gallerists who filled out the questionnaire believed that the aesthetics of global contemporary art will be increasingly diversified (49 per cent). Forty six per cent are convinced that the aesthetics of the threshold countries will achieve a greater influence – clearly more than in Basel, where only 30 per cent were of this opinion. In contrast only six per cent (Basel 14 per cent) believe in the continued dominance of Western aesthetics. Here we can clearly see how the local involvement in a globalizing market can contribute to specific location dependent perceptions.

In regard to the influence of various factors on the prices of works of art the gallerists attributed great importance to exhibitions in public museums (56 per cent) and purchases by powerful collectors (51 per cent). The prestige of the gallery was regarded as less relevant by the interviewees in Hong Kong (44 per cent) than by their counterparts in Basel (58 per cent). Here too it must be pointed out that the choice of the galleries participating in the original fair in Basel is clearly much more restrictive and their composition undoubtedly more elitist, so that we can speak of different levels of prestige of the galleries represented at the two fairs.

In their assessment of the causes for price increases in the past the gallerists give first place to the money-driven dynamics of the art market. Here "capital investment and market speculation" are seen as being "very much" responsible (47 per cent, nine per cent points more than in Basel), followed by the "demand for art from emerging countries" (47 per cent) and "new groups of purchasers with high incomes" (46 per cent). However, 44 per cent attribute the rise in prices to the "increased quality of the art production". Only 28 per cent of those interviewed in

Hong Kong mention the "growing market power of auction houses" as an important reason (in comparison to 39 per cent in Basel). Whereas the comparatively low significance attributed to auctions might seem at first sight surprising (perhaps their role is so taken for granted that it does not need to be specifically emphasized), the other statements on this question clearly reveal the special nature of the emerging Asian market.

All in all the opinions expressed by this group of actors give a very coherent overall picture, which is characterized not least by a marked optimism in regard to its future prospects in a globalized art world. But it remains nonetheless clear that in spite of the spectacular developments in the Asian art market the fair in Hong Kong will continue to be a kind of side-stage or junior partner of the original fair in Basel. When singular goods are concerned, whose origin is a decisive factor determining their primarily symbolic value, then the brand contemporary art, like the brands of global luxury goods and their mints, is and probably will, in the medium term, remain associated with the Western metropolises.

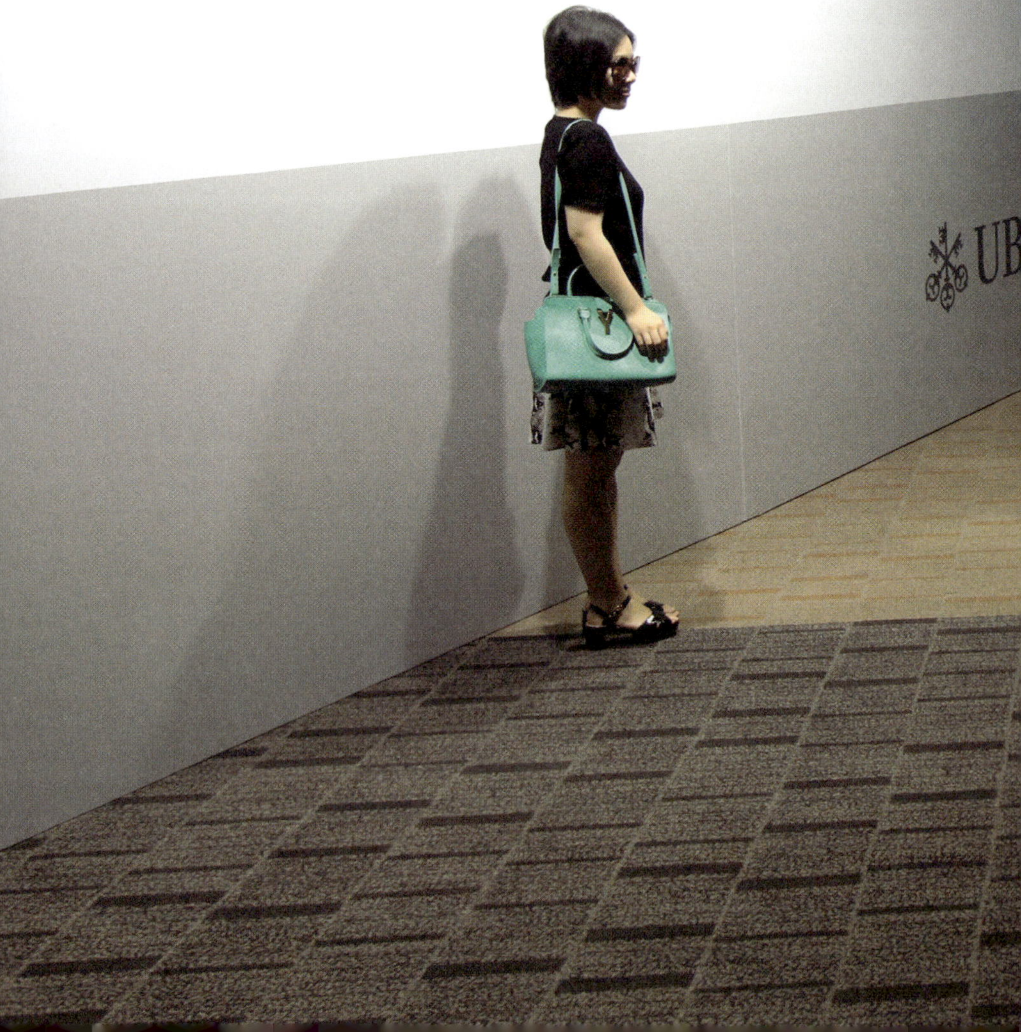

Art | Basel
UB

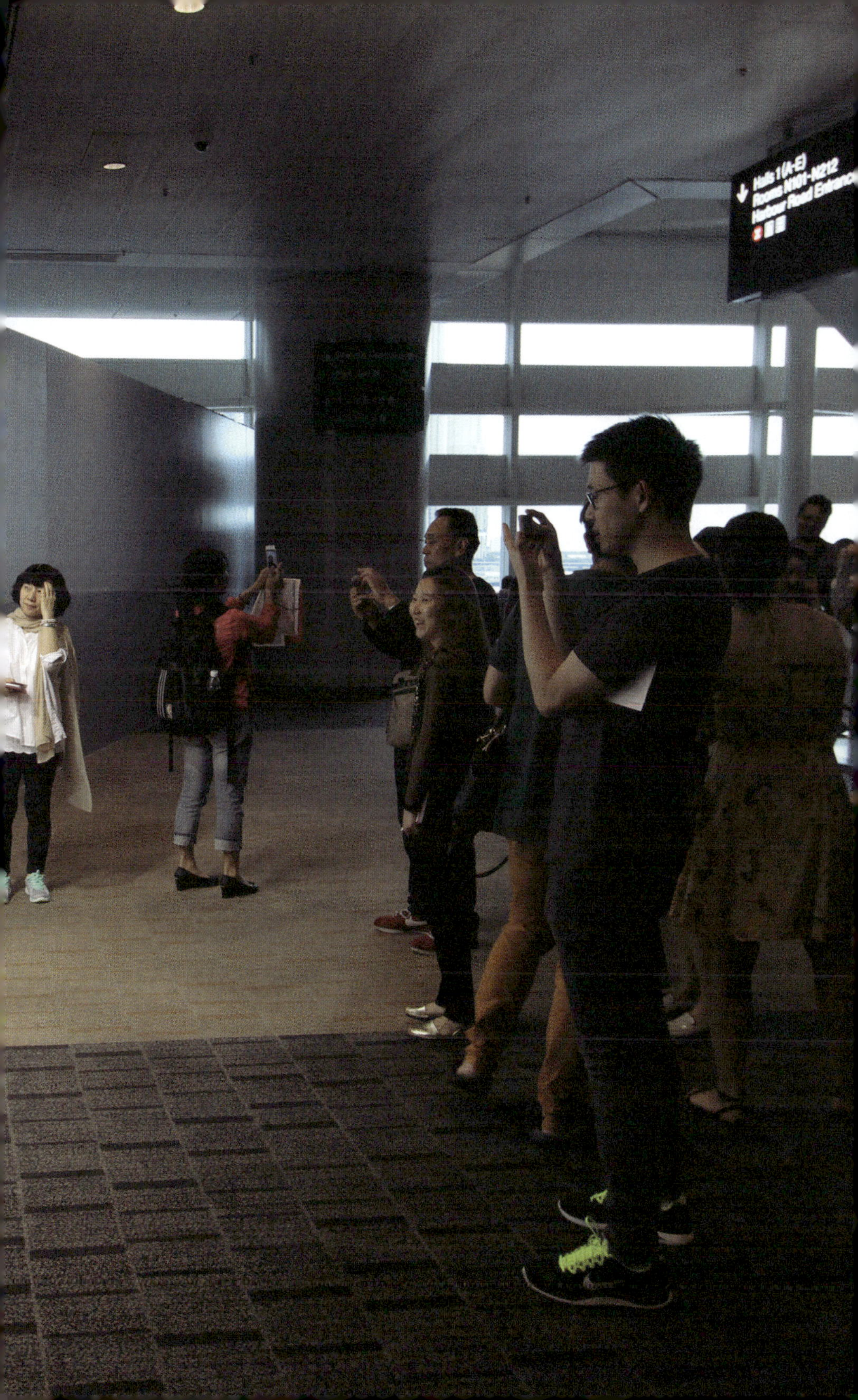

Halls 1 (A-E)
Rooms N101-N212
Harbour Road Entrance

Contemporary art and its Eastern public

After our presentation of a series of statements by the actors in the Chinese art world we will now let the non-professional actors, the public at the Art Basel in Hong Kong, briefly have their say. Although the art fair is obviously organized as a primarily commercial undertaking for the suppliers and buyers of art works, the "rank and file", the visitors interested in art who do not intend or lack the financial means to buy art, are also a part of the event. They participate out of curiosity or love of art, but as extras they are nonetheless indispensable for the successful production of the show. In March 2015 almost 60,000 people visited the Art Basel in Hong Kong and at the time we did our field work the figure was even over 65,000.

For easily comprehensible socio-historical reasons the public there is less familiar with contemporary art and its reception and consumption than those interviewed in the years before at the Art Basel in Basel and in Miami Beach. However, the around three dozen guests interviewed at the Art Basel in Hong Kong in regard to their impressions and assessments were also enthusiastic about the abundance of insights into the world of contemporary art. They all praised the perfect organization of the fair and particularly the strong presence of art from the Asian region, although some of them felt that the Asian galleries should have been even more strongly represented than the art dealers from the West. In particular, the mainland Chinese we interviewed regarded the presentation of less usual art genres – from sculptures to installations and video art – alongside the customarily dominant paintings as a great advantage of this event. All of the interviewed persons felt that the visit to the fair was worthwhile.

In contrast to the findings of the previous interviews in Basel and Miami Beach, however, there were statements which indicated a certain disorientation and frustration in the face of a cultural pattern – the way of dealing with contemporary art and its presentation –, as this was not part of the customary repertoire of cultural practice in this region and was not readily available in the form of habitualized aesthetic-intellectual competence.

For example an around thirty-years-old visitor from Xian reports: "Art Basel is very professional, in terms of details and services, more organized and international." At the same time he thought that the fair was "a bit bombarding, too overwhelming for ordinary audiences, there is too much information." In addition he also suggested that the organizers "could improve the route of visit. Now it is rather messy." By this he meant that it would be better if there were a planned visiting route for the art fair that one could follow in order to view the works more effectively. A woman from Singapore who accompanied her son to the fair expressed her new impressions in similar words: "I wished there were more elaborations for each art piece. For me sometimes the elaborations are not enough. I can't catch what it is all about." Another visitor noted: "And also art should be free but the way people are going around, it should be more organized, like the alley, sometimes they are parallel, sometimes you can go through, you could miss out pieces. You could miss out a lot of important things, the way the route is set. They are displaying large pieces that are hard to see when there are 50 people around." And a woman from mainland China added: "I think it seems messy at the beginning. I walked around and I felt disorientated. Maybe it is just me though."

The statement by a young visitor from Quangdong, an accountant by profession, reveals the expectations she had in regard to the presentation of art and the way the fair differed in this respect: "The works are represented based on galleries so it is quite messy for me since I do not have much understanding of art works. It is not really suited for visitors; maybe the buyers would like this arrangement. I would rather prefer to categorize the works on the basis of styles or genres. It is like a carnival. It would be great if the art fair makers could have a theme, but I guess it is more of a sales fair than an exhibition."

These different references to a widespread discomfiture on account of the over-stimulation resulting from the presentation of a mass of art works in a way felt to be unstructured, confusing and unsurveyable points to a sociologically interesting relationship between the availability of specific cultural capital and the claim to and the competence for an autonomous mode of appropriating art. As early as the 1960s the study of a research group led by Pierre Bourdieu on the public attending various European museums revealed that visitors with only a small amount of cultural capital emphasized, in exactly the same way as the Asian interviewees quoted above, that they desired a clearer, pedagogical-didactical introduction to their encounters with cultural goods and more specific aids for the understanding and interpretation of the art works on view, whereas visitors with more cultural capital rejected this kind of didactic support as out of place and superfluous. Like many of the Asian visitors to the art fair in Hong Kong they called for explicit instructions in the form of clearly designated routes and explanations of the art works presented at the fair.

A further indication of the so called "civilization gap" resulting from the conditions of delayed "contemporaneity" and of the need to catch up in the development of the specific cultural competencies and dispositions required for dealing with the singular goods of art is clearly manifested on many of the walls of the exhibition booths in Hong Kong. There are many little "Don't touch" signs designed to keep visitors less acquainted with the etiquette of the "White Cube" at a distance from the works of art. A comparative observation of the events in Basel, Miami Beach and Hong Kong reveals clear, culture-specific behavioral patterns in the ways of dealing with the institution of the art fair and its objects in a different regard. These include, not least, the omnipresent use of smart phones, in particular for taking selfies with the works of art in the background. This practice, criticized by some of our interviewees as being "in bad taste", is much less common in Miami Beach and Basel, but it seems to fit in almost seamlessly with the social habits of the visitors to the Art Basel in Hong Kong. The atmosphere often calls to mind the funfairs at which small groups of friends amuse themselves, turning the event into a kind of leisure activity with entertainment for all the family. The practice was severely criticized by some of the actors from the art world we interviewed and was anything but a welcome sight for the gallerists at the fair.

How matter-of-course the combination of a visit to the fair with family leisure pursuits was can be seen by casting a glance at the location of Art Basel, the Convention Center in the harbor of Hong Kong, where onlookers could gaze in amazement at a gigantic yellow rubber duck by the Dutch artist Florentijn Hofman. Although the rubber duck quickly ran out of air and shrank into a small heap of plastic it enjoyed much greater publicity and a wider success among the public than the works of art which could be seen in the background. In discussions in the foyer of the exhibition organized by the Asia Art Archive, in which we took part, the invited experts frequently criticized this symbol of popular (bad) taste as an eyesore in front of the gates of the elitist fair.

In our discussions with the experts they repeatedly referred to the need to catch up by means of "aesthetic education", which – as they expressly emphasized – should start in early childhood in order to develop sensitivity and competence in dealing with contemporary art and to achieve a sustainable socialization in this respect. The strong presence of elites accompanied by their offspring in the halls of the fair in Hong Kong seems to point precisely to this ambition to overcome the deficits in regard to the cultural pattern of love of art imported from the West.

Intercultural differences between the events in Hong Kong, Basel and Miami Beach are also revealed to the observer in regard to both the presentation of the show and the ways of encountering the culture on offer. The Art Basel in Basel is clearly much more discreet and distinguished than the Art Basel in Miami Beach with its stylized chicness and media hype. In contrast to both, the public at the Hong Kong Convention Center was clearly less excited, more everyday and less prone to life-style oriented self-presentation even in the periods reserved for the VIPs. At the opening of the fair, in contrast to the often inconsiderate pushing and shoving of the Western VIP collectors in Basel and Miami Beach, there was no tendency to hustle and bustle, no sign of routes through the fair prepared in advance, designed to lead collectors eager to make purchases down the shortest and quickest paths to the objects of their desire and to get them there before potential competitors. There was also no indication that the big business of the galleries took place in the very first hours or even minutes after the opening of the fair. Instead the Western gallerists depict a behavioral pattern of the buyers which was for them both unusual and disturbing. Throughout the entire day customers potentially interested in buying a work of art would turn up several times at the exhibition booth and ask about the price.

Finally a further striking difference in the social uses of art is revealed by the comparison of the three locations. Whereas in Miami Beach and even more so in Basel the "art lovers" we interviewed revealed a clear tendency towards a cultural condemnation and stigmatization of art auctions, Hong Kong presented a picture of truly harmonious coexistence. In 2013 a big auction of contemporary art by Christie's auction house took place in the Convention Center parallel to the Art Basel. The public moved regularly and casually from one site of the art trade to the other without any noticeable inhibition or feeling they were breaking a taboo. What is more, the manager of the Art Basel in Hong Kong was no less unproblematic in his approach to a competitor so often decried in the West. The talk here was of meaningful "synergies" in such a concentration of two art events and of an important time-saving factor for the entire clientele of Asian collectors.

Paradoxically, or possibly not, the Asian visitors to the Art Basel in Hong Kong are a socially selected population with an above average educational capital, which is, however culture specific and contextually dependent. In this respect it reflects the outcomes of the interviews already carried out in Basel and Miami Beach. It is not a lack of formal educational capital as such which creates the need for clearer guidance through the abundance of cultural goods. What we see here is, rather, a kind of "missing link" in the canon of legitimate educational goods, which inevitably makes contemporary art seem unusual and even consternating in the absence of a specific view and particular competence in deciphering art works deriving from an aesthetic disposition which the Western cultural elites had developed during a 150 years-long tradition of dealing with modern and contemporary art.

We are dealing, therefore, with newcomers who call for support and guidance in view of their lack of familiarity with this kind of art. This is expressed, for example, in the inability of some of the interviewees to recall the names of the galleries they had visited or the artists who had impressed them. A young women from Shenzen reports: "I took some pictures of the works that interested me, but I can't remember the names of the works or the galleries representing them, I don't have that habit." She added that she seldom attends exhibitions and apologizes with the remark: "I'm too lazy."

The emerging love of art and the process of gaining familiarity with the canon can also be discovered by tracing the spread of knowledge about established works and artists. Within the framework of a small additional empirical study some of the visitors were shown a small selection of "blue chip" works of art of Western (Van Gogh and Picasso, Rothko, Warhol and Koons) and Asian (Qi Baishi, Zhang Daquian) provenience and asked whether they knew the works or could name the painters. It turned out that the interviewees were best acquainted with the classical representatives of Western modern art (Van Gogh and Picasso with 70 per cent and 50 per cent respectively), whereas only a small minority knew the works of Rothko and Koons. In contrast, our interviewees from mainland China were seldom in a position to identify the reproductions of Chinese works of art which are relatively well-known in the West on account of the media reports on the spectacular prices achieved on the market by the originals. Only one in six knew the works of Qi Bashi or Zhang Daquian. It seems, therefore, that the spectacular market value of a work of art achieved at an auction is not enough to put it on the road to becoming an icon, whereas the emblematic representatives of Western aesthetics are easily able to exercise their hegemonial influence in the Far East.

It is worth noting here that the most easily accessible artworks of Impressionism with their pleasing motives typically achieved the greatest resonance among the inexpert consumers of art. During a visit to a Monet exhibition in a shopping mall in Shanghai we were able to see how strong the attractive power exercised by this kind of middle brow "blockbuster" art on the Chinese public was and how readily the visit to the exhibition harmonized with the acquisition of Monet-inspired consumer articles in a nearby sales room. At the same time, and probably not by chance, huge reproductions on billboards in the town drew attention to a here hitherto completely unknown Chinese artist whose style and motifs obviously worked like variations on the aesthetics and themes of Monet.

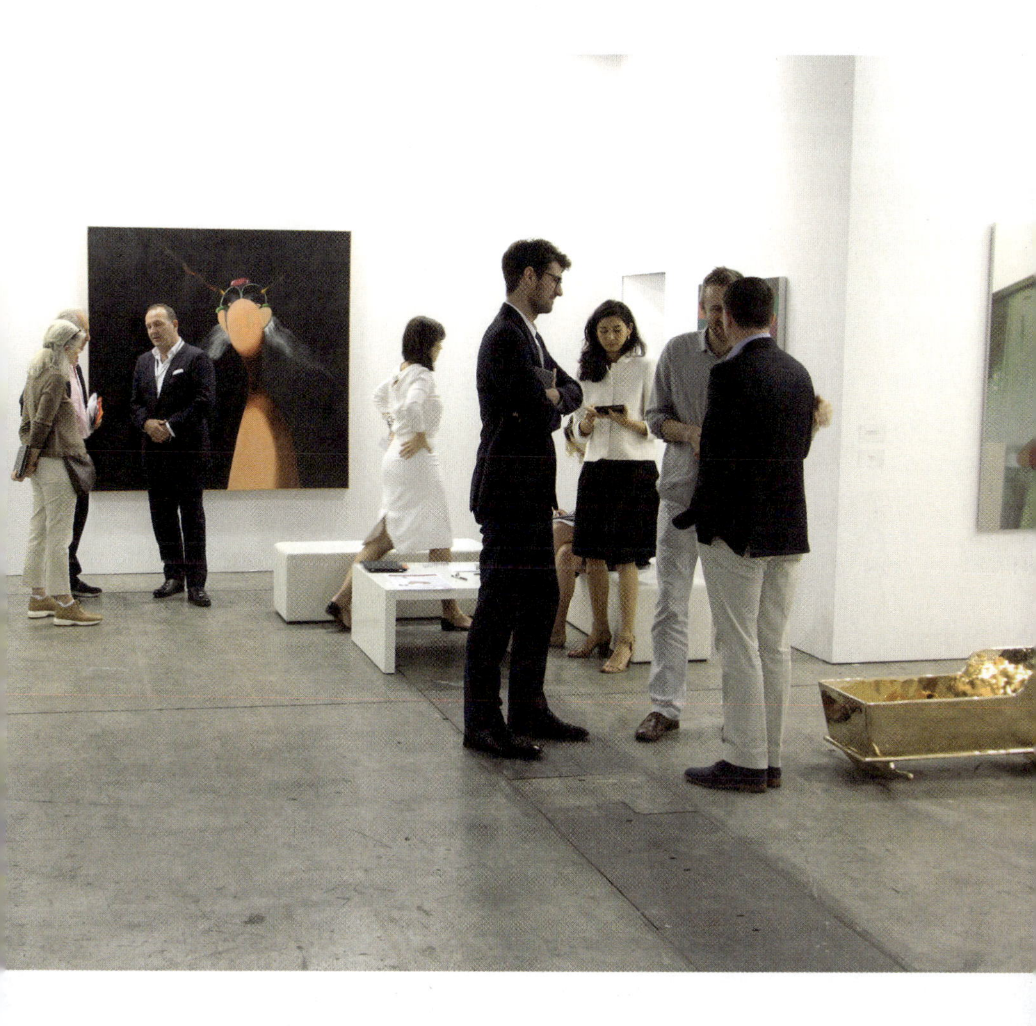

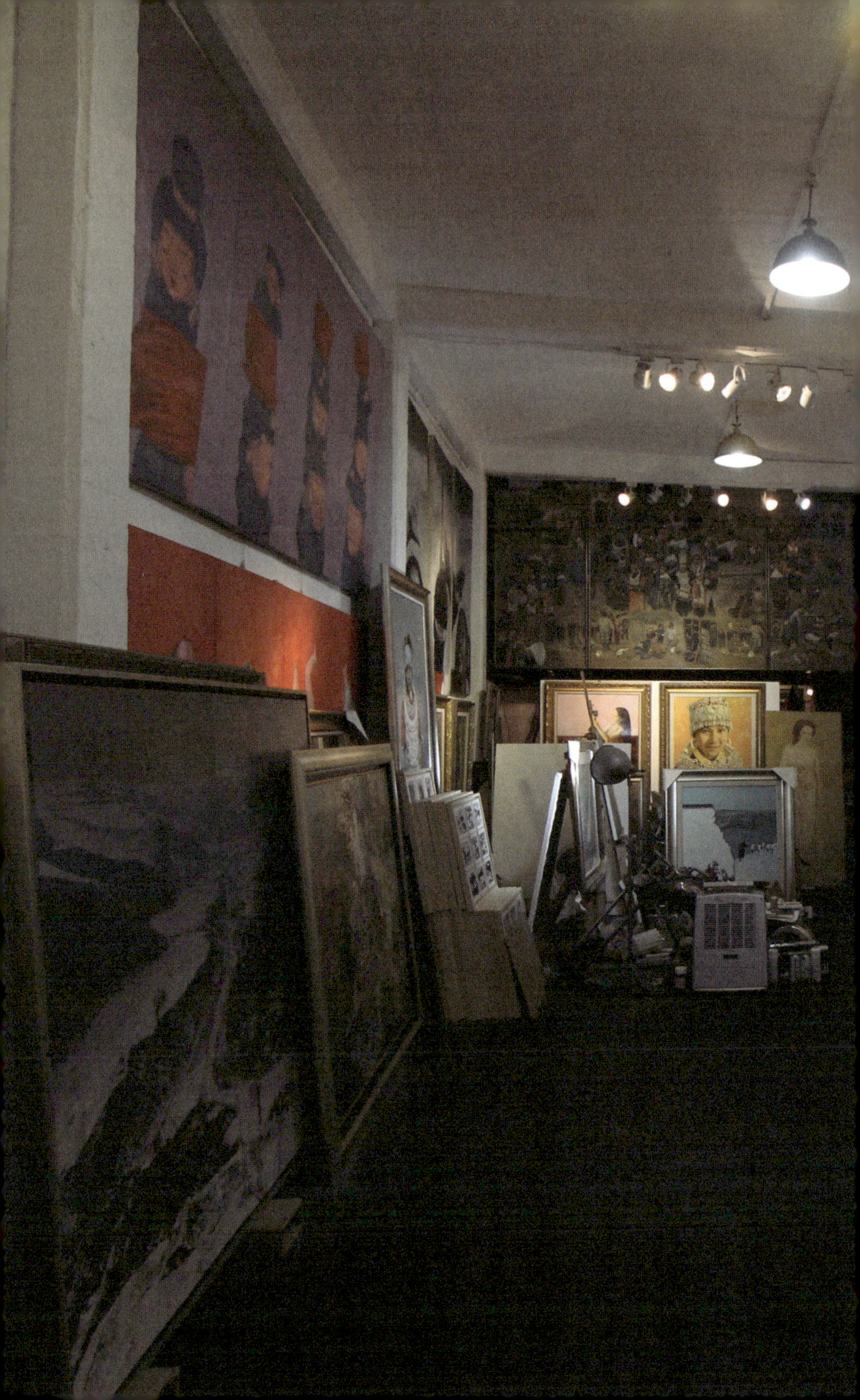

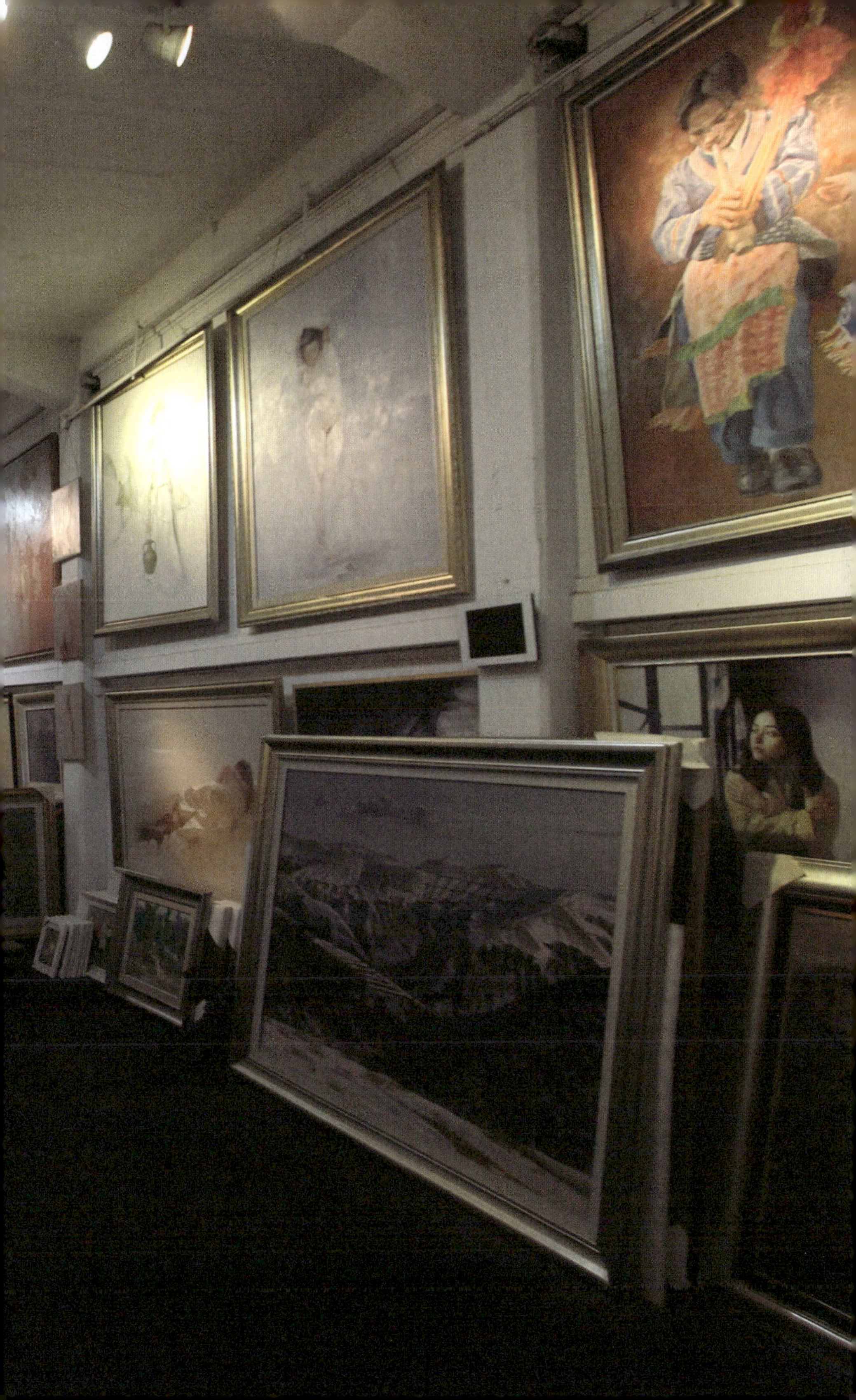

A world turned upside down

The birth of an art field under the aegis of the (global) art market

A common form of the ethnocentric misjudgment and distortion of alien and distant social realities and cultural phenomenon results from seeing and judging them through the glasses of our own ingrained patterns of perception and interpretation. In essence such "touristic errors" reveal more about the observer, his cultural codes and social norms than about the object of his observations, which is simply assimilated without reflection into the accustomed patterns. In this way genuine curiosity about and encounters with foreign culture is rendered improbable and a confirmation of existing stereotypes and prejudices likely.

The pictures of this region of the world mediated by our dialogue partners in the West (see the chapter "Prospective territorial occupations") seems to be nourished primarily by the hyped up Western media reporting on the turnover of the art market in China, which has made a giant leap forward within a few years from being a marginal, grey zone to becoming a first-class growth area of the global art trade. Although these spectacular indicators of a rapid inclusion of China in the global art market have proved unreliable and the Chinese market has in the last few years turned out to be unstable and highly dependent on economic trends, this seems as yet to have scarcely any effect on the generalized gold-rush fever and euphoric mood. The conviction of gallerists, collectors, curators and art critics that the Far East is the growth market of the future seems completely unshaken. This is clearly shown in the in-depth interviews and the surveys we undertook in Basel, Miami Beach and Hong Kong. The large numbers of rich and newly rich collectors, the numerous opportunities such an emerging market offers and the need to stake one's own claims on it: these are the common stereotypes which always occur in conversations about Asia and especially about China.

But what do these circumstances and phenomena look like when seen at close quarters? How are they seen, interpreted and judged by the relevant local actors and experts? In what complex social practices and cultural contexts are these apparently so objective market data and the accompanying dynamics embedded? The question is not simply whether the spectacular rise of the Asian and the Chinese art market might turn out to be a flash in the pan, whose impressive radiant powers diminish the closer one gets to it. Much more fundamental questions must be asked about the Asian art scene as such, about its status and significance within the so hotly discussed and eagerly invoked global art market.

In the 60 interviews and conversations we conducted a large number of approaches and positions were thematized, discussed and occasionally analyzed in more depth. Many questions were raised and some, albeit careful and only provisional, answers given. The interviews collected in this book and many of the unpublished dialogues speak in the first place for themselves. They can only provide a few starting points for discourse which must be continued and intensified. In their standpoints and their assessments of the structures, changes and transformation processes and their consequences and challenges the interview partners sometimes differ widely, as each of them argues from a particular standpoint – on the one hand as art dealers, gallerists, curators or artists and on the other hand on the basis of their origins and cultural background. Nonetheless an attempt will be undertaken here to present a comprehensive view of the most important aspects.

In this concluding observation it is necessary, first of all, to emphasize once again what all the actors in the East and South East Asian art world expressly and unisono pointed out: as a monolithic social-cultural entity Asia is no more existent than is the West. Just as Michel Leiris uses the telling title "Afrique fântome" when speaking about Africa in his classical ethnological and demystifying travel report, we too can fittingly speak in our context of an "Asie fântome" in order to underline the massively ethnocentric simplifications and distortions typically applied to this huge region from the distance of the West. Our local interview partners seem to have felt a great need to warn against and to eliminate this fundamental misunderstanding and lack of comprehension. In contrast to the Western actors of the art world, who usually simply thematize this region as a market to be conquered, the Asian actors are directly involved in the markedly divergent art worlds of the various Asian countries, regions and cultures, whose development is the prime object of their interest. They also seem to be inspired by an, albeit rather different, pioneering spirit. For them, in contrast to the actors from the West, this region of the world is not an unknown territory waiting for the discovery of its treasures and marketing opportunities, but rather an extremely lively art world in its own right, and is undergoing a process of developing and blossoming in which many of them are participating or wish to do so.

This fundamental divergence in the positions and perspectives of the two groups which meet in the expanding art market hub of Hong Kong leads to no less fundamental communication problems. Apparently the actors are speaking about the same object, but mean, on the one hand, a terrain whose occupation by the established global players promises profit, and, on the other hand, a blossoming autochtonous site of original regional and local art production.

Those who are directly involved as gallerists or collectors in the local or regional art field tend to adopt a standpoint which respectfully takes the cultural particularities of each region into account and identifies and differentiates between lines of tradition and specific aesthetic codes. The global view of distant sales markets has neither the cultural competence nor the sensitivity needed for this approach. As representative of the statements of many of our dialogue partners we can quote one of the most distinguished experts on the Chinese art market, who recently realized yet again how slight his knowledge of this huge cultural area was when he heard of prices amounting to millions paid for the works of a Chinese artist completely unknown to him, whose fame was presumably restricted to one particular Chinese province. Other dialogue partners emphasized the radical differences in the aesthetics of artists from Hong Kong, mainland China or Indonesia, who were sweepingly subsumed under the heading of contemporary art and who, in each particular case, attracted the interest of different groups of collectors. And in regard to the motives for the relatively recent practice of art collecting in this huge region many of the collectors we interviewed emphasized how important for them the search for the cultural identity of a region as expressed in its art was.

In general it seems to be the case that the dynamics of the rising regional and local markets for contemporary art are closely tied to the economic growth of each particular country and to a growing national self-awareness, so that art in a certain fashion becomes a reservoir for the symbolic means of expressing national identity or at least the sense of regional or local belonging. In this context contemporary art acquires a completely different status and different functions than the traditional or classical art goods. The latter represent the transgenerational patrimony and in a certain fashion look backwards, whereas contemporary art symbolizes and demonstrates the fact that one is keeping pace with the times and is willing and able to compete on equal terms with the dominant hegemonial powers in the world of cultural exchange as in the analogous case of newly acquired economic importance. The dynamics of the art world described here is thus embedded in complex socio-historical transformation processes. And although it enjoys a relative autonomy over the important economic factors in the current shifting geo-political setting, under the given circumstances this autonomy is clearly much more restricted than in Western countries with their more than a hundred-years-old pre-history of given conditions.

GLOBALIZATION AND MODERNIZATION AS CATCHING-UP DEVELOPMENT

In the course of globalization Asia has experienced rapid economic, social and cultural changes in the past two decades. As a result of its growing economic power the region has become an engine of growth for the world economy, which many observers already regard as the gravitational center of the 21st century. In particular the East Asian states China (with Taiwan) and South Korea have experienced a boom which continues unabated to this day. The South East Asian countries Thailand, Indonesia, Singapore and Malaysia, which were severely shaken by the Asian crisis at the end of the 1990s, have caught up enormously and now count among the winners of the globalization process in the region. In spite of all the evident problems these countries still face the entry of the region into a new age seems pre-determined. Today one third of the global added value is already generated in Asia, without taking Japan into account. China, which is now the most powerful economic force in Asia, will probably overtake the USA as the biggest national economy in the world within the next few years. The powerful growth has also increased the prosperity of the region and the number of people with improved living standards is growing in spite of serious inequalities. According to the predictions the middle-class in Asia will rise to around a billion people by 2020.

Due to its economic success and its massive economic and social upheavals China stands without doubt in the focus of interest. The rapid modernization process is characterized by the integration of China into the world economy, material growth, increasing consumption and a gigantic boom in urbanization. And the economic rise of a national economy obviously also accelerates the interest in the globalized art world of the regions concerned.

The cultural transformation undergone by the art trade parallel to the processes of modernization in the country must be seen against this background. The hitherto scarcely heeded Chinese contemporary art, which could be seen for the first time at international biennials and exhibitions in the 1990s, became a factor to be taken seriously in the global art world after the turn of the century. In spite of its complexity and highly heterogeneous contexts the Western understanding of contemporary Chinese art suffers from a systematic distortion which continues to exist up to the present day. Contemporary Chinese art is mostly reduced to and interpreted as a symbol of freedom in an authoritarian system.

The rise of the Chinese art market and of Chinese art to which we have frequently referred both reflects and symbolizes profound commercial changes in the global field of art. In the course of the last few decades the art trade has opened up new sales markets in regions which, at least in regard to art, were characterized by their peripheral situation. China's rapid rise to the status of a global player in the art market and the high growth rates for the trade in art in Brazil, India, Mexico, Russia and the Arab world are witnesses to a territorial and structural transformation of the art world.

In contrast to the globalization of the world economy the globalization of the art world was until recently clearly limited in scope. The dominance of the US-American and the European art scene was unbroken, as was manifested above all in the supply and demand in the art market, but also in the conditions for the reception of art, the language of the art world, art criticism and the exclusively Western art historical canon. And although numerous studies[1] show that this ascendancy continues to exist, the global

---

1 | See for example Buchholz, Larissa/Wuggenig, Ulf (2004): Cultural Globalization between Myth and Reality: The Case of the Contemporary Visual Arts. In:

turn has nonetheless led to a readjustment of the relationships of power and to a differentiated view of the continuing processes of change. The art world has become fragile in spite of the North American and European hegemony and the gate-keeping of its professional actors.

In harmony with the ideological promises of neo-liberal politics and with the economy globalization now seems to be asserting itself in the art field as well – specifically through the art market. If we leave aside the biennalization of art, we can encounter this globalization nowhere more clearly than in the trade with art. The growing economic power of the emerging or developing economies is the driving force behind the international art market and it involves a power struggle over resources, claims and markets. The primarily economic expansion has not only shifted the geographical borders of the art trade and changed its practices. In the course of the world-wide economic globalization the number of so-called high wealth individuals has massively increased, creating a clientele of millionaires and billionaires from the so-called take off countries, who are increasingly present on the expanding art market as the buyers of traditional, modern and contemporary art.

Western modernism with its universalist codex has never attempted to conceal its claim to economic, political and cultural hegemony. In this context art always plays a role which should not be underestimated. What was regarded as modern or even avant-gardist was always subject to modification by developments and the course of time. This seems to apply in equal measure to the age of globalization, which, like capitalism, is a product of the Western modern age. Whoever fails to move with the times falls by the wayside. Inclusion and exclusion touch upon the self-understanding of the art world not only in the emerging economies but also in the developed Western states themselves.

Our dialogue partners provide a detailed insight into the development of an emerging, highly dynamic and rapidly changing art scene, characterized particularly by an expanding art market, a low but growing density of art institutions and an unbelievable number of young aspiring artists. A part of these stories is closely associated with the economic rise of China, which has also provided for an exponential growth of the

Art-e-Fact, 4. Lind, Maria/Velthuis, Olav (eds.) (2012): Contemporary Art and Its Commercial Markets: A Report on Current Conditions and Future Scenarios. Berlin: Sternberg.

art market in recent decades. The nature and the speed of the political, economic, social and cultural transformations experienced by China since the end of the Mao era determines the conditions for the current and the further development of the art world and gives it its own particular stamp. It also profoundly influences the relationship between artists, their cultural inheritance, their understandingof the present and their vision of the future.

According to the statements of the actors the rapid social development of China in particular has thoroughly ambivalent consequences for Chinese art and the Chinese art world. As the majority of our dialogue partners report, the speed of art production matches the speed of change. Not only the artists but also all the other actors such as curators, critics, collectors or the public interested in art have scarcely any time for thought or reflection. They can only react to the accelerated developments in order to keep up with them.

COMMERCIALIZATION AND INSTITUTIONALIZATION OF THE ART SCENE

Many changes today occur under the aegis of capitalism. Many actors in the West, above all, seem to be truly dazzled by the boom in the Chinese art market. According to their estimates China is the future market of the art world pure and simple – regardless of whether it is critically received or simply positively welcomed. Among the important market actors in particular there is a pioneering spirit which no-one can or will evade. Gallerists even justify financial losses by arguing that they must be in at the beginning in order to stake their claims.

To all appearances attention is predominantly directed towards economic factors and economic success. This enables galleries to cooperate indirectly with up and coming artists, who in turn need the galleries in order to make progress in their artistic careers. But this does not mean that artistic development is totally neglected. Well known commercial galleries in particular search for established artists whose works can be easily sold and who act more skillfully in the promotion of their careers. On the other hand it is reported that numerous young artists prefer to be represented by renowned Western galleries rather than to be cared for by smaller, ambitious program galleries under Chinese management, even though this would be more advantageous for their future artistic development.

Since the beginnings of the modern art market private art traders in the West have always seen themselves as the patrons and promoters of art rather than as dealers and marketers of art.[2] In China, however, the auction houses, which sell art for record prices, continue to play a dominating role, which has, not least, led many galleries to keep an eye on investment opportunities with prospects of economic profit when choosing their artists. In contrast to the auction houses, however, the galleries remain indispensable for an art trade which holds the balance between artistic and economic interests.

In this connection the role of the museums must also be mentioned, as they as institutions occupy a central position in the art trade and the art world. As new museums are sprouting up in record time in China one of the most important questions to be asked will concern the criteria these houses follow outside their functions in regard to the art-interested public. Will they, like the auction houses and galleries, be mainly guided by economic values and market trends or will they be developed and curated in accordance with the discourses of the science, history and criticism of art? In view of the large number of museums it is highly doubtful, according to the statements of some of our dialogue partners, whether the museums will in the near future take on an important role similar to that of their counterparts in the West. It is not for nothing that they place their hopes on already existing institutions with an international reputation such as the Rockbund Museum in Shanghai, the Central Academy of Fine Arts Art Museum (CAFA) and the Ullens Center of Contemporary Art (UCCA) in Beijing or planned flagships such as M+ in Hong Kong.

If one is to believe the statements of the local actors China has successfully become a part of the international art world. But the country still owes its visibility in the global art world above all to the powerful growth of the art market and the high prices achieved on it. Of course there is a remarkable number of young artists, above all in the metropolises such as Hong Kong, Shanghai, Beijing, Nanjing or Xian. But the positive development is partly hindered by the substantial difficulties of the art

---

2 | See for example Thurn, Hans Peter (1994): Der Kunsthändler. Wandlungen eines Berufes. Munich: Hirmer.

institutions of the state. The actors repeatedly complain about the lack of public museums, exhibition halls, non-commercial foundations and non-profit facilities, which are of enormous importance for the visibility of Chinese art. All of our dialogue partners emphasize unisono that such an infrastructure is one of the most important preconditions if the Chinese art scene is to acquire international status. The long term institutionalization process of the kind we know in the West is only in its infancy in China. Even the existing facilities such as the academies have not as yet gone through a historical development similar to that of their counterparts in the West. Consequently comparisons with Europe at the beginning of the 20th century are not seldom made.

Our dialogue partners complain again and again that with few exceptions there are virtually no public museums which could provide an overview of modern and contemporary art in China. The exhibitions of the museums financed by the state continue to pursue strongly political or educational goals. Although numerous semi-public or private museums have arisen in the very recent past, with few exceptions they do not follow a curatorial principle or have any art historical or scientific ambitions. Here an academic basis is evidently lacking and the collecting activity is often guided by considerations of investment or social prestige. In addition the borders between public and private institutions are unclearly drawn and often call for political and economic compromises. In order to cover their costs the private museums are often dependent on state support or sponsoring. This phenomenon is well-known in the West and has become particularly apparent following China's entry into the market economy. The suspicion is frequently expressed that some of the newly established private museums are simply architectonic prestige objects designed to increase the value of the property and to promote luxury neighborhoods. Many of the private museums which were established during the two building waves after 1990 have in the meantime closed again and have been put to different uses.

As some of our dialogue partners report, most of the private museums cannot in any case be compared with Western collections and by no means correspond to the Western concept of collection and museal presentation. Even the few books on the contemporary development of art forms in China do not attempt to find or develop a professionally well-founded art historical consensus. It seems necessary, therefore, to promote more strongly the young and emerging, scientifically oriented, art critical and curatorial generation in the country and to build up the necessary infrastructure to achieve this end. The lack of qualified personnel ranging from museum directors or curators and art historians to administrative staff further restricts the ability of the existing institutions to act effectively. Severe competition for personnel and a high fluctuation among the staff are consequences which are felt even by respected institutions such as the Ullens Center for Contemporary Art, whose top management changed every two years.

The boom in Chinese art is scarcely visible in the old centers of the art trade. From an artistic point of view contemporary art in China has scarcely been received to this day in the Western art world, if one ignores the familiar names such as Zhang Xiaogang, Zeng Fanzhi, Li Shan, Fang Lijun or Yue Minjun from the first generation of Chinese artists, who in the course of the political and social upheavals of the mid 1980s made their way as artists slowly, accompanied by numerous reversals, and were variously labeled according to taste as the Chinese avant-garde or as representatives of so called cynical realism or political pop.

But it is no less interesting to see what was ultimately filtered out of the entire range of Chinese art production by the structures and mechanisms of the art world and so achieved a degree of international publicity. According to our interview partners art production in China is fundamentally more differentiated than is suggested by the impressions successfully conveyed to the Western art world, which are mostly oriented on the current taste in art of a Western and nowadays increasingly cosmopolitan elite. Chinese contemporary art is mainly conceived in the terms of the Western narrative, and, conversely, the West needs this narrative in order to find access to Chinese art. This is the conclusion of an interview partner, which may at first sight seem banal but nonetheless hits the nail on the head.

The predominant image of a necessary catch up development both at the institutional level and in the equipment of the recipients with the necessary cultural capital, as it is expressed in the interviews, is highly ambivalent. It is oriented largely on the norms, standards and rules which have characterized the field of art since it achieved relative autonomy in the Western hemisphere. They ought, it is said, to be implemented as swiftly as possible so that China can be included in this art field. This process strongly recalls the implementation of the rules of liberalization and free trade of the West by transnational institutions such as the IWF, the World Bank and the WTO in the course of economic globalization.

Discussions on how far commercialization has affected the conditions for the production and distribution of art or on the influence of price increases on the creative work of the artists are not today in the center of focus. Instead our interview partners brought up questions about the function of art in China, Chinese self-awareness and, not least, the educational level of the public.

WHEN THE MARKET RULES ART: THE TWO FACES OF THE ART WORLD REVISITED

There is a danger that fundamental misunderstandings will arise in dealing with the semantics of such a well-established concept as globalization if there is a lack of differentiation in regard to the levels at which processes are described. It seems necessary, for example, to distinguish between narrations about the art world in terms of the structural levels to which they refer. Are we dealing with the art market as such or with the field of art when we talk of contemporaneity and a globalized art world? If we consider the undoubtedly existent and even massively expanding state of the trade with the symbolic goods of art and takes the exploding turnover of the auction houses in China as an indicator for such a diagnosis, the concept of globalization seems to be a completely fitting label. But if, instead, we enquire about the social structures in the field of the production and consecration of art, the establishment of its legitimacy and aura and the promotion of the career of the artists through these instances of consecration and certain recognized educational procedures etc., a clearly different, more complex and even contradictory picture of the events results.

The developments of the recent decades clearly show that the trade in art has in the meantime reached almost all the important metropolises in the world, even though these locations may hitherto have been scarcely visible on a world map of the history of contemporary art. Wherever economic capital endeavors to be converted into symbolic capital and profane material wealth seeks for legitimacy in the form of cultural noblesse the operational system of the art market with its diverse institutions soon comes into play. However, the locations where this symbolical capital is produced and goods which usually have only a minimal material value are equipped with a priceless aura by means of a kind of symbolic consecration are few in number and highly selective in nature.

The relevant locations on the globe of the art world reflect the crystallizations of a laborious socio-historical dynamics. They are places in which generations of actors have worked – cooperatively or competitively – to create networks of institutions and ensembles of collective practices, aesthetic codes and social uses of symbolic forms of expression which interact and so supply this universe with a specific symbolic capital and endow it with visibility and legitimacy as a relatively autonomous social field. They are places such as Paris, the "capital of modernity" (Walter Benjamin) which themselves present "modern myths" (Roger Caillos), serve as projection surfaces and models in the international context and become radiating international poles of attraction for lovers of art. In such places what can be described in the terms of the sociologist Pierre Bourdieu as "fields of art" are formed and function as prototypes and models. Only after the "long durée" (Fernand Braudel) of the socio-historical emergence of a relatively autonomous field gravitating around a specific good, the symbolic capital of art, can such a highly symbolic place develop that aura which is then transferred to the actors active in that field.

Such a field of art cannot be conjured up out of thin air in the short term by the mere accumulation of wealth and the accompanying demand or even by means of state regulation, as is attempted in some of the oil-rich desert states or booming emerging industrial regions. It is, instead, built upon the congealed history of the long-term collective endeavors and investments of all the interested actors participating in it. Depending on the national context in each case, this history is not only characterized by massive asynchronies, but also directly reflects international symbolic relationships of power. This means that national fields of art production which develop early can also establish themselves in a transnational context as an avant-garde and as a model, as in the already mentioned case of Paris as a prototype or as was manifested after the Second World War by the establishment of the cultural hegemony of the United States with New York as its center. From the fact that in recent years the global art trade has achieved its greatest turnover in China it can by no means, therefore, be concluded that parallel to this development globally recognized sites for the consecration of the production and distribution of art have also been established. Successful assertion on the global art market is by no means automatically accompanied by the recognition of a location as a transnational art field. "What money cannot buy" is precisely this specific symbolic capital: without itself being consecrated a location cannot become a site of consecration; without aura no aura can be radiated, without magic no enchantment.

This is precisely the context for a point made several times by our interview partners from the Far East. Although the art market is booming and the region occupies top positions on the global world market for art, it nonetheless plays at best only a secondary role in the international field of art. As the interviewees emphasized again and again, the region lacks the institutions necessary for the existence of an autonomous field of art and for the exercise of the powers of consecration. What is more, in contrast to some of the emerging countries in Latin America, for example, China possesses no tightly knit national network of artists, galleries, auction houses and collectors, state institutions such as academies, public and private museums, biennials and art fairs, or curators, art critics and other relevant actors and professional groups. Some of our dialogue partners explained this by reference to the particular political development of China. Not only the art market but also the entire art scene was in a state of suspension and subject to state supervision and control before the opening up of the country. The dynamic growth of the art market and the art scene only began after the turn of the century.

As we have already stated, the museum landscape is in the initial stage of development, but it does not yet possess the critical mass, public presence and visibility to contribute to the emergence of a public equipped with the cultural capital needed by contemporary art in order to achieve resonance and a broad impact. The public education facilities cannot fulfill this function either. In our Western civilization the educational system – and in particular the upper levels of the schools – have functioned for more than a century as instances for the mediation of art and have familiarized entire generations with the specific aesthetics of modernism and late modernism. For readily comprehensible historical reasons such educational functions can scarcely be taken over in the short term by other cultures.

In the interviews it was also frequently emphasized that the countries of the region, and above all China, did in fact have specific art academies for the training of artists. However these academies, which can look back on a centuries-old tradition, have always produced an elite of artists with certified competencies, who were committed to specifically codified aesthetic ideals. The form of perfection they teach, for example in regard to certain artistic genres such as calligraphy or techniques such as copying, must be envied for its virtuosity, but it nonetheless runs counter to the artistic ethos of singularity, distinctiveness and autonomous creativity demanded by contemporary art. The situation is only slowly changing with the appointment of contemporary artists as teachers in the academies, who can familiarize the young generation of artists with the specific codices of contemporary art.

Against the background of this historically explicable lack of many of the elements of an art field it is easy to understand why our informants all emphasized that young artists from the region had to gain experience as travelling journeymen in places and institutions on the map of the art world which possessed the necessary resources for the legitimate mediation, certification and consecration of artistic capital. This compulsion to migrate is accompanied by the danger that these talented young artists might not return to their home country after their initial sojourn in the promised lands of the art world, even though several of the interview partners emphasized the strong attachment of the young generation of artists to their countries of origin and underlined that they would look for artistic recognition precisely in their home country. Furthermore, the institutions of art criticism and curatorship have scarcely been developed or established in an emerging national or regional art scene which has developed late and often under unfavorable political conditions. This is a further handicap in the process of catching up in the development of an art field comparable to that of Western regions.

Last but not least the late and hesitant development of a gallery system probably shares a degree of responsibility for the specific structures of the art field in this region. Regardless of whether they are commercial, semi-commercial or non commercial, galleries of a Western kind have no tradition in China. The Chinese art trade was always characterized by direct purchasing from the artist. Even today a great part of the artistic production is still sold by the artists themselves in their ateliers and workshops or brought to one of the numerous auction houses for sale. Before 1991 auctions were forbidden; the first gallery, the Red Gate Gallery, was also opened in 1991, revealingly enough by an Australian.

Our dialogue partners again and again emphasize the enormous influence of the auction houses. They explain it by reference to the specific social psychology of market behavior under the given socio-historical conditions, namely the delayed development of a field of contemporary art together with its characteristic cultural patterns, social rules and practices. The numerous auction houses, including the big players from the West, had already occupied, not to say virtually monopolized, the terrain of the art trade even before the autochthonous galleries began to show their presence. The latter had a difficult time in the face of these powerful competitors, who seemed to enjoy a range of obvious advantages in the eyes of an as yet unpracticed and inexperienced art public in general and of an emerging community of collectors of contemporary art in particular. As was frequently reported, these include above all the transparency of the price formation at the auctions, whereas the fixing of the prices for art works bought at galleries seems less transparent and is largely based on trust. Trust, however, is capital which can only be accumulated gradually on the basis of experience with previous successful transactions, whereas the open market with its exemplary demonstration of competition at auctions plainly shows everyone the relationship between supply and demand. On this point the author of an article in a Swiss economics periodical writes: "However, the infrastructure which supports every art system is deficient: an established museum structure, pioneering exhibitions, curators and also the criteria for the judgment of art – all of these are lacking. The vacuum has been filled up to now by the auction houses such as Poly International Auction (since 2005) and, of course Christie's and Sotheby's."[3]

At the same time, in view of the slight degree of legitimation of the gallery as an institution in the Eastern art market, the argument put forward by many buyers and collectors seems plausible and even convincing, namely that the 50 per cent of the proceeds of sales which usually ends up in the pocket of the gallerist represents an unnecessary and easily avoidable waste of money when compared to the much lower charges of the auction houses. The market power of the auction houses, which is incidentally demonstrated by the maintenance of luxurious exhibition rooms in the style of the big galleries of Western provenience, is at the same time a handicap for the development of a gallery system which would feel particularly obliged to serve the primary market and to provide a programmatic orientation.

---

3 | Brigitte Ulmer (2007): Kunstmarkt: Goldrush in China. In: Bilanz. Das Schweizer Wirtschaftsmagazin, 9.11.2007.

Galleries are more than purely commercial undertakings; they traditionally also serve to discover and encourage young artists, and to bring them to the notice of the public during the first stages of their careers – a function which no other institution of the art field, let alone of the art market in the narrow sense, is even remotely capable of fulfilling so efficiently. It is indeed reported that some of the auction houses in the meantime also serve the primary market for young artists and accept the works of unknown artists alongside their established candidates and blue chips. But this involves the danger that young artists will be quickly promoted with a lot of hype and just as quickly dropped again and forgotten.

The precarious situation of the gallery system in China seems to be improving gradually. In the meantime a number of galleries exist which have succeeded, after years of intensive endeavor, in building up a stock of collectors as clients, even though they are also faced with direct competition from the big galleries from the Western metropolises such as Gagosian, Pace or White Cube, which are streaming into the country. Gagosian, for example, has a branch at one of the noblest addresses in Hong Kong, the Pedder Building, for which it pays an extremely high rent – a rent which in the opinion of our dialogue partners can scarcely be justified by the turnover achieved.

Since the Art Basel entered the Asian art market in 2012 with its take-over of the Hong Kong Art Fair the lack of balance between the market dominance of the auction houses and the relatively marginal existence of the gallery scene seems to have been rectified to some degree. It should not be forgotten, however, that the Art Basel itself practices a kind of global gatekeeping by only admitting galleries to the fair which meet certain (Western) norms and standards. But whereas in the West it continues to maintain a clear distance from the auction system frowned upon by traditional collectors, it has, significantly, come into close touch and cooperates with the auction houses in Hong Kong under the circumstances sketched out above. In 2013, for example, a big auction was carried out by Christie's in the Convention Center at the same time as the Art Basel. It was possible to observe how a freely fluctuating public moved effortlessly and seemingly uninhibitedly from one minute to the other between the exhibition space of a noble art gallery at the fair and the fully packed auction room.

What does the pattern of collecting in such an emerging economy look like? As we know, taste, motives and behavior often differ very widely from the familiar notions of the Western art world. Although the collection of art has a long tradition in the East and South East Asian regions, it was concentrated for a long time on classical art and antiquities, which is scarcely surprising in view of the absence of an autochthonous and autonomous period of modern art and the late development of a field of contemporary art. Even today the market for classical art commodities is still a powerful economic factor and remains competitive in the face of alternatives from the West.

In most of the countries apart from Japan and, to a certain extent, South Korea the collection of contemporary art is still a relatively unusual cultural practice which it takes time to get used to. This is particularly true of China where, together with antiquities and porcelain, traditional ink and brush paintings were mainly collected, which were founded on an autonomous artistic tradition. The opening up of the country to contemporary art trends only began in the 1990s. The subsequent astoundingly swift growth of interest in contemporary art is attributed by our local interview partners to various factors. They refer, on the one hand, to the model role of Western elites, with whom the representatives of the new money among the Eastern economic elites are trying to catch up for reasons of prestige and the legitimation of their social status. They also emphasize that contemporary art is seen as a particularly stylish form of symbolic capital, in which considerable economic resources are invested in order to achieve social benefits in the shape of recognition and distinction.

In the talks it was also pointed out that newcomers to the field of collecting contemporary art could also fall back on the services of Western enterprises such as the art consulting unit of the UBS. A younger Hong Kong art collector informed us that he had recently participated in a seminar held by the UBS in Switzerland in which he was not only introduced to the finer points of collecting and its economic aspects but also had the opportunity to meet artists in their workshops and, not least, to make network contacts with other collectors all over the world. To our knowledge there is a great demand for such coaching and development aid among the latecomers to the world community of collectors.

During the Art Basel in Hong Kong our participant observation enabled us to discover at close quarters how intensive the exchange of information can be on such occasions between the aspirants from the emerging economies and the established collectors of Western provenience. At all events the staff of the art consulting unit of this Swiss bank see in their offer of services an attractive instrument for the acquisition of discerning customers from the wealthiest layers of society in these regions. They emphasize that they are offering precisely what money alone cannot buy, namely special connoisseurship and expertise in dealing with art and in acquiring access to the exclusive circle of the Western collectors' community. In other words such an undertaking skillfully takes advantage of a backlog demand in order to function as a kind of exchange platform for the conversion of the abundance of economic capital into social and symbolic capital. A bulletin of another big Swiss bank states this relationship in all clarity: "The new Chinese millionaires all desire status symbols which represent their newly achieved wealth." And again: "Chinese businessmen travel to Europe and the USA, where they meet Pinault, Arnault or the Rockefellers, and must recognize that it is not enough just to be rich, but that one must also buy and collect works of art.", says François Curiel, the president of Christie's in Asia.

From a sociological point of view the enormous attractive power which the symbolic capital of art acquisition and art possession exercises over the new money and the social climbers can be put in a nutshell in the words of Pierre Bourdieu: "Of all the conversion techniques designed to create and accumulate symbolic capital, the purchase of works of art, objectified evidence of 'personal taste', is the one which is the closest to the most irreproachable and inimitable form of accumulation, that is, the internalization of distinctive signs and symbols of power in the form of natural 'distinction', personal 'authority' or 'culture'. The exclusive appropriation of priceless works is not without analogy to the ostentatious destruction of wealth; the irreproachable exhibition of wealth which it permits is, simultaneously, a challenge thrown down to all those who cannot dissociate their 'being' from their 'having' and attain disinterestedness, the supreme affirmation of personal excellence."[4]

It has been pointed out to us again and again that the strategy of using art commodities as objects of investment for the purpose of making a profit is far less stigmatized or looked down upon in this region. Some of the Asian collectors we interviewed by no means concealed the fact that they regularly resold works of art at a profit, a conduct clearly disapproved

---

4 | Bourdieu, Pierre (1984) [1979]: Distinction. A Social Critique of the Judgement of Taste. Cambridge: Harvard University Press, p. 282.

of among the collectors we interviewed in Europe and the USA, which would lead to a revocation of the status of a genuine collector. But here too changes are happening and the narration which emerges from our interviews suggests that the young generation of collectors from the East is in the meantime moving closer to the decades-old ideal type of the collector in the West with his credo "L'art pour l'art" and has internalized and habitualized the explicit and the implicit rules of art so profoundly that the hitherto existing coarse and fine differences in the etiquette and social uses of art will soon pale into insignificance. On the other hand, in spite of these indications of convergence and the leveling out of differences, the strength of the tendencies towards the self-assertion of cultural identity through distancing and distinction from hegemonial models should not be underestimated.

Why should the cultural specifica of the artistic traditions in this huge geographical region, such as ink painting, not be preserved in the evolution of an aesthetic code of contemporary art of a Chinese kind? Or find expression in a hybridization of differing techniques of different origin? The further development of the Eastern art world will probably depend, not least, on whether the producers of art, among whom we primarily include all the actors of the primary market with its sphere of limited production, succeed in emancipating themselves from the powerful big players of the global art market and assert themselves by acquiring the measure of autonomy needed if art is to be justifiably seen as more than a luxury good – a condition and a claim which might appear all too illusory and romantic under the conditions of a completely unfettered and deregulated capitalism.

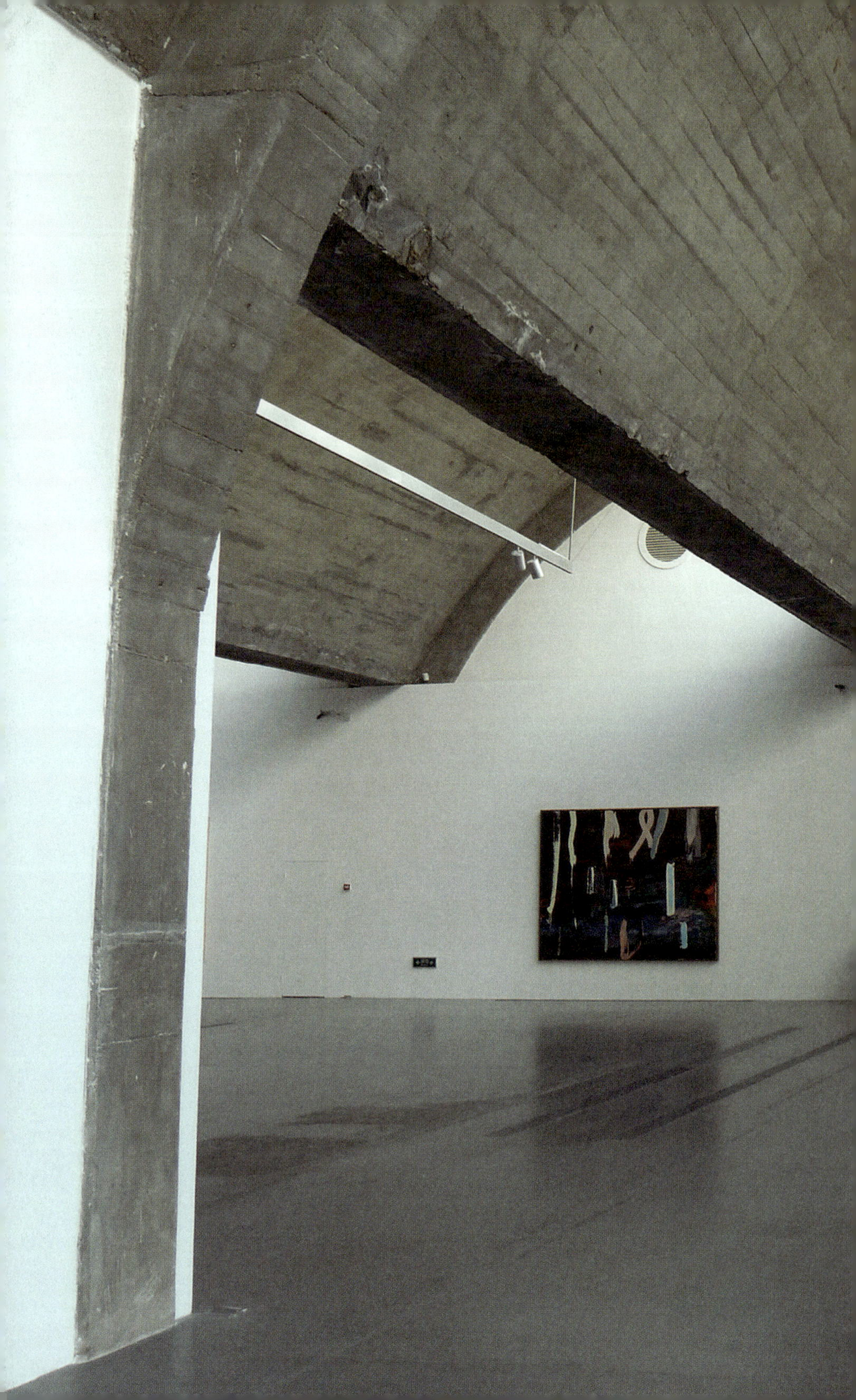

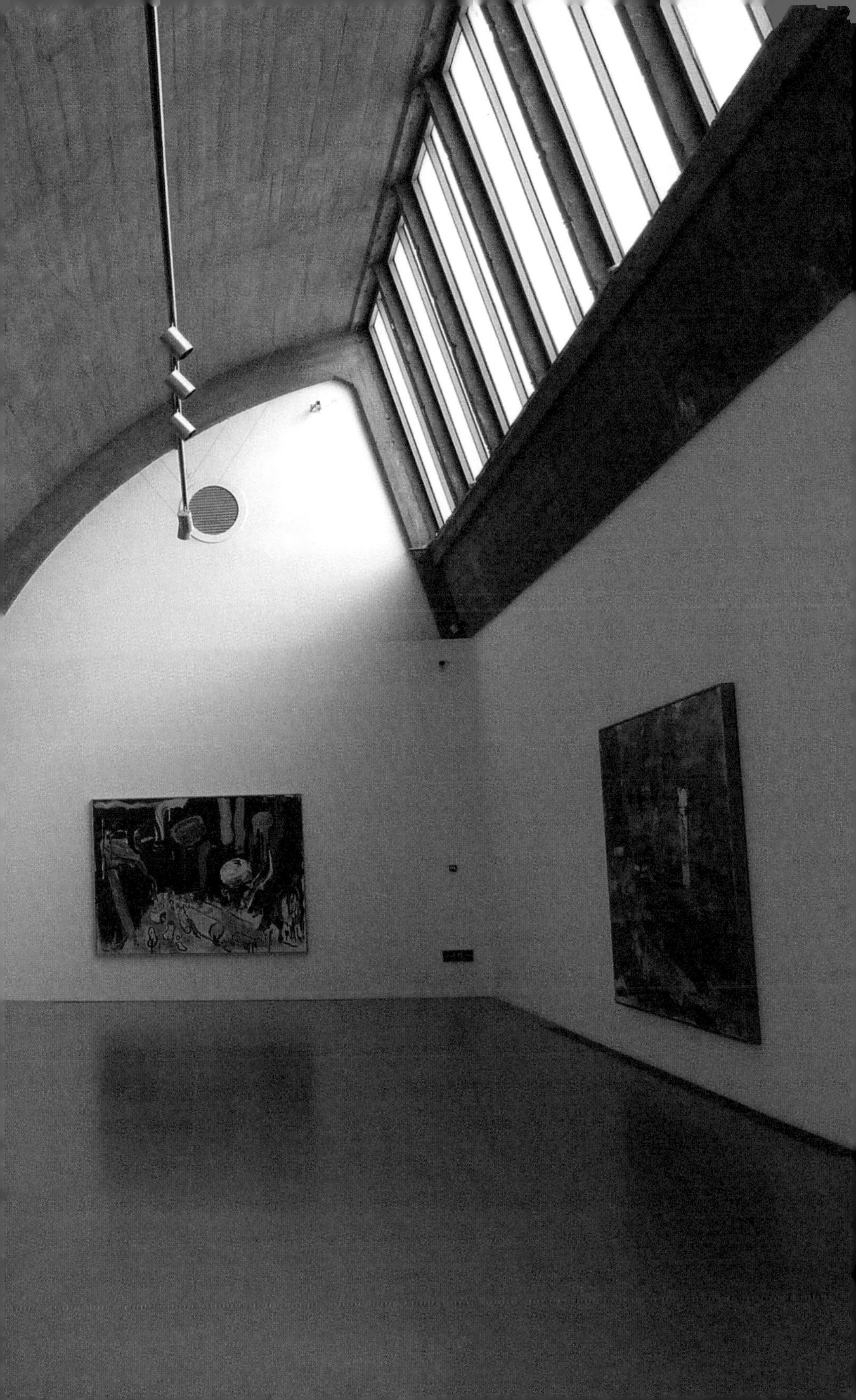

Appendix

ACKNOWLEDGMENTS

We wish to express our special thanks to various institutions and persons who have contributed to the realization of this book.

The Research Committee of the University of St. Gallen provided the initial financing for a pilot study which formed the basis for the preparation and presentation of a research application to the Swiss National Science Foundation.

The SNSF funded this project for a period of one year and then approved an extension for a further three months in view of the abundance of the collected data.

Eric Yau, Kwan Sin Joyce Mok, Meng Wang, Marta Baniukiewicz, Tina Willner and Yeung Suet Ying Clarisse were indispensable colleagues in the field research in Hong Kong.

Finally our thanks are due to the management of the Art Basel and particularly to Annette Schönholzer, who generously and uncomplicatedly opened the doors of the world of the Art Basel to us as "outsiders", in spite of the risk that the sociological radiography of this world could only be had at the expense of its demystification.

INTERVIEWS

In the context of the project more than 60 detailed interviews were recorded. The discussions with the staff of the Art Basel in Hong Kong, with the directors of public and private museums and collections, with curators, with gallerists and collectors, auctioneers and artists provide an instructive insight not only into the "workings" of the contemporary art market but above all into the way it is perceived by the participating actors.

For these discussions we are among other thankful to: Nadim Abbas (Hong Kong) • Tobias Berger (Hong Kong) • Robert Ceresia (Shanghai) • Jane Chao (Hong Kong) • Colin Chinnery (Beijing) • Hallam Chow (Hong Kong) • Chung (Hong Kong) • David Clarke (Hong Kong) • Katie de Tilly (Hong Kong) • Francois Ghebaly (Los Angeles) • Benjamin Hampe (Singapore) • Karin Handlbauer (Vienna) • Lorenz Helbling (Shanghai) • Ferdie Ju (Shanghai) • Michelle Lau (Hong Kong) • Leung Chi Wo (Hong Kong) • Sylvain & Dominique Lévy (Paris) • William Lim (Hong Kong) • David Lin (Taipei) • Gu Ling (Shanghai) • Alan Lo (Hong Kong) • Meg Maggio (Beijing) • Edouard Malingue (Hong Kong) • Adnan Z. Manjal (Jeddah) • Urs Meile (Beijing) • Ming Ming (Shanghai) • Sueo Mizuma (Tokyo) • Shinji Nanzuka (Tokyo) • Hans Ulrich Obrist (London) • Robin Peckham (Hong Kong) • Cedric Pinto (Singapore) • Magnus Renfrew (Hong Kong) • Fabio Rossi (Hong Kong) • Andrée Sfeir-Semler (Hamburg) • Eva Shiu (Singapore) • Vidya Shivadas (New Delhi) • Nick Simunovic (Hong Kong) • Karen Smith (Beijing) • James Solway (Shanghai) • Jonathan Stone (Hong Kong) • Honus Tandijono (Hong Kong) • Rudy Tseng (Taipei) • Henrietta Tsui (Hong Kong) • Choy Chun Wei (Kuala Lumpur) • Lim Wei-Ling (Kuala Lumpur) • Audrey Yeo (Singapore) • Hugh Zimmern (Hong Kong)

The Authors

Franz Schultheis is Professor of Sociology at the University of St. Gallen and President of the Fondation Bourdieu. He is co-editor of Pierre Bourdieu's writings.

Erwin Single has studied sociology, communication sciences and journalism and works as a freelance journalist in Berlin.

Raphaela Köfeler has studied International Affairs at the University of St. Gallen. She lives in Asia and is doing research about the art worlds of Hong Kong and Singapore.

Thomas Mazzurana has studied Business informatics and Sociology. He is a research associate at the Institute of Sociology at the University of St. Gallen.

PICTURE CREDITS

Photograph by Raphaela Köfeler on page
105
Photographs by Thomas Mazzurana on the cover and on pages
6/7 – 14/15 – 30/31 – 58/59 – 71 – 72/73 – 82/83 – 91 – 98 – 99 – 122/123 –
130/131 – 144/145 – 152/153 – 160 – 161 – 196/197 – 216/217 – 224/225 – 233
– 234/235
Photographs by Erwin Single on pages
13 – 57– 115 – 169 – 170 – 171 – 184/185 – 207 – 256/257

Cover and pages 30/31 and 122/123: *Inside the Long Museum West Bund in Shanghai. The museum was founded by the Chinese collectors, Liu Yiqian and his wife, Wang Wei, and houses one of the largest private collections in China.*

Page 6/7: *Street scene with Art Basel advertising in Hong Kong.*

Page 13: *The gallery Pace Beijing in the 798 Art District in Beijing.*

Page 14/15: *Opening of the second edition of the Art Basel in Hong Kong on May 14th 2014.*

Pages 57, 144/145, 160, 161, 256/257: *At the 798 Art District in Beijing in the Chaoyang District. Established in 1995 it is now home to many galleries, art institutions, bookshops and fashion labels.*

Pages 58/59 and 234/235: *Inside and outside the M50 Art District, Shanghai's most famous art district with many galleries and non-profit organizations located in the eponymous Moganshan Road.*

Pages 71 and 72/73: *Inside the Yuz Museum in Shanghai. The museum was founded by Indonesian-Chinese billionaire collector Budi Tek and opened in May 2014.*

Pages 82/83, 91 and 130/131: *At the Wong Chuk Hang Art Night, a satellite event to the Art Basel in Hong Kong with many participating galleries, art spaces and artist studios located in Wong Chuk Hang, Ap Lei Chau, Tin Wan and Aberdeen.*

Pages 98, 99, 152/153 and 169: *The Caochangdi Art Village in Beijing, home of domestic and international art galleries like the Galerie Urs Meile.*

Page 105: *Public art by Dutch artist Florentijn Hofman on the occasion of the Art Basel in the harbor of Hong Kong in May 2013.*

Page 115: *In the CAFA Art Museum in Beijing, one of the most important art institutions in Asia.*

Pages 170 and 171: *The Ullens Center for Contemporary Art in the 798 Art District, an independent, not-for-profit art center founded by the Belgian collectors Guy and Myriam Ullens and opened in November 2007.*

Page 184/185: *In front of the Rockbund Art Museum in Shanghai, located in the former Royal Asiatic Society building completed in 1933 near The Bund waterfront.*

Page 196/197: *An exercise class at the China Central Academy of Fine Arts (CAFA), an art academy under the direct charge of the Ministry of Education of China.*

Page 207: *A gallery in Hollywood Road in Hong Kong, an area with many galleries and antique shops.*

Pages 216/217, 224/225 and 233: *At the Art Basel in Hong Kong.*